Praise for *Listening to Prestige*

"Written with a contagious enthusiasm and a breezy style that newcomers to jazz will find particularly rewarding, *Listening to Prestige* is a valentine to one of the foundational labels of post-war jazz. Tad Richards highlights scores of now-classic recordings by Miles Davis, Sonny Rollins, Thelonious Monk, Yusef Lateef, Jack McDuff, and countless others, while also opening a window on the modus operandi of Prestige's founder Bob Weinstock and the stylistic changes coursing through jazz from the late '40s through the early '70s."

— Mark Stryker, author of *Jazz from Detroit*

"When it comes to jazz, this is one of the rare books that we actually need, that does not cover the usual ground with the usual suspects. Prestige Records, for all the attention it has received from audiences, is not well known in the historical sense. Every jazz fan has these records, which is important, but few know the inside story, the complex process of the jazz independent label in the era before independent labels became as common as recording projects. And Tad Richards is the writer to do this, with a firm grasp of jazz's historical succession, the bebop era, and the musical needs of musician and audience. Read this book."

— Allen Lowe, saxophonist and historian who has recorded with Julius Hemphill, David Murray, Doc Cheatham, and Marc Ribot

Listening to Prestige

Listening to Prestige

Chronicling Its Classic Jazz Recordings, 1949–1972

TAD RICHARDS

excelsior editions
State University of New York Press
Albany, New York

Cover image of the 1950's Prestige record label; in the public domain.

Published by State University of New York Press, Albany

© 2025 State University of New York

All rights reserved

Printed in the United States of America

No part of this book may be used or reproduced in any manner whatsoever without written permission. No part of this book may be stored in a retrieval system or transmitted in any form or by any means including electronic, electrostatic, magnetic tape, mechanical, photocopying, recording, or otherwise without the prior permission in writing of the publisher.

Links to third-party websites are provided as a convenience and for informational purposes only. They do not constitute an endorsement or an approval of any of the products, services, or opinions of the organization, companies, or individuals. SUNY Press bears no responsibility for the accuracy, legality, or content of a URL, the external website, or for that of subsequent websites.

EU GPSR Authorised Representative:
Logos Europe, 9 rue Nicolas Poussin, 17000, La Rochelle, France
contact@logoseurope.eu

Excelsior Editions is an imprint of State University of New York Press

For information, contact State University of New York Press, Albany, NY
www.sunypress.edu

Library of Congress Cataloging-in-Publication Data

Name: Richards, Tad, author.
Title: Listening to Prestige : chronicling its classic jazz recordings, 1949–1972 / Tad Richards.
Description: Albany : State University of New York, [2025]. | Series: Excelsior editions | Includes bibliographical references and index.
Identifiers: LCCN 2025020826 | ISBN 9798855804942 (hardcover: alk. paper | ISBN 9798855804966 (ebook) | ISBN 9798855804959 (pbk. : alk. paper)
Subjects: LCSH: Prestige Records (Firm). | Jazz—History and criticism.
Classification: LCC ML3792.P74 R53 2025 | DDC 781.65/149—dc23/eng/20250721
LC record available at https://lccn.loc.gov/2025020826

For Pat . . . 'nuff said

Contents

Preamble: How This Book Came About		ix
Introduction: Bob Weinstock and Prestige		1
Chapter 1	Postwar Independent Jazz Record Labels	3
Chapter 2	Weinstock's Beginnings: New Jazz	7
Chapter 3	Early Artists on New Jazz	12
Chapter 4	The Birth of the Prestige Label	19
Chapter 5	The First Jazz on LP	26
Chapter 6	Wardell Gray, James Moody, and King Pleasure	34
Chapter 7	Miles Davis	40
Chapter 8	Thelonious Monk	50
Chapter 9	Enter Rudy Van Gelder and Recording More Monk	56
Chapter 10	The Modern Jazz Quartet	66
Chapter 11	Cover Art, and a Dual Role for Esmond Edwards	75
Chapter 12	Sonny Rollins	82
Chapter 13	Miles Davis Back and Ready to Work: The Contractual Marathon	102

Chapter 14	Changing Times and Technologies at Prestige	112
Chapter 15	Other '50s-Era Prestige Recording Artists	119
Chapter 16	Miles's Sidemen and John Coltrane	143
Chapter 17	Mose Allison and Yusef Lateef	157
Chapter 18	A New Era: Soul Jazz	171
Chapter 19	Prestige's Satellite Labels	183
Chapter 20	Soul Jazz Organists	190
Chapter 21	Moving On: Free Jazz and Eric Dolphy	196
Chapter 22	Dolphy's Peers at Prestige	210
Chapter 23	Booker Ervin	217
Chapter 24	Stars of the Early '60s	221
Chapter 25	Final Days	241

Epilogue	249
Acknowledgments	251
Works Cited	253
Index	257

Preamble

How This Book Came About

This book had its genesis about ten years ago in an ongoing conversation about jazz with my friend, the painter Peter Jones, about the decade we came of age in, and discovered a passion for music in: the 1950s. It was a passion that set us apart from most of our contemporaries in a way that was succinctly captured by Barry Levinson's 1982 film *Diner* and its character Shrevie, played by Daniel Stern. Shrevie and Beth (Ellen Barkin) are recently married, and their marriage is already in trouble, because Beth has a habit of pulling a record out from his collection, playing it, and not reshelving in—or, worse yet, reshelving it in the wrong place. Shrevie has everything arranged alphabetically and by category: jazz, pop, rock and roll, folk, rhythm and blues. To Beth, it's all just music—nice to listen to but nothing to obsess about. To make matters worse, she would never quiz him on music trivia, like the flip sides of hit 45 rpm records.

We were that way. We were the guys who knew all the flip sides. And we never grew out of it. Now we debated whether it was worth getting a subscription to Spotify, because sure they gave you access to an unheard-of catalog of great and obscure jazz records, but they didn't give the personnel on each cut.

And heading into our social security years, we still challenged each other to list, from memory, all the jazz artists who recorded for Capitol or EmArcy, or all the musicians who were still alive who had played with Bird. And we kept coming back to one thing. Top 40 radio in those days was a hit-or-miss proposition, shoveling you a lot of pap—Eddie Fisher, the Crew-Cuts, Fabian—that you had to put up with to hear the good stuff.

But the jazz of that era—the jazz on the records we could afford to buy, the cuts that were played on Symphony Sid—it was all good. We couldn't think of a single record that had let us down.

But was it really all good?

I decided to put it to the test.

I couldn't really listen to every jazz recording from the 1950s. But maybe every recording from a representative label?

Which brought me to Prestige. There were other labels, certainly. I didn't want to choose a major label like Columbia. The independents would have more variety, take more risks. And there were some good ones. Atlantic, surely my favorite rhythm and blues label, but a jazz pioneer too. Verve, Riverside . . . and of course Blue Note.

Blue Note and Prestige were right there together at the center of New York jazz, and New York was the center of jazz. All the tributaries—New Orleans, Chicago, Kansas City—had been leading inexorably toward the Big Apple. So if I was really going to take the pulse of the music of a decade, these two labels were the place to start.

But which one? Two things shaped my decision making. First, a lot had already been written about Blue Note. There were books on its history. And precious little about Prestige.

Second, a more personal reason. Prestige felt like home base to me. The first three jazz albums I ever bought were all Prestige artists (John Coltrane, Mose Allison, King Pleasure/Annie Ross). As I thought back to my early years of passionate collecting, it seemed as though the Prestige label turned up over and over again.

And that was the beginning of my blog, *Listening to Prestige*. Thanks to the internet, and particularly the Japanese website jazzdisco.org, I had a discography and session log for every Prestige session. I began in 2014, and ten years later, when Richard Carlin of SUNY Press suggested I write a history of Prestige Records, I had gotten well past my original goal of testing Peter's and my theory about the '50s, and was halfway through the next decade. And I hadn't found a bad record yet.

This book is also titled *Listening to Prestige*, and its perspective is a little different from that of the column. It's the story of the birth, the robust life, and eventually the death of an important independent jazz label: its chronology, its mission, and how the changing roster of the label reflected the changing styles and tastes in jazz over two decades. But the music is still at the center of it, and I've drawn extensively on ten years of blogging. All of the "Listening to Prestige" sidebar sections are blog entries, or parts of blog entries. All of those blog entries included the date and place of the recording session, the personnel, and the tunes cut that day, and that information is included with each sidebar. The blog itself can be found at http://opusforty.blogspot.com.

Introduction

Bob Weinstock and Prestige

The Prestige story starts with an eight-year-old kid. Bob Weinstock inherited his love of jazz from his father, Sol, a shoe salesman. His earliest memory was going out to a flea market with his father and coming home with a stack of jazz records they had bought for nine cents apiece. That was the beginning of his collecting career, and by the age of fifteen he had his own mail-order record business, advertising in trade magazines.

In 1946, at the age of eighteen and with his father's support, he opened his first record store in Times Square, near the Metropole Café, a midtown jazz club presenting traditional jazz artists—the music he and his father had collected, the music he sold in his store. The store became a hangout for Metropole musicians on their break, and soon for other musicians as well. Weinstock was becoming known in jazz circles. But he was still an innocent in many ways.

Just how innocent, he was about to find out. One day Alfred Lion, the owner of the established jazz record label Blue Note, stopped by and told the younger man, "You've got to listen to this."

Weinstock listened with a growing sense of wonder. "What is that?" he asked.

"That's Thelonious Monk, and it's called bebop."

Weinstock was hooked, from the first bebop record he heard. He wanted to be part of it. He wanted to sell it in his store, but that wasn't all. He wanted to record it.

He did, and he kept doing it for two decades. The history of Prestige Records is the history of the development of jazz through one of its most fertile periods, and in this book we'll follow that development through the lens of one scrappy independent record label.

There's a lot to be said about racial and economic injustice in the story of American music. Did Bob Weinstock treat musicians fairly? Much has been written about the economic exploitation of musicians, particularly Black musicians, during this era, and there's no question but that it is a terrible stain on American cultural history, just as it is on American social history. The TV series *The Sopranos* featured the memorable character of a gangster (loosely based on music business personality Morris Levy) who had gotten rich in the 1950s by cheating and exploiting young Black musicians. In his book *Jazz and Justice: Racism and the Political Economy of the Music*, Gerald Horne, a professor of history and African American studies at the University of Houston, offers a searing exposé of the jazz industry, and does not spare Weinstock or Prestige. Similarly, *At the Vanguard of Vinyl: A Cultural History of the Long-Playing Record in Jazz*, by Darren Mueller, singles out Weinstock for particular opprobrium. These are just one side of the story, and there are many who would argue against holding Weinstock up as an archetype of exploitation. Miles Davis is just one musician whose recollection of his experience with Prestige is mostly favorable.

In any case, that will not be the focus of this book. I don't know enough to do it justice. And ultimately, important as it is, it's not what I want to write about. I came to Prestige Records as a seventeen-year-old new convert to jazz, confronted with a catalog that opened my eyes, and my ears, to a world of beauty and passion and creativity and intellectual challenge, and that's what I will be focusing on in this book: the music, and its place in the cultural history of the American Century in music, one of the greatest creative eras this world has ever known.

Chapter 1

Postwar Independent Jazz Record Labels

It was a propitious time to be starting an independent record label. The postwar manufacturing boom, fueled by innovation and the availability of materials previously prioritized for the war effort, made the manufacture of 78 rpm records a growing business. Record pressing plants had been owned by, and only available to, the big corporate record labels like RCA Victor, Columbia and Decca. Now anyone could get a record pressed, although distribution was still a problem.

This had made for an unprecedented boom in the independent record label business. And there was an untapped market just waiting to be addressed.

The early record business was aimed at an upscale market. Phonographs were a status symbol, made of mahogany, sold in furniture stores. In 1920, when songwriter Perry Bradford couldn't find a white singer to record his new song "Crazy Blues," he suggested cutting it with a Black singer, an idea that was met with jeers. Who would want to listen to a colored singer? Who would buy such a record? But when, against the current wisdom, the recording of "Crazy Blues" became a best seller, it was a revelation. Black people bought records! Owned phonographs! And the 1920s saw a boom in blues recording that gave careers to Bessie Smith, Blind Lemon Jefferson, and others, until the 1929 crash and the Depression caused a retrenchment among entertainment providers, and the Black entertainers were the first to be cut loose.

There were exceptions. Bessie Smith continued to record in the 1930s. Robert Johnson's brief recording career was in that decade. Black dance bands like Jimmie Lunceford and Erskine Hawkins made records (although Hawkins's signature song, "Tuxedo Junction," became a runaway hit only when Glenn Miller recorded it). But by and large, the Black audience for music was being ignored.

And that audience was there, and growing. The Great Migration brought Blacks to northern cities, the defense industry opened up employment opportunities, and a new Black class, segregated from but not dissimilar to the white middle class, was emerging. Much has been written about this new demographic, but perhaps nothing as pungent and absorbing as Walter Mosley's first private eye novel, *Devil in a Blue Dress*. For a nonfiction memoir, I recommend Johnny Otis's *Upside Your Head! Rhythm and Blues on Central Avenue*.

New styles of music were evolving to meet the demands of the new populace: amplified, hard-driving modifications of Delta blues in Chicago, small group swing in Los Angeles, bebop in New York. An entrepreneur who could get these new sounds on record could do very well, and those entrepreneurs were emerging, even as World War II was raging, and even more so directly after the war. Savoy, Excelsior, and Exclusive began in 1942; Apollo and Black and White in 1943; King and Gilt-Edge in 1944; Modern and Philo (which became much better known as Aladdin) in 1945; Specialty and Mercury in 1946. Atlantic started in 1947, as did Aristocrat, which would change its name to Chess, and Down Beat, which was not connected to the magazine and would undergo a couple of name changes before settling on Swing Time, which was the first label to record a young Nat "King" Cole soundalike named Ray Charles. All of these labels—and there were many more—were primarily focused on what was becoming known as "race music." King Records, started by Syd Nathan in Cincinnati, was a "hillbilly" label (serving another underserved demographic) and expanded to the race market when Nathan saw the possibilities for sales there.

The race market was a niche one. There weren't the big bucks that the major labels could make with performers like Glenn Miller and Frank Sinatra, but there was a living, sometimes a pretty good one. This was music you could dance to, or cry to, or orchestrate a seduction to. There was another form of music developing in this same time period, also coming out of the Black musical community, that you couldn't do any of those three things to (as is illustrated in the movie *Jerry Maguire*, where the hotshot young yuppie sports agent is given a Miles Davis/John Coltrane recording to play as an aid to making love, but after a few bars he yanks it out of the cassette player and throws it in the trash). But modern jazz was making history; its pioneers were artists of the first rank, and that music needed to be preserved on record too.

Blue Note was the first of the jazz independents, and the longest-lasting—it's still around. It was formed in 1939 by two German Jewish immigrants, Alfred Lion and Max Margulis, with this mission statement: "BlueNote Records [as Lion originally called it] are designed simply to serve the uncompromising expressions of hot jazz or swing, in general." But Lion and Francis Wolff, another German émigré who joined the label early on, had alert ears, and in 1947 they turned to bebop, recording Thelonious Monk. Bob Weinstock first learned about modern jazz from Alfred Lion. As he told Michael Jarrett, when interviewed for *Pressed for All Time: Producing the Great Jazz Albums*: "The man was a genius. He went from New Orleans jazz up to the latest modern things: Cecil Taylor and Ornette Coleman. He was my real mentor."

Dial began in 1946, as a pure jazz label. It is best known for its recordings of Charlie Parker, but founder Ross Russell had a solid commitment to modern jazz, and released some important records. But that didn't last long. In 1949 Russell abruptly switched the label's focus to classical, and not long before it folded in 1954, he had switched again, to calypso. Weinstock recalled that *"Ross Russell, who recorded Bird on Dial, he shaped my philosophies of life."*

Norman Granz, founder of Jazz at the Philharmonic, is best known for his Verve record label, founded in 1956, and the label for many of jazz's luminaries. But he had begun recording his JATP concerts in 1945, leasing the recordings first to Asch/Disc Records and then Mercury, before regaining ownership of the masters and releasing them on his Clef label in 1953. Weinstock said of Granz: "Because I produced Miles and Rollins, Trane, Monk, and Milt Jackson, people thought I was a real modernist. What they didn't understand was that I also loved the Norman Granz stuff. Granz knew two things: swing and play pretty. He made such good records. He was a hero. One of the first things that really got me excited when I was in high school was his Jazz at the Philharmonic." Savoy recorded some modern jazz, including some of Charlie Parker's seminal sessions, but they were more and more focused on rhythm and blues. Aladdin recorded Lester Young, Coleman Hawkins, and Gene Ammons, but they were really a rhythm and blues label. Mercury, which was formed in 1945, was an all-purpose label, but starting in 1947 they did have a very active jazz division, headed at first by producer/jazz enthusiast John Hammond. A subsidiary Mercury label, EmArcy, was all jazz. Atlantic was started in 1947, and although founder Ahmet Ertegun was a jazz lover, and they would later become important players in the jazz field, their early recordings, outside of sessions by Ellingtonians Rex Stewart and Johnny Hodges, eschewed jazz. In fact, their early recordings were all over the place, until success with the small group swing of Joe Morris turned them in a rhythm and blues direction. Atlantic would have the biggest commercial success of any of the independent labels, until by the end of the decade they had budgets to compete

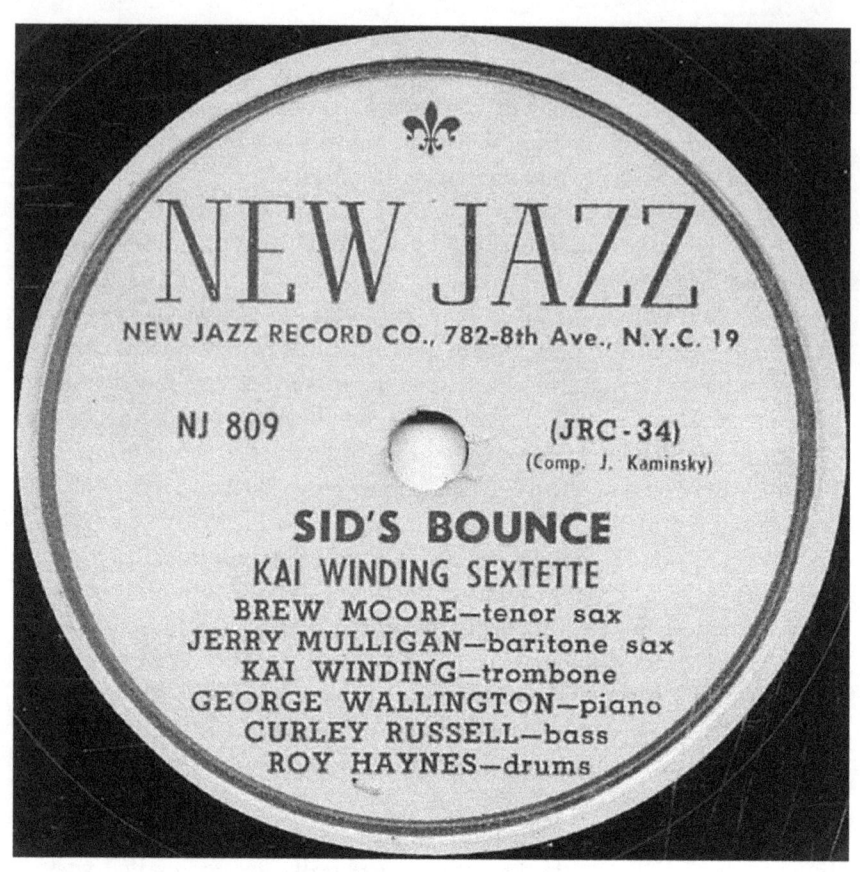

with the major labels. Fantasy began in 1949 on the West Coast, primarily to record Dave Brubeck. The other significant West Coast jazz label, Pacific Jazz, was a later arrival, in 1952.

And that was it. There was precious little modern jazz being recorded by anyone when Bob Weinstock decided to start a label. He was encouraged by bebop pioneer Kenny Clarke, who was a regular at Weinstock's store and had gotten to be friends with the young man. Clarke told him he could get him all the stars of bebop he could handle. On January 11, 1949, twenty-year-old Bob Weinstock entered the studio with a quintet led by Lennie Tristano, for his first step on the venture that was to be his legacy: recording this new jazz. And that was the name he first gave to his record label: New Jazz.

Chapter 2

Weinstock's Beginnings

New Jazz

You didn't need much to start an independent label in the 1940s. When Art Rupe began Specialty, his office was a cigar box on someone else's desk. Studio time could be rented, records could be pressed at the new postwar plants. Distribution had traditionally been handled in-house by the major labels, and some independents set up their own distribution networks. Art Rupe financed his two brothers in a distribution business. Others relied on the new independent distributors who were springing up, answering a need in the same way that the fledgling record companies were answering the need for a new kind of music. Bob Weinstock, who had run both a record store and a mail-order business, was more savvy than many new entrepreneurs about the distribution side of the business. So the only problem was finding the talent, because at the root of it, whether a record label succeeded or not depended on making records that people wanted to hear.

When the talent pool was modern jazz, and your base of operations was New York, there was plenty of talent. With Kenny Clarke's help, along with the help of other musicians he had befriended from the record store, and with a telephone, Weinstock set out to find them. And they were right around the corner. The heyday of 52nd Street as a bebop mecca was almost over, but it was not quite dead yet. Weinstock had begun frequenting the Royal Roost, just off Swing Street at Broadway and 50th, and maybe he had been there in September 1948, when a new and experimental nonet joined the bill, opening for Count Basie. The nonet was not a hit with Basie fans, and although Capitol issued some of its performances on 78 rpm records, they were poorly received critically and commercially. The musicians for that first club date were Miles Davis (trumpet), Mike Zwerin (trombone), Bill Barber (tuba), Junior Collins (French horn), Gerry Mulligan (baritone saxophone), Lee Konitz (alto saxophone), John Lewis (piano), Al McKibbon (bass), and Max Roach (drums). When the recordings made in 1949–50 (with slight changes in the personnel) were finally released by Capitol on a 1957 LP release called *Birth of the Cool*, they were rightfully hailed as one of the most important musical events of their era.

Whether or not Weinstock heard Konitz with the nonet, he did get to know him, and, according to his recollection to Dom Cerulli in a 1957 *Down Beat* interview, Konitz and other Royal Roost regulars put the bug in his ear—started pestering him, as he recalled it—to start his own label, so that somebody would be recording them.

The pestering seemed to pay off, and in 1949, he was ready. He would have, as he told Michael Jarrett in a 1995 interview, "loved to have recorded Dizzy Gillespie and Bird. They were, to me, the greatest at the time—the pioneers of bebop and the best of bebop. Unfortunately, they were tied up. I couldn't get them." So he asked his friend Lee Konitz for advice on where to start, and Konitz, unsurprisingly, said, "Me. I'd like to record. I've never recorded. But it would be better for everybody if Lennie Tristano would be the leader. He has more name power. I feel more secure doing my first recording with Lennie as the leader."

Blind from age nine and a musical prodigy, Tristano was born and raised in Chicago. He studied at Chicago's American Conservatory of Music starting in 1938. He graduated in 1943, continued for a master's that he never completed, and began playing with local bands, and also teaching—a dual role that he would continue when he came to New York in 1946, gradually shifting his focus more into teaching. Lee Konitz was one of his students, as was Emmett Carls, who would start a band with Tristano and do a recording session—the first of Tristano's "Lost Sessions," though it would eventually be found, and can be heard on YouTube. Carls went on to play with Stan Kenton and Benny Goodman, and, most intriguingly, in the Chico Marx Orchestra, which the comedian fronted and played piano with when he wasn't making movies, but was mostly led by Ben Pollack.

Tristano first stayed on Long Island at the home of Chubby Jackson's parents. He had met Jackson in Chicago, when Jackson was touring as the bassist with Woody Herman's band. Jackson introduced him to guitarist

Billy Bauer, another Herman alumnus, and the two hit it off right away, not without a certain initial bemusement on Bauer's part. As Bauer recalled, "He says 'here's what we'd do. No rhythm guitar. No melody. So let's play.' . . . Now I'm not supposed to play the melody, I'm not supposed to play rhythm. So he says, 'Just play something.'" Bauer found something, because he and Tristano were to play together for several years.

Tristano began teaching privately almost as soon as he arrived in New York, and a sort of salon began to coalesce around him, rivaling the sort-of-salon that had grown around Charlie Parker, whom he met soon after his arrival. The two men took each other's measure, and Parker said of Tristano, "I'd like to go on record as saying I endorse his work in every particular. . . . He has a big heart and it's in his music. . . . He's a tremendous acclimatizer." And still, he barely existed on record.

Tristano's reputation in 1949 was at its zenith among musicians, but almost nonexistent among a wider public—certainly the record-buying, radio-listening public. Tristano's recording career before the Prestige session can be followed on Tom Lord's ultracomplete database of recorded jazz, starting with a session titled "The Lost Sessions," and on the Japanese discography database jazzdisco.com. Of particular interest is an entire recording of Tristano and Charlie Parker together, including a session with just the two of them, accompanied by Kenny Clarke playing with wire brushes on a Manhattan phone book, in Tristano's apartment.

It's interesting to look at the backgrounds of the musicians on Tristano's Prestige session. Guitarist Billy Bauer, though he found a kindred spirit in Tristano, had a swing and big band background, having played with Jerry Wald, Woody Herman, Benny Goodman, and Jack Teagarden. Drummer Shelley Manne started in a big band, then played and recorded with a number of Ellington sidemen, as well as with Coleman Hawkins and Don Byas. After his move to the West Coast, he showed great versatility, playing in every setting from Dixieland to movie soundtracks to the avant-garde. Bassist Arnold Fishkind played with Jack Teagarden, Bunny Berigan, even the dance band of Les Brown. And even during the years of his association with Tristano, he was also playing with Charlie Barnet and Benny Goodman.

This is all par for the course for the early modern jazz pioneers; they had to come from somewhere. Tristano and Konitz are the unusual ones, in that they came to modern jazz pretty much from day one. Konitz grew up admiring Benny Goodman, but his first big band job, as a temporary replacement for Charlie Barnet in the Teddy Powell orchestra, reportedly made Powell bang his head against a wall in anguish when Konitz started playing. He was not cut out to be a swing musician. And Tristano really was always the cerebral, difficult modernist he's famous for being. So in a way Bauer, Fishkind, and Manne had to learn not to swing, or not to rely on swinging.

The recording's success helped launch the new label. From the Jarrett interview, Weinstock remembers: "It was a smash hit in jazz circles. All the critics gave it five stars. Stores all over the United States would call up and order it. I was swamped with orders. They even sent their checks for the record to get it quickly. 'Here, we're enclosing so-and-so. Send me the records at once!'"

Not long after the Prestige sessions, in May 1949, Tristano took this same group, with the addition of his other prize pupil, Warne Marsh, to record three different sessions for Capitol. Two 78 rpm singles came out of these sessions, the second of which, "Intuition," was the first of Tristano's investigations of "pure improvisation," anticipating by a decade free jazz, or the spontaneous improvisation of Keith Jarrett.

Weinstock is not exaggerating the critical impact of his Tristano recordings, or their significance in announcing to the world the arrival of an important new jazz label, at a time when it was sorely needed. In that respect, he could hardly have chosen a better inaugural artist. He may, however, have been a little rosy in his memory of having a smash hit. Certainly, it must have seemed that way to a twenty-year-old passionate about jazz and flush with the excitement of having his own label, recording a virtually untapped genius of modern music and having his accomplishment recognized. On the other hand, Oscar Peterson, on hearing the record on a *Down Beat* blindfold test, commented: "Musically it's a fine record. Commercially I don't think it holds much value; the public isn't up to that standard in music."

Not all that many people were going to buy any modern jazz record. By 1949, bebop was starting to reach a broader audience, but it certainly wasn't achieving mass acceptance. Charlie Parker and Dizzy Gillespie were still controversial figures, their music widely thought of as incomprehensible. Today, theirs is the music of the mainstream, and it's hard for a younger listener to understand why it was thought of as difficult. However, Lennie Tristano, with his pure improvisation, complex turns of phrase, and almost fetishistic disregard for the melody can still be a little daunting. So one can only imagine how many listeners in 1949 would have been left scratching their heads.

Chapter 3

Early Artists on New Jazz

Weinstock named his label New Jazz, but perhaps not all of it had to be quite that new. In his next few recording sessions, he tapped musicians who were closer to the mainstream, although—mostly—still modern. The one exception was Dixieland star Jimmy McPartland, presumably drawn from the Metropole roster, who made two 78 rpm old jazz records for New Jazz, featuring his young bride Marian, who before too long would shed Jimmy but keep his name.

But Weinstock, even at twenty—or perhaps especially at twenty—had a remarkable consistency of vision. He had formed his record company on the epiphany that had been thrust on him by Alfred Lion in the form of a Thelonious Monk record (not to mention those pesky musicians at the Royal Roost), and he honored that vision. By comparison, look at another label that started around the same time, and was destined for greatness: Atlantic Records. Ahmet and Nesuhi Ertegun were gentlemen of taste and vision, but the artists that they recorded during the first half of their first year are all over the map. There's virtually no one that you'd find on their roster a couple of years down the line, until they signed Joe Morris in the fall. But it seems Weinstock always knew what he wanted and went after it.

If he needed musicians with a modern sound and a little more mainstream appeal, he needed to look no further than that long narrow catwalk behind the bar of the Metropole Café, a stage that appeared to be designed more for strippers than jazz combos, and indeed that would be what the club featured in its declining years. But musicians did line up along that odd bandstand, sometimes quite a lot of them. Bill Crow recalls playing there with the whole Woody Herman orchestra.

Herman was a star. The 1940s, for him, were an unbroken string of hit records. But along with his crowd-pleasing arrangements, he had in his Second Herd some exceptional players in the modern idiom, and his saxophone section had received particular acclaim for their recording of a tune by Jimmy Giuffre, "Four Brothers." The four brothers in Herman's band were Zoot Sims, Serge Chaloff, Herbie Steward, and a megastar in the making, twenty-year-old Stan Getz.

One of them, baritone sax man Serge Chaloff, led a group on March 10, 1949, that traded on the Herman name, as Serge Chaloff and the Herdsmen. It was a good cross section of the Second Herd, and an all-star combo by any measure, featuring Red Rodney, trumpet; Earl Swope, trombone; Al Cohn, tenor sax; Serge Chaloff, baritone sax; Terry Gibbs, vibes; Barbara Carroll, piano; Oscar Pettiford, bass; Denzil Best, drums.

Chaloff came from a musical family. His mother, a renowned professor at the New England Conservatory of Music, numbered Leonard Bernstein, George Shearing, Keith Jarrett, Herbie Hancock, and Chick Corea among her students. He had begun playing the baritone saxophone out of admiration for Ellingtonian Harry Carney, and had begun to achieve recognition in a number of big bands during the early 1940s—the formative years of bebop. Chaloff was drawn to 52nd Street, and his mastery of the bebop idiom on a formidably difficult instrument earned him the nickname of "the white Charlie Parker."

In 1949, Chaloff was at the zenith of his career. He won his first *Down Beat* poll on baritone sax in that year, and followed it with wins the next two years. After that, Gerry Mulligan took over, and no one else was ever close again. Chaloff's career was undermined by heroin addiction and ill health. His last recording, on February 11, 1957, was a reunion of the Four Brothers, with Al Cohn taking Stan Getz's place. He died in July of that year, his reputation shrunk to the point that when his Prestige sessions were rereleased on CD, they bore the name of "Oscar Pettiford Sextet."

Four days later, a second Herman group was assembled, this one led by Terry Gibbs. In those days, before it was decided that jazz was too serious for such frivolities, you could still have fun with titles of tunes and names of groups, so this one was billed as Terry's New Jazz Pirates. Terry and the Pirates were Gibbs on vibes, plus Shorty Rogers, trumpet; Earl Swope, trombone; Stan Getz, tenor sax; George Wallington, piano; Curly Russell,

bass; Shadow Wilson, drums. These tunes also saw CD release under a different name, not so much because of diminution of Gibbs's stature as the incredible rise of one of his bandmates: they became known as *Early Stan*.

Even then, Getz was starting to move to the forefront, as Weinstock neatly bracketed his new label's beginnings with the most inaccessible and the most accessible of contemporary jazz stars. The next session, on April 8, was billed as Stan Getz and his Four Brothers (Al Cohn, Allen Eager, Brew Moore, Zoot Sims, tenor sax; Getz, tenor, baritone sax; Walter Bishop, piano; Gene Ramey, bass; Charlie Perry, drums). Another superstar in the making was the arranger for the session, Gerry Mulligan.

Additional Getz sessions for Prestige in 1949 included:

- May 12, a session variously billed as Al Haig Sextet featuring Stan Getz and Stan Getz and the Al Haig Quintet. The bebop piano pioneer and the rising sax star were joined by Jimmy Raney, guitar; Gene Ramey, bass; Charlie Perry, drums. The sextet tracks added Carlos Vidal, congas.
- June 21, the Stan Getz Bop stars, with Haig and Ramey, and Stan Levey on drums.
- July 28, the Al Haig Sextet (rereleased as *Stan Getz with Al Haig*), featuring Getz, Haig and Raney; Kai Winding, trombone; Tommy Potter, bass; Roy Haynes, drums; Blossom Dearie, vocal.

The piano players most commonly associated with the bebop movement are Bud Powell and Thelonious Monk, but none is more ubiquitous than Al Haig. Between 1945 and 1954, he played on something like one hundred sessions, many of them with Charlie Parker and Dizzy Gillespie. His 1951–53 work with Getz marked the end of an era for him; after that, he seems to have fallen out of favor, and he spent the next couple of decades mostly playing in undistinguished cocktail lounges, until a move to Europe in the 1970s sparked a resurgence of interest in him.

Jimmy Raney would be a semiregular with Prestige throughout the 1950s. In addition to his work with Getz and Haig, he recorded two albums under his own name (one as coleader with Kenny Burrell) and did sessions with Bob Brookmeyer and Barbara Lea.

Getz remained with Prestige for a few more sessions, into the early 1950s, as styles and recording techniques changed. Particularly appealing was a June 21, 1950, session with a quartet including two Woody Herman alumni, Tony Aless on piano and Don Lamond on drums. Both had recently been playing with Chubby Jackson, another ex-Herdsman who was a fine bass player and bandleader, but who later achieved more fame as a kiddie TV host. The bass player, Percy Heath, came from two even more exclusive organizations: one, a jazz-playing family, and two, the legendary World War II all-Black flying corps, the Tuskegee Airmen. They cut four songs, as was typically the case in that era: two two-sided 78s. The first LPs had been issued in 1949, as had the first 45 rpm records, but such innovations were slow to reach the independent labels. In this case, it was four ballads, each of them showcasing Getz's romantic side.

One of the joys that the great balladeers like Stan Getz bring to jazz is their way with classic songs from what has come to be known as the Great American Songbook. These are vivid and memorable melodies, with chord changes and melodic structures that lend themselves to jazz interpretation and improvisation. But they're more than that. They're songs, with the emotional and thematic power that only a song can deliver. Lester Young said that he always heard the words to a song in his head as he played it. The fictional Dale Turner, played by Dexter Gordon in the movie *Round Midnight*, has a moment when he realizes he's losing his ability to produce the music he wants to, and says, "I forgot the words." I don't know if Stan Getz played the words in his head when he recorded a ballad, but he captures that feeling in these records.

In "You Stepped Out of a Dream," it's that rapt wonder that only the person you've suddenly, unreservedly fallen in love with can evoke. Written by Nacio Herb Brown and Gus Kahn, it was originally sung by Tony Martin for the 1941 musical *Ziegfeld Girl*, to the visual of Lana Turner descending a staircase. "My Old Flame," written by Arthur Johnston and Sam Coslow, brings sweet nostalgia, regret. "The Lady in Red," by Allie Wrubel, is bright, vivacious, sparkling, and in "Wrap Your Troubles in Dreams," by Harry Barris, Ted Koehler, and Billy Moll, Getz captures the dreamy optimism that comes out of sadness. You wouldn't have to wrap your troubles in dreams and dream your troubles away if you didn't have troubles.

All these songs are about loss, and about an at best evanescent reality, and Stan Getz was a poet of loss, right up to that iconic girl walking across a beach in Brazil, looking straight ahead, not at you. Here he gives us loss that you have to dream away, but you never really can. The fading memory of an old flame. The girl who steps out of a dream—she's Lana Turner—and you'll never have her. She'll never really detach from that dream. Even the vivacious, snazzy lady in red: You'll never have her either.

It's amazing how much music this new label called New Jazz recorded in 1949, and how many great musicians recorded for this twenty-year-old kid. Weinstock can't have been paying much in 1949; by most accounts, he *never* paid much. But there was so much music going around, and such a hunger to record. Here's a partial list of the artists who recorded on New Jazz in 1949 alone, in addition to the ones already named:

- Brew Moore
- Clark Terry
- Coleman Hawkins
- Duke Jordan
- Fats Navarro
- J. J. Johnson
- James Moody
- John Lewis
- Kai Winding
- Kenny Dorham
- Max Roach
- Sonny Rollins
- Sonny Stitt
- Wardell Gray

Weinstock also recorded a considerable number of Swedish musicians, because James Moody was over in Sweden at the time. Don Lanphere, forgotten today but an up-and-comer in the 1940s scene, recorded for New Jazz in 1949 with Duke Jordan and Fats Navarro. He would lose his battle to drugs, go back home to the Pacific Northwest, clean up, and become a legend on his home turf. His other claim to fame is that he hosted a basement jam session that was attended by Charlie Parker and Lanphere's then girlfriend, Chan Richardson, who ended up marrying Parker.

The early New Jazz sessions set certain patterns that Weinstock was to follow throughout his career. First, as mentioned, he didn't pay a lot, but jazz has never been the first place you'd go if your goal was raking in the big bucks. Second, he didn't know a lot about producing a record, so he pretty much let the musicians do their thing. This was fine. The Woody Herman musicians had a lot of experience playing together, under a tight taskmaster. The other musicians assembled from the denizens of the Royal Roost or Kenny Clarke's phone book knew each other from the scene. This approach fit with what Weinstock loved about jazz: the jam sessions, the spontaneous creativity. As the years went on, as New Jazz became Prestige, as he gained experience as a producer, and later as he hired other producers and bowed out of the recording aspect of the business, he held to those early principles. He didn't pay for rehearsal time (this also jibed with his principle of not paying a lot of money). He didn't encourage a lot of takes. All of this led to records that have been criticized in later years, by a newer generation that came to put more of a premium on perfection, as being sloppy, careless, slapdash. Others have praised the spontaneity that became a Prestige hallmark. But no one, I think, would want these records unmade, the jazz of this era unrecorded.

Chapter 4

The Birth of the Prestige Label

The first records under the Prestige label were a James Moody session, released in 1949, although New Jazz singles continued to be released until 1951; the first long-playing records released by a Weinstock company, in 1950–51, came out under the New Jazz label (rereleased in short order as Prestige).

The new long-playing record format had been introduced by Columbia in 1948. The records were made from vinyl, which could handle microgrooves, allowing a lot more information to be stored. A ten-inch 78 could hold about three minutes' worth of music, maybe four if you pushed it, but a ten-inch vinyl LP, played at 33 1/3 rpm, would hold ten to fifteen minutes. And at the same time, Columbia also introduced a twelve-inch LP, which could hold up to twenty-one minutes per side.

New Jazz and the other independent labels stuck to the ten-inch format at first; it was not until 1955 that Prestige released its first twelve-inch LP. This may have been due to practical considerations: there often just wasn't enough material for the larger format. The early LP releases, naturally enough, were rereleases of existing sessions. New Jazz started with the most inaccessible/most accessible bookends they had recorded in those early days: Lennie Tristano and Stan Getz. Recording sessions, in the pre-LP days, typically consisted of four tunes—enough for two two-sided 78 records. New Jazz had done one of those sessions with Tristano, and two two-song sessions with Tristano acolytes led by Lee Konitz. That added up to eleven minutes and fifty-seven seconds of Tristano, 13:36 of Konitz: just enough for two sides of a ten-inch record album (so-called because they took the place of an album-sized collection of 78s). The same was true with Stan Getz. One side of the New Jazz LP *Stan Getz, Volume 1* contained the four songs recorded by the "Stan Getz and his Four Brothers" octet; the other had two of the songs from June 21, 1949, by the quartet billed as "Stan Getz Bop Stars" and two from the ballad session of exactly a year later, leaving enough for a *Stan Getz, Volume 2*, which followed shortly.

In between the two Getz LPs was an album by Sonny Stitt and Bud Powell. Powell was the architect of bebop piano, a key figure in shaping the music and central to a number of bebop's seminal recordings. A beating at the hands of police in 1945 led to brain damage and recurring bouts with mental illness, but 1949–50 were years of relative stability and a lot of work with different combinations of musicians, much of it for Blue Note but a fair amount for other labels, including New Jazz/Prestige. Sonny Stitt would go on to amass one of the largest catalogs of any jazz performer, with over one hundred albums issued under his name as leader, but in 1949–50 that was all still ahead of him. He had been on the scene from bebop's early days, drawing attention as the alto saxophone player who sounded the most like Charlie Parker and recording two sessions for Savoy as coleader of a group called the Bebop Boys (which included Powell).

A switch to tenor began his development of a sound and identity all his own. A prison term on a drug-related charge interrupted his progress, so his December 11, 1949, session, with a classic bebop rhythm section of Powell, Curly Russell, and Max Roach, can be said to be his real debut as leader on a jazz recording. A second four-song session with the same group came as the calendar rolled over to a new year that would be the start of a red-letter decade for jazz in toto and Prestige in particular. Those two sessions would comprise the New Jazz album *Sonny Stitt and Bud Powell*. It was New Jazz catalog number 103, and the following year it would be rereleased as Prestige 103, the difference being that between 1950 and 1951, it had occurred to their marketing division (which was Bob Weinstock, still a one-man company) that they could put a picture of Stitt on the album cover. By 1956, when twelve-inch LPs had become the standard and record stores were starting to cut out ten-incher sections, the eight songs with Powell had been augmented by four tracks from an earlier session led by J. J. Johnson, and the album was retitled *Sonny Stitt, Bud Powell, J. J. Johnson*.

Stitt continued to record for Prestige throughout 1950. One session that particularly stands out took place on March 5, as Weinstock assembled a group composed of Stitt on tenor and baritone saxes, Duke Jordan, piano; Tommy Potter bass; and Jo Jones, drums. Bill Massey (trumpet) and Eph Greenlea (trombone) played on two tracks, and the group backed up singer Teddy Williams on two others. And then there was the other saxophone, for what was billed on the album releases as the Battle of the Saxes: Gene Ammons. As a battle, it was more of a love match. The two proved ideally suited to each other, so much so that they returned to the studio together five more times in 1950, and three in 1951. Stitt would go on to record for various different labels but would return to Prestige in the early 1960s to record again with Ammons.

As for Gene "Jug" Ammons, he literally never left; he remained with Prestige, one of the label's most popular artists, for the entire length of his career, and the entire length of the label's career as well—longer, in fact. Weinstock sold Prestige to Fantasy Records in 1972, and after that, it became strictly a reissue label, with the exception of Gene Ammons, who continued to cut and release new music on Prestige until his death in 1974. Ammons was twenty-four when he came to Prestige, but he had already developed a reputation, and done his share of recording. He had recorded with Billy Eckstine and Woody Herman—and with his father, boogie-woogie master Albert Ammons. He had recorded quite a bit under his own name, for Mercury and its jazz subsidiary EmArcy (in 1947), and for Chess and its subsidiaries Cadet and Aristocrat (in 1948–49). He had a bad heroin problem that resulted in two prison stretches, but he was Prestige's most constant talent throughout the label's history.

The March 5 session also broke new ground in that more than the traditional four tunes were recorded. Counting two songs accompanying vocalist Teddy Williams, which were released separately under Williams's name, they recorded eight. So perhaps they were looking ahead toward an album. If so, it was a very tentative look. In fact, when *Gene Ammons vs. Sonny Stitt—Battle of the Saxes* was released in 1951, only four of the March 5 tunes were used, just as if it had been a standard 78 rpm session.

One more interesting fact about the ten-inch *Gene Ammons vs. Sonny Stitt—Battle of the Saxes* LP: it was the first Prestige record to include, on the packaging, their new office address: 754 10th Avenue, NYC, on a stretch of Manhattan real estate that became a central location for a variety of independent labels.

The Birth of the Prestige Label | 21

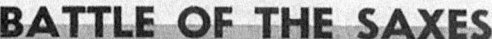

Listening to Prestige:
Gene Ammons and Sonny Stitt, six sessions, 1950–52

Recorded in New York, March 5, 1950, studio unknown

Bill Massey, trumpet; Eph Greenlea, trombone; Gene Ammons, tenor sax; Sonny Stitt, tenor, baritone sax; Duke Jordan, piano; Tommy Potter, bass; Jo Jones, drums

Tracks recorded: Bye Bye; Let It Be; Blues Up and Down (takes 1–3); You Can Depend on Me (takes 1 & 2)

Two classic bebop tenors, playing off a loose structure that gives plenty of room for improvisation, trading lines of unequal length back and forth with casual intricacy that leaves me wondering "how do they do it?" But mostly just appreciating that they're doing it. We know it wasn't rehearsed, because Bob Weinstock didn't allow for rehearsal, and in any case, you couldn't really rehearse that sort of improvisational give and take. I guess you could write a chart; I'll take twelve bars and then you take four and then I'll take four and then you take eight but I'll overlap the last one . . . but I don't think so.

Oh, and maybe I'm not the musical dunce I think I am . . . or maybe I'm not the only one. The reviewer of the Stitt-Ammons sessions on one contemporary web site says "at times, when [Stitt] and Gene Ammons are dueling on tenors, it's difficult to tell the difference between them," whereas another reviewer enthuses about "the contrast between Stitt's swift, complex phrases and Ammons's gruff passion" (how's that for bebop meets R&B?). I'm with the second guy.

Recorded April 26, 1950, same location

Same personnel with Bennie Green replacing Eph Greenlea, Art Blakey replacing Jo Jones, Stitt only on baritone

Tracks recorded: Chabootie; Who Put the Sleeping Pills in Rip Van Winkle's Coffee?; Gravy (as Walkin'); Easy Glide

This is an odd session, particularly as regarding the vocal, if you can call it that, on "Sleeping Pills," where it sounds as though the whole band is singing along, and they're making no attempts at harmonizing or jazz styling; they sound like a bunch of Irishmen in a pub.

If this sounds negative, it is and it isn't, mostly isn't. My guess is that both the Basie-style ensemble playing on "Chabootie" and the novelty "Sleeping Pills" vocal—which really is fun to listen to once you get over the shock—were aimed at jukeboxes. Prestige probably needed some jukebox play—I doubt that they'd had a hit since "Moody's Mood for Love," although they'd put out some great music. George Benson, when he was criticized by jazz purists for his pop records, maintained he was still playing jazz; he said that if he put strong, poppish hooks at the beginning and end, he could play anything he wanted in the middle. And that's true of both of these songs.

"Chabootie" starts out with a lengthy swing-era ensemble chorus, but then Stitt enters with one of Charlie Parker's signature licks, given a new timbre on the baritone sax, and they're off from there, with some absolutely lovely solo work, and some pepper from Blakey. The same is true on "Sleeping Pills"; the solos on that number are definitely not the work of drunken Irishmen.

The Birth of the Prestige Label | 23

Recorded January 16, 1951, in NYC, studio undisclosed

Bill Massey, trumpet; Matthew Gee, trombone; Junior Mance, piano; Ammons; Stitt (on tenor and baritone); Gene Wright, bass; Teddy Stewart, drums

Tracks recorded: Around About One A.M.; Jug; Wow!; Blue and Sentimental

They kept developing the septet sound. There's no arranger listed for this date—presumably it's either Ammons or Stitt, or both—but the arrangements are the best I've heard, and I've been listening to a lot of this band. "Wow!" is my reaction to almost all their ensemble work; it is tight and adventurous. "Jug" does amazing call-and-response work between the soloists and the ensemble, at that breakneck pace that only the top beboppers could handle; and the pace is just as fast, the changes just as tricky, when the ensemble is playing. And don't forget these are Prestige sessions, so Weinstock was paying for no rehearsal time, and precious few retakes.

Recorded January 31, 1951, NYC, studio undisclosed—two sessions

Session one: Stitt (alto); Charlie Bateman, piano; Gene Wright, bass; Art Blakey, drums

Tracks recorded: Liza; Can't We Be Friends; This Can't Be Love

Session two: Massey; Al Outcault, trombone; Stitt (tenor); Ammons (baritone); Bateman; Wright; Blakey.

Tracks recorded: New Blues Up and Down Parts 1 and 2

A 1940s comic strip showed Nancy, as she washed the dishes, muttering to herself that Sluggo was driving her crazy listening to beep-bop. Just then, she dropped a huge armload of dishes on the floor, and Sluggo called out from the next room, "Hey! Play some more of that beep-bop!" So you had to be hip to love "beep-bop," but maybe you needed a little help, too; these guys were as hip as they come, and as good as they come, but also user-friendly.

Recorded August 14, 1951, NYC, studio undisclosed

Stitt (tenor); Clarence Anderson, piano; Earl May, bass; Teddy Stewart, drums

Tracks recorded: Down with It; For the Fat Man; Splinter; Confessin'

One thing I've noticed about all these sessions so far in our Prestige history. We have yet to hear a bass solo, not much solo drum work, and not even all that much in the way of piano solos. I'm guessing these sessions were all done with one mike. Certainly, they were all in mono, and Weinstock was teaching himself how to produce and engineer a recording session; don't forget how young he was when he started Prestige. The Rudy Van Gelder years were yet to come, but this stuff still sounds good, and we're lucky to have it. But for this session, perhaps he figured out a different mike placement, because there are some real piano solos by Clarence Anderson.

Recorded March 24, 1952, NYC, studio undisclosed

John Hunt, Massey, Joe Newman, trumpet; Stitt (tenor); John Houston, piano; Ernie Sheppard, bass; Shadow Wilson, drums; Humberto Morales, timbales

Tracks recorded: Cool Mambo; Sonny Sounds; Blue Mambo; Stitt's It

The mambo craze finds Sonny Stitt, and it's a match made in *cielo*. This is a blazing hot session, and my favorite of it is "Cool Mambo," composed by Bill Massey. Mambo meets bebop, and my only regret is that there isn't a video of a couple of great Latin dancers, or a whole dance floor, dancing to this. Bebop is often considered the antidance music, but you couldn't prove it by this session. It's cool, it's hot, it's frantic, and it doesn't let up.

The Birth of the Prestige Label | 25

Chapter 5

The First Jazz on LP

The first session to have been planned with an LP in mind seems to have featured a twelve-piece band led by Chubby Jackson. They assembled on March 18, 1950, and recorded eight tunes, all of which appeared on the ten-inch *Chubby Jackson and His All Star Band*. It was released in 1950 on New Jazz and in 1951 on the new Prestige label, number 105 in the catalog, following Tristano and Konitz, the two Getzes, and Stitt and Powell. There wasn't anything in the way of album cover art, but it had the logo of the scalloped semicircle with the saxophone and the name of the new record label.

But if it was planned as an LP, that planning was still a little short-sighted. The long-playing record was to revolutionize recorded jazz, as musicians and producers began to realize that jazz improvisers no longer needed to be limited by the three minutes or so that a 78 rpm record—or its trimmer, sexier 45 rpm cousin, also beginning to make its appearance with the new decade—offered. This session was certainly planned with the 78 singles market as its main target, and all eight of the tunes were released as four single records.

Jackson, besides having introduced Billy Bauer to Lennie Tristano, had a creditable career in the field of jazz, and an interesting second career as the host of several Saturday morning kiddie TV shows, but his name has faded into obscurity, and with it, this album, which is a shame, because it really did live up to its all-star band billing. It featured Don Ferrara, Howard McGhee, Al Porcino, trumpet; J.J. Johnson, Kai Winding, trombone;

Charlie Kennedy, alto sax; Georgie Auld, Zoot Sims, tenor sax; Tony Aless, piano; Chubby Jackson, bass, leader; Don Lamond, drums. And one more name, a musician who would ascend to the upper reaches of jazz's Olympus: Gerry Mulligan, baritone sax. If this aggregation had been called the Gerry Mulligan Big Band, might it have earned it more respect? At this stage of his career Mulligan was better known as an arranger than as a saxophone player, and although there's no arranger credit given, several of the tunes certainly bear the Mulligan stamp.

Mulligan, like Stan Getz, was just passing through, and Prestige is not much more than a footnote to his illustrious career. He had done an early session with Kai Winding, who had been part of the nonet with whom Mulligan, Miles Davis, and Gil Evans had begun to forge the cool sound. He brought a ten-piece band into the studio on September 21, 1951, making Prestige the label for his first ever session as leader of his own group. It would be released in 1953 as the *Gerry Mulligan All Stars*. One of the musicians on the date was Gail Madden, maracas, who has her own footnote in jazz history. She was, by some accounts, the person who first suggested to Gerry that he put together a quartet without a piano. And she was—as his girlfriend at the time—the person who suggested they move to California. The rest is history, but not the history of Prestige.

Who was the artist who first went into the studio with the freedom of a long-playing record in mind? For Prestige, it was a young musician who had already broken new ground with a series of recordings for Capitol that no one listened to and who would go on to blaze one new trail after another in a storied career. We will have much more to say about Miles Davis later on. But as Bob Weinstock later recalled in an interview with Michael Jarrett,

> I said, "Miles, we're going to stretch out."
> He said, "You mean we're just going to play?"
> "As long as you want almost—within reason."
> He said, "Okay, who should I use?" "
> "You seem to love Sonny Rollins." If you look at the early ones, Sonny's on a lot of them.
> He asked, "What about this young guy, Jackie McLean? He's pretty good, too, if we're going to stretch out."
> "Yeah, I've heard him," I said. "He's good."
> So Miles and Sonny stretched out. That's how it went.

On October 5, 1951, the lineup was Jackie McLean on alto sax; Sonny Rollins, tenor sax; Walter Bishop, piano; Tommy Potter, bass; Art Blakey, drums. They started off the set with a George Shearing tune, "Conception." When they wrapped it up, it had taken four minutes and three seconds. Could it have fit on a 78? Yeah, just barely. But the second cut, "Out of the Blue," a composition credited to Miles, ran 6:15, and now we were in uncharted territory, a fact noted by Ira Gitler in his liner notes (liner notes on the back of an album were also a fairly new phenomenon):

> This album gives Miles more freedom than he has ever had on record because time limits were not strictly enforced. There is opportunity to build ideas into a definite cumulative effect. These sides sound much more like air-shots than studio recordings.
>
> Upon the wonderful rhythmic foundations of Art Blakey's drums, Tommy Potter's bass, and Walter Bishop's piano, tenorman Sonny Rollins and altoman Jackie McLean are able to enjoy some of the unlimited time for their solo efforts . . .
>
> Here are New Sounds at greater length. Listen to them at great length.

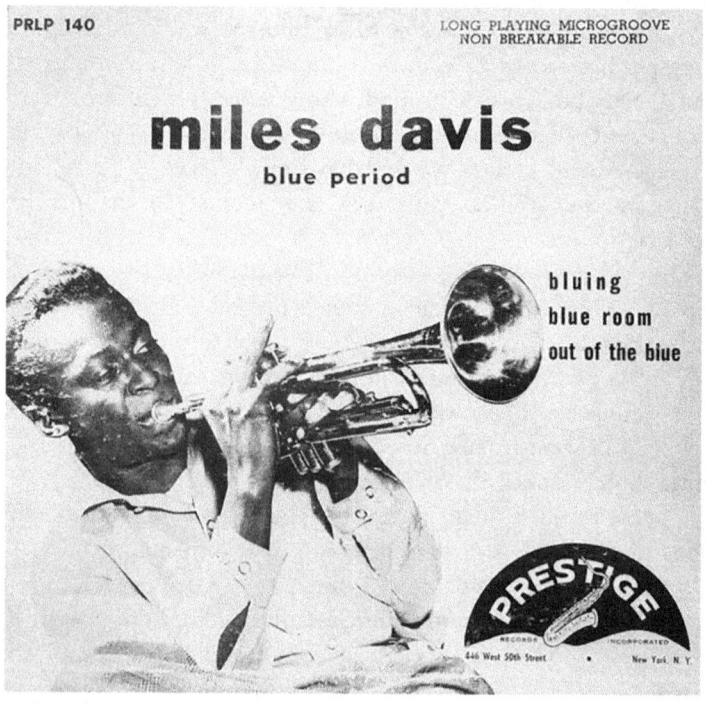

The rest of *The New Sounds* album were two standards, "My Old Flame" (6:36) and "It's Only a Paper Moon" (5:23); and "Dig" (7:33), a tune also credited to Miles but actually written by nineteen-year-old Jackie McLean.

"Out of the Blue" and "Bluing," along with "Blue Room" from an earlier session, were released on a second album, *Blue Period*. "Bluing," at 9:54, took up one whole side of the album, surely a jazz recording first.

> **Listening to Prestige:**
> **Two Early Miles Davis sessions**
>
> Recorded at Apex Studios, NYC, January 17, 1951
>
> Miles Davis Sextet: Miles Davis, trumpet; Bennie Green, trombone; Sonny Rollins, tenor sax; John Lewis, piano; Percy Heath, bass; Roy Haynes, drums
>
> Sonny Rollins Quartet: Rollins; Davis (piano); Heath; Haynes
>
> Tracks recorded: Morpheus; Down; Blue Room (Take 1); Blue Room (Take 2); Whispering
>
> I Know (Sonny Rollins Quartet)

As bebop, according to some, was bopping its last throes at Birdland, Miles Davis was in the studio, doing his bit to help it along. Now, it is not my intention to draw a series of lines in the sand between bebop, hard bop, and cool school. I couldn't if I wanted to, and I wouldn't want to anyway. My belief is that the great strength of the American century in music lay in its blurred lines. The dialogue was ongoing and insistent, the voices sometimes clashing, sometimes harmonizing, but always in the family. In this session, Rollins is playing solidly within the bebop tradition—and so are the others, even John Lewis, who had been with Miles for the *Birth of the Cool* and was shortly to chart his own independent course. But Miles, particularly on "Morpheus," is going very much in the direction he had started to chart with the nonet.

This doesn't make for a mismatch: All these musicians are on the same page, albeit with sometimes different calligraphy. That's the beauty of a small group framework with strong individual soloists: each can add a different voice. And one would be remiss not to comment on the work of yet another important hand on "Morpheus": Roy Haynes.

Even in jazz, where the melody gets left behind quickly for the uncharted roads of improvisation, a good melody matters a whole lot.

"The Blue Room" is a 1926 composition by Rodgers and Hart, most notably recorded before this by the Dorsey Brothers, Benny Goodman, and Perry Como. It is given a new look by Miles, and he makes it achingly beautiful on both takes. He goes back even farther in time for "Whispering," a 1920 composition by Vincent Rose (best known for "Avalon" and "Blueberry Hill"), and brings it beautifully into the modern era, too. The last cut on the January 17 session featured Sonny Rollins as leader, but this will be discussed in detail later.

The Davis tunes were released on two 78s, on an EP, on a couple of ten-inch LPs, a trumpet compilation and one called Miles Davis Blue Period. All of these cuts appeared later on twelve-inch LPs, including "The Blue Room" on a record called Miles Davis and John Coltrane Play Richard Rodgers.

Recorded March 8, 1951, NYC, studio undisclosed

Lee Konitz Sextet

Miles Davis, trumpet; Lee Konitz, alto sax; Sal Mosca, piano; Billy Bauer, guitar; Arnold Fishkin, bass; Max Roach, drums

Tracks recorded: Odjenar; Ezz-thetic; Hibeck; Yesterdays

The guy in the bar in Harlem, or 18th and Vine in Kansas City, putting his nickels into a jukebox was most likely going to be playing Amos Milburn or Louis Jordan—or the Ink Spots or Nat "King" Cole or Mr. B. if his tastes ran smoother—but there'd be nickels for Sonny Stitt and Gene Ammons, too. Jazz was no longer America's popular music, but it was hip and it was hot, and once you got used to the rapid tempi and counterintuitive melodic twists, it sounded good. And today, to the jazz lover at least, that music is mainstream. It remains fresh and inventive, but it's familiar, just like home.

On those same jukeboxes, very few nickels would summon up Lee Konitz and Miles Davis. Over sixty years later, this music still presents a challenge to the ears. Don't forget, while the Birth of the Cool recordings had been made two years earlier, they didn't get widely heard until Capitol released the album in 1958, and even then the music sounded advanced. Don't forget that Miles was not able to keep his nonet together, to get more club dates or recording sessions, because their gig at the Royal Roost had not been a big draw. This session, with Lee Konitz and the Lennie Tristano gang (Sal Mosca playing the Tristano role), is harder to listen to than Birth of the Cool, which sounds mainstream these days. Possibly the difference is no Gerry Mulligan arrangements. Possibly Davis and Konitz, stung by the rejection of what is now generally regarded as their masterpiece, decided to go for an even more intensely challenging experience.

In any case, one has to be fairly certain that Bob Weinstock knew he was not getting a Gene Ammons jukebox toe-tapper when he brought these guys into the studio, so more credit to him. If Weinstock had been looking to make money more than he was looking to make from jazz, he would have been out signing the next Amos Milburn, or maybe some of these new vocal harmony groups like the Clovers that his rival Atlantic was snatching up. Or maybe it came to him in a dream that Miles was shortly to form a quintet with John Coltrane and make music that was advanced and intoxicatingly listenable all at the same time.

Digressing once again, and back to the jazz and race topic, I was thinking about my first experience hearing jazz in a club—the Donald Byrd–Pepper Adams Quintet at Small's Paradise in Harlem—and I started wondering how many other jazz ensembles had been co-led interracially. J. J. and Kai were the first that came to mind; the Thad Jones-Mel Lewis Orchestra; the Clarke-Boland Big Band, if one extends the search to France; Mulligan meets Monk, Mulligan meets Ben Webster. Byrd would also lead a quintet with Phil Woods. And those were all I could think of. My friend Morris Holbrook adds the Art Farmer/Jim Hall Quartet and the Clark Terry/Bob Brookmeyer Quintet. Certainly there has never been a shortage, at least since Benny Goodman broke the color barrier, of groups made up of both Black and white musicians, but not many that I could come up with, with a Black-white coleadership.

This one is under the nominal label of Lee Konitz Sextet, so maybe it shouldn't count either, but certainly Miles is a coequal partner. The tracks from the session have also been released, at varying times, under the Davis name, and allmusic.com lists these recordings as being by the Miles Davis/Lee Konitz Sextet. In fact, Konitz and Davis collaborated a lot; the 1948 nonet sessions are sometimes listed as the Miles Davis/Lee Konitz Nonet, and they also recorded some sides in '48 as the Lee Konitz/Miles Davis Quintet.

Anyway, the music. In my discussion of the Miles Davis Sextet sessions of January 17, I noted that it seemed to me that Miles, although playing on an essentially bebop-oriented session, was introducing something different, something more from the Birth of the Cool tonality. I wasn't exactly sure how to describe that, and I'm still not, but I found this master's thesis online, from Leonardo Camacho Bernal, a student at the University of North Texas (noted for its jazz program). I learned a lot from reading it, and I plan to go back and read more of it. It's called Miles Davis: The Road to Modal Jazz, and it traces the development of the sound that would come to fruition on the Kind of Blue album. Here's what Bernal has to say about Birth of the Cool:

> Most of the bases of the cool style were not common in jazz small ensembles: the classical Western music influence; the instrumentation and orchestration; the fusing of varied tones of the instruments. The influence of classical composers such as Stravinsky and Debussy helped Evans, Mulligan and Lewis, arrangers on this project, to create that sound density and color richness in their arrangements that started to be identified as the sound of the cool style.
>
> Moreover, all the musicians who performed in this project had their particular and personal features, which were extremely important to the creation of a new jazz style. Each had his own tone color, articulation, rhythm, and an individual approach to improvisation. Their playing also featured the plain sound with no vibrato, smoother timbre, and dry tone. Most of the players had been formed by Thornhill's and Herman's bands, and had been influenced by musicians like Young and Tristano, which gave them the perfect tools to start a new style.
>
> On the other hand, Miles Davis came from the best of the bebop school. After being in New York for a while, he started working with Parker's quintet where he was playing trumpet with some of the masterminds that created and developed bebop: the alto saxophonist Charlie Parker and the trumpeter Dizzy Gillespie. They taught him how to approach the virtuosic features of the style. At the same time, Davis was jamming and hanging out with musicians such as Evans, Mulligan, and George Russell, a theorist and composer who started introducing Davis to classical Western music. At that time, Davis's project was the best approximation of cool style. "Davis's nonet was originally seen as the smallest unit capable of reproducing the flavor of Thornhill's big band of the mid-1940s," according to Mark Gridley. This was the starting point for Davis to pull together musicians and concepts to create a new way to play jazz in his quest for new colors, textures, and a new sound.

So, we're not at the modal point yet—that's still a few years away—but we're starting out on the road to it, with a way of combining sounds that's new and groundbreaking. It combines Miles's unique and visionary approach to music—he's not quite twenty-five at this point, but that's well past prodigy age and into his mature period as a jazzman—and the influence of Gil Evans, Lennie Tristano, and the composer of two of the tunes recorded on this session, George Russell. Russell composed "Odjenar" and "Ezz-Thetic," the latter of which became one of Konitz/s signature pieces. Konitz composed "Hi-Beck," and the fourth song, "Yesterdays" (Max Roach sitting this one out) is a Jerome Kern standard.

The interplay between Konitz and Davis is intense, intricate and in a way simple, with one of them taking the sort-of-boppish melody line, and the other playing a somewhat discordant and always compelling harmony. The contributions of Tristano protege Sal Mosca and Billy Bauer are also notable. They may not have been prime jukebox fodder, but they were released on 78 under both the Prestige and New Jazz labels, mixed in with Konitz/Bauer duo sides.

Chapter 6

Wardell Gray, James Moody, and King Pleasure

Three key artists in Prestige's early years helped established the label as an up-and-comer in the jazz world: Wardell Gray, James Moody, and King Pleasure.

Wardell Gray

When remembering some of the significant musicians on Prestige in the first couple of years, it's impossible not to touch on Wardell Gray, who recorded in New York in the label's birth year of 1949, in Detroit's hotbed of jazz in 1950, and then in a few sessions on the West Coast from 1950 to 1953. Among musicians, he was known for his wide-ranging intelligence, able to discuss politics, literature, existentialism. He was a passionate supporter of the NAACP at a time when jazz musicians were not noted for social consciousness. A mentor to younger musicians, he frequently counseled them on the importance of staying away from drugs. But ultimately he was tempted, and quickly fell prey to addiction. He died of an overdose in 1955. Gray's stature in the jazz world can perhaps best be summarized by Benny Goodman's response to him. Goodman had been quite vocal in his rejection of bebop and its practitioners. Then, after hearing Gray, he said, "If Wardell Gray plays bop, it's great. Because he's wonderful." Goodman became a convert to the new music, and even formed his own bebop group around Gray, but soon abandoned it when audiences made it clear that bop was not what they wanted to hear from the King of Swing.

Gray worked regularly in the 1940s, recording most often with Earl Hines, Billy Eckstine, and Woody Herman. He did one session leading a quartet in Los Angeles in 1946, but that went unreleased until after his death. He did one notable 1947 LA session with Charlie Parker for Dial, which included "Relaxin' at Camarillo." Probably his most famous session of those early West Coast years was his duet with Dexter Gordon on "The Chase," which Jack Kerouac waxes rhapsodic over in *On the Road*, and which became the biggest seller in the Dial catalog, outstripping even Parker.

Arriving in New York in 1948, Gray worked with Count Basie and Benny Goodman. Then on November 11, 1949, he got his first chance to record as a leader with Prestige, making one of the most important records of his short and underrecorded career. He led a quartet with Al Haig, piano; Tommy Potter, bass; Roy Haynes, drums. They recorded four songs, one of which was "Twisted," about which we'll have more to say later.

A 1950 touring schedule with Count Basie found him in Detroit, playing at the Blue Bird Inn, a club at the epicenter of a regional scene that produced a staggering number of major jazz talents. Live recordings at the Blue Bird have been lost, but Gray did go into the studio with the club's house band to make his second session for Prestige. It's a major addition to the Gray canon, and a rare opportunity to hear some of Detroit's finest unsung musicians.

Arriving on the West Coast later in 1950, Gray reconnected with Dexter Gordon, who had also recently returned to the area. They produced a recorded jam session in which the two of them were joined by Clark Terry, trumpet; Sonny Criss, alto sax; Jimmy Bunn, piano; Billy Hadnott, bass; Chuck Thompson, drums. They backed up singer Damita Jo on one song that was released on the Xanadu label, then went into two extended jams, "Jazz on Sunset," which was based on "Move," the Denzil Best tune that had been recorded by the Miles Davis–led nonet in the *Birth of the Cool* sessions, and "Kiddo," based on Charlie Parker's "Scrapple from the Apple." These sessions represented a series of firsts for Prestige: It was their first West Coast recording, as Weinstock was just starting to establish a beachhead there, one that he would not hold for long. It also was the label's first live recording, beginning what was not to become a significant trend: there were a few others, but Weinstock, especially after he teamed up with Rudy Van Gelder, seemed to prefer the studio. And it was the first Prestige album to have one tune take up the whole of each side.

There was one more LA session with Gray as leader, held on January 21, 1952, and featuring Art Farmer, trumpet; Hampton Hawes, piano; Harper

Cosby, bass; Lawrence Marable, drums; Robert Collier, congas. It was Farmer's recording debut, and he would later say of Gray, putting into words what so many younger jazz musicians felt: "Wardell was one of the nicest people I ever have known and he was like a big brother to me. He never hesitated to tell me what he felt I needed to know. I can't think of anything about this man as a man or as a musician to find fault with. It's just too bad that he didn't live long enough for the rest of the world to hear him."

In early 1953, Weinstock sent vibraphonist Teddy Charles, a close friend, out to LA to establish a West Coast office for Prestige. As Charles recalled it, "The first thing Bob wanted me to do was record Wardell Gray." There were three sessions with Gray, but these were end times for the erudite saxophonist. There are only a few more scattered recordings before his death.

James Moody

Prestige would become known as one of the most prolific of record labels, in part because Weinstock's no-rehearsal, don't-go-overboard-on-alternate-takes philosophy meant that you could schedule a lot of sessions. In those first few years, he hadn't revved up enough connections or production experience to make a large output possible. He partially filled out the catalog by leasing a number of European records, chiefly from Sweden. The country was producing some quite creditable home-grown talent, including records from the likes of Arne Domnerus and Bengt Halberg, and attracting some first-rate American expatriates, with quite a number of recordings by Swedish groups led by one expatriate in particular: James Moody. Moody was a young tenor sax player who had made one record for Blue Note before choosing the expat life in Europe to get out from under the yoke of American racism.

The early days of bebop were famous for musical and intellectual rigor, very consciously aimed at dispelling the vaudeville and Hollywood stereotype of the shuffling, malaprop-spouting buffoonish darky. But that didn't mean the beboppers were bereft of a sense of humor, and one of the ways it showed up was in the whimsical titles that they gave to their compositions. Some were inside jokes; Charlie Parker's "Relaxin' at Camarillo" conjuring up images of a spa or a seaside resort and not what it actually was: the mental institution to which Parker had been remanded while in California. Others were fond of puns: "A Night on Bop Mountain" or "Flight of the Bopple Bee." Or puns on their names, or the names of friends. Lee Konitz did both, with "Subconscious-Lee" on the one hand, and on the other

"Ezz-thetic," a tribute to the heavyweight champion and skillful amateur jazz bassist Ezzard Charles.

James Moody loved puns on his name: "Moody and Soul," "Just Moody," and "Blue Moody." But when he recorded the song that was to become his signature, and one of the most popular jazz standards of all time, on October 12, 1949, with a group of Swedish musicians, he initially put the pun in the wrong place, calling it "I'm in the Mood for Bop." It was an inspired improvisation, starting with a little descending phrase. Moody would say in an interview years later that he was playing the tune on an unfamiliar instrument, the alto saxophone, and those were just a few notes he had played to try to get the feel of the instrument. They might just as easily have been cut off the final recording. But they weren't, and in 1952, singer Eddie Jefferson was inspired by that little descending riff to put words to it—"There I go, there I go, there I go, there I go, there . . . I . . . go." The lyrics Jefferson wrote to the rest of the Moody improvisation played with the concept of being in the mood for love, improvising around the words the way Moody improvised around the melody. The original recording had a brief piano solo by Thore Swanerud, and Jefferson wrote a second part, a woman's cool commentary on the moody lover's passion, winding it up with Moody's coda, written as "James Moody you can come on in now and you can blow now if you want to . . . we're through."

King Pleasure

Jefferson performed the song in a club where another singer, Clarence "King Pleasure" Beeks, was tending bar. Pleasure liked the song, and asked Jefferson if he could do a version of it. That version was recorded on February 19, 1952. It doesn't appear that Bob Weinstock saw this as a particularly important session. Pleasure recorded only two tunes, enough for one 78. He was backed up by Teacho Wiltshire, a rhythm and blues bandleader who was doing some A&R work for Prestige, with a band made up of equally unknown musicians, and released as "Moody's Mood for Love." Lots of independent record companies came and went in the late '40s and early '50s. It was a new business model, highly speculative. By 1952, Prestige was on the ropes, in danger of going under. They needed a smash hit, and with "Moody's Mood for Love," they had it. It finished the year at number 15 on *Billboard*'s rhythm and blues chart, and is considered a landmark in the style of jazz singing that has come to be known as "vocalese."

Surprisingly, Prestige didn't bring Pleasure back into the studio until December, and with another group of musicians mostly associated with that small group swing music that was in those days relegated to the somewhat disreputable rhythm and blues labels, led by tenor saxophonist Charlie Ferguson. They recorded eight songs, most of which went unissued, except for "Red Top," based on a Gene Ammons solo. Ammons's recording also featured a trumpet solo by Gail Brockman, which was given to a twenty-three-year-old recent émigré from Detroit, Betty Carter, whose previous career had been driving Lionel Hampton crazy by insisting on singing bebop with his traditional swing ensemble. "Red Top" was another hit, placing at number 17 on the *Billboard* year-end chart. The flip side of that record was "Jumpin' with Symphony Sid," Lester Young's tribute to the jazz disc jockey, which has gone on to be considered another classic of vocalese.

When they brought King Pleasure back into the studio, in September of the following year, they had graduated him to the A list of jazz performers: John Lewis, piano; Percy Heath, bass; Kenny Clarke, drums; and a vocal trio led by Dave Lambert, who had recently been asked to do the choral arrangements to a follow-up album to the popular *Charlie Parker with Strings*. The result, *Charlie Parker with Voices*, was universally panned, but Lambert was still a respected vocal arranger, as he would show the world later on with his Lambert, Hendricks, and Ross trio recordings. The new all-star group did a September 29 session that produced two nonhits, "Sometimes I'm Happy" and "This Is Always." But for a Christmas Eve session with just a trio—Lewis, Heath, and Clarke—Pleasure brought in lyrics to a lesser-known Charlie Parker tune. Bird had recorded "Parker's Mood" only once, in a 1948 session for Savoy (with John Lewis on piano). His mood that day had been bluesy and elegiac, and Pleasure brilliantly captured that feeling in his lyric. Released in 1954, when Parker was near the end of his life (he died in March 1955) but still alive and not at all pleased to hear what everyone regarded as an elegy for him, the song was on every jukebox and inescapable. It has become a classic of vocalese, and I for one have asked that it be played at my funeral.

If Weinstock didn't exactly jump on a King Pleasure bandwagon (there would be one more four-song session in December 1954, with a seven-piece band led by Quincy Jones, and vocal backing by Eddie Jefferson and Jon Hendricks), he did take notice enough of the success of "Moody's Mood" to ask a twenty-three-year-old singer he ran into at a party if she could do anything like that. "If he had asked me if I could fly, I would have said yes," Annie Ross would recall later. The niece of Broadway star Ella Logan,

Ross had been a fourteen-year-old prodigy whose composition "Let's Fly" had won a nationwide songwriting contest and been recorded by Johnny Mercer and the Pied Pipers. But now she was at a stalled-out point in her career. She went home that night with a stack of Prestige 78s and found inspiration in two Wardell Gray records, "Farmer's Market" (written by Art Farmer) and "Twisted." These were recorded as part of a four-song session with Teacho Wiltshire (George Wallington played piano on two cuts); Ram Ramirez, organ; Percy Heath, bass; Art Blakey, drums. "Twisted," with its clever sendup of psychoanalysis, has become a jazz standard, recorded by Bette Midler, Amy Winehouse, and many others. Weinstock was not all that interested in vocalese, and Ross went on to other projects. She was part of the vocal ensemble Dave Lambert put together for the ill-fated *Charlie Parker with Voices* album.

Dave Lambert was an early champion of the possibilities of the voice in modern jazz. Another experimenter was singer/lyricist Jon Hendricks, who was already dissatisfied with the conventional chorus-chorus-bridge-chorus structure of most popular songs. He had felt a whole world open up to him at the moment he first heard "Moody's Mood for Love" on a jukebox. The two of them and Ross had worked together once before, on an unreleased 1950 session with Mary Lou Williams. Joining forces again (and recording a version of "Twisted" among other things), they would become the preeminent jazz vocal group of the 1950s.

Weinstock, in the meantime, had moved on. He was recording a lot of new acts, but one in particular—a musician widely regarded as washed up, another casualty of the drug wars: Miles Davis.

Chapter 7

Miles Davis

Miles Davis had come up with the right sound, at the wrong time and place. His new sound, a break from bebop and a new direction in jazz, was worked out in workshops in Gil Evans's basement apartment on 55th Street. It employed new instrumentation, new arrangements, and a whole new approach to jazz. The Davis nonet debuted at the Royal Roost on 52nd Street to a resounding lack of interest. If it could not succeed on 52nd Street, then where? Fifty-second's tiny clubs were the birthplace of modern jazz. But maybe the nonet's sound was a little too modern for the modernists; maybe they were starting to get a bit too comfortable with the conventions of bebop; maybe the hipper-than-hip audiences had become resistant to change.

The recordings that the group made on Capitol had not sold, and Capitol was not interested in anything more from Davis. The newest major label, Capitol had the resources to plug a new sound, the distribution network to get records on the shelves, the clout to get them played on the air. But not these records. The nonet sides were released on 78, then shelved, not to be issued on LP until 1957. The nonet disbanded, and one of its chief architects, Gerry Mulligan, took the sound out to California, where it was reincarnated as "cool jazz" or "West Coast jazz," and found a following.

Davis was disheartened, cut adrift, mired in self-doubt, and, to top it all off, increasingly dependent on heroin. New York had chewed him up and spit him out, and he and his heroin habit drifted to the Midwest. He spent time in his hometown of St. Louis, then in Chicago and in Detroit, which had perhaps the most vibrant progressive jazz scene outside of New York.

He played in clubs when he could get a gig, and when he could borrow a horn, his own having long since been traded for the white powder he could cook up and shoot into his arm. And borrowed horns had a distressing habit of turning up in pawnshops, a reputation that preceded him in one instance. Lars Bjorn and Jim Gallert tell the story in their book *Before Motown: A History of Jazz in Detroit, 1920–1960*: "Davis's desperate straits did indeed lead him to borrow Lonnie Hillyer's trumpet. Hillyer lived in the neighborhood and was only fourteen at the time. Billy Mitchell recalled how Mrs. Hillyer walked up to the stage and took her son's trumpet right out of Davis's mouth. 'If he's such a great trumpet player, how come he does not have his own trumpet?' she announced to the baffled audience." It seemed the only one interested in Miles Davis in 1950 was Bob Weinstock, who recalled in an interview with James Rozzi:

> Miles had vanished after he did those Capitol sides with the Nonet. Nobody knew where he was. Somebody had said that he may be at home in East St. Louis, so while I was in Chicago on business I tracked him down. His father was a dentist, so I knew that his number would be in the phone book. I had met Miles at a Dial session where he recorded with Bird, but he didn't remember me. Anyway, he said if I'd send him money to get to New York, he'd be happy to record. I said that I was interested in doing a series of recordings, and that I wanted to sign him to a contract. He said alright, just get him to New York and we'd talk about it then.

If no one knew where Miles Davis was, no one except Bob Weinstock seemed to want to know. As Davis says in his autobiography, "The critics were beginning to treat me like I was one of the old guys, you know, like I was just a memory—and a bad memory at that—and I was only twenty-six years old in 1952." Davis attributes this, at least in part, to a racial bias prevalent at the time, and while it may seem far-fetched at first to think of racism as dominating this field that we think of as the great contribution of Black culture to the American experience, he's not so far off:

> A lot of white critics kept talking about all these white jazz musicians, imitators of us, like they was some great motherfuckers and everything. Talking about Stan Getz, Dave Brubeck, Kai Winding, Lee Konitz, Lennie Tristano, and Gerry Mulligan like

they was gods or something. And some of them white guys were junkies like we were, but wasn't nobody writing about that like they was writing about us. They didn't start paying attention to white guys being junkies until Stan Getz got busted trying to break into a drugstore to cop some drugs. That shit made the headlines until people forgot and went back to just talking about black musicians being junkies.

Now, I'm not saying here that these guys weren't good musicians, because they were; Gerry, Lee, Stan, Dave, Kai, Lennie, all of them were good musicians. But they didn't start nothing, and they knew it, and they weren't the best at what was being done. What bothered me more than anything was that all the critics were starting to talk about Chet Baker in Gerry Mulligan's band like he was the second coming of Jesus Christ. And him sounding just like me—worse than me even while I was a terrible junkie. Sometimes I found myself wondering if he could really play better than me and Dizzy and Clifford Brown, who was just really coming on to the scene.

What were the critics, and the people who followed those critics, thinking in 1950? The *Down Beat* poll winners for that year, with the two exceptions of Charlie Parker and Oscar Peterson, were all white. Stan Kenton beat out Count Basie and Duke Ellington as bandleader, Maynard Ferguson topped Davis and Dizzy Gillespie and Harry Edison on trumpet, and so on down the line. And this is not just by chance. According to the book *Race Music: Black Cultures from Bebop to Hip-Hop*, by Guthrie P. Ramsay, *Esquire* Magazine created something of a firestorm in 1943, when it began its Critics' Poll, because it made the unusual move of including Black critics on its panel. Their winners included Louis Armstrong, Coleman Hawkins, Art Tatum, Billie Holiday, and Cootie Williams. They had a fair selection of white winners too, but even so, they were attacked. One publication, *Jazz Record*, accused them of practicing reverse Jim Crow, and added that "the top men for small hot-jazz band work today are predominantly white men!" And Stan Kenton, of all people—he who won far more polls than he probably deserved to—complained that the 1956 *Down Beat* critics' poll had created "a new minority group, white jazz musicians."

The 1956 Readers' Poll was still heavily white, although Kenton was no longer winning. That year there also were separate readers' and critics' polls. In the sax section, the critics chose Benny Carter, Lester Young, and

Harry Carney; the readers went with Paul Desmond, Stan Getz, and Gerry Mulligan. No argument at all with either set of selections, but one can't help but note the difference. At least it's not the *Playboy* jazz poll, where Doc Severinsen regularly beat out Miles Davis and Dizzy Gillespie.

In 1950, the only jazz clubs listed in the *New Yorker*'s Goings On About Town section were Eddie Condon's and Jimmy Ryan's, 52nd Street's white Dixieland havens. In January 1951, they included Birdland, but none of the other modern jazz spots like the Royal Roost. They did include the Village Vanguard, but it was not an exclusively jazz spot in those days. Their feature that month profiled arty-folky tenor Richard Dyer-Bennett. Birdland was featuring a Dizzy Gillespie Sextet, a Lester Young quartet, and Dinah Washington, in what their commentator described as "what may be the death throes of bebop." It's hard to figure out exactly what he meant by that, but I'm guessing this was not a forward-looking jazz savant who had heard the Miles Davis Nonet and seen the future. More likely it was the wishful thinking of a moldy fig who would really rather have been in the company of Jimmy Ryan or Eddie Condon, who famously said, referring to one of bebop's more adventurous chordal variations, "We don't flat our fifths—we drink 'em."

It was up to the small independent labels—the small entrepreneurs like Alfred Lion and Bob Weinstock and Orrin Keepnews of Riverside Records, who loved jazz (and who also couldn't afford to compete with the big labels for Benny Goodman and Stan Kenton and Dave Brubeck)—to make sure that Black artists like Thelonious Monk, Art Farmer, Art Blakey, and the nearly forgotten (in 1952) Miles Davis were preserved on record during their peak of creativity.

Davis's career was long and adventurous, with many twists and turns, changes in personnel, changes in musical direction, and complete reinventions. But for many jazz fans, he is most vividly associated with two ensembles so celebrated that they came to be known as The First and Second Great Quintet: John Coltrane–Red Garland–Paul Chambers–Philly Joe Jones; and Wayne Shorter–Herbie Hancock–Ron Carter-Tony Williams. The FGQ became a sextet with the addition of Cannonball Adderley. In a career that spanned five decades, Davis had the Great Quintets for a little over three years each, but they do loom large in the public perception. The FGQ was formed at the end of his Prestige years, and when people think of "Miles Davis on Prestige," they're generally thinking of those recordings. But when Weinstock brought Davis to New York, it was with a different idea: "So, our basic idea was just to make records with different people, to record with the best people around. That's what we did until the end, when he had the quintet. . . . But everything up to that point developed from where we would sit down and talk about it. Miles would mention who was in town, who he would like to record with. I'd say who I'd like to hear him record with. We'd kick ideas around." It's possible that their association was not quite as collaborative as Weinstock remembered it. Davis's recollection of their studio sessions together, in his autobiography, contradicts Weinstock's assertion: "I went over to record my first date as a leader for Prestige. I hired Sonny Rollins, Bennie Green, John Lewis, Percy Heath, and Roy Haynes for the date. Bob Weinstock, the producer, didn't like the idea of my using Sonny because he didn't think he was ready, but I talked him into it and even convinced him that he should give Sonny his own record date, and he did on that same day." Miles added about Weinstock's function in the studio:

> We got along all right, but he always wanted to tell me what to do, how to make *my* records, and so I used to tell him, "I'm the musician and you're the producer, so you just work on the technical side and leave the creative shit to me." When he didn't quite get that, I would just say, "Fuck you, Bob, get the fuck out of here and leave us alone." If I hadn't done that, we wouldn't have had Sonny Rollins, Art Blakey (and later, Trane and Monk) playing the shit they were playing because Bob wanted them to play and record differently than they did for those sessions for Prestige.
>
> Most white record producers just wanted to always make the shit sound whiter, and so in order to keep it black, you had to fight them every step of the way. Bob wanted to do some tired shit, some pseudo-white shit. But he changed after a while—I can say that much for him.

Everyone is the hero of their own story, and the haze of memory may have made Bob Weinstock more of an active creative collaborator with Miles Davis than he really was. But on the other hand, Miles was also inclined to be the hero of his own story, and his grudging acceptance of Weinstock's creative contribution ("But he changed after a while—I can say that much for him") is interesting. His serious complaints about Weinstock have to do with money and his contractual obligations, and those are mostly legitimate ones that every artist had against every independent record label owner in the '40s, '50s, and '60s.

But whoever thought of what, the point is that for the first four years of Davis's time with Prestige, we do find him making music in a variety of situations, with various combinations of the best jazzmen around; this is an extremely valuable, too often overlooked, part of his musical development, and his musical history. We've already discussed a couple of those sessions: Miles with Sonny Rollins and Bennie Green, Miles with Lee Konitz and Billy Bauer.

Davis had come back to New York to change his life and reboot his career, but he'd brought the worst of his life along with him: his heroin addiction. Here he credits Weinstock for taking a chance on him: "Bob Weinstock knew I was a junkie, but he was willing to take a chance that I would eventually come around." Miles went back to the Midwest, to St. Louis, to ask his father for help. His father convinced him to go to the US Narcotic Farm in Lexington, Kentucky, which was a prison that you could be sent to by a judge, but you could also commit yourself to voluntarily. His father drove him to Lexington, but at the last minute Davis balked.

During this second Midwestern retreat, Davis sat in at a local St. Louis club called the Barrel, with a band led by saxophonist Jimmy Forrest. The tapes from a live recording of this session sat on Prestige's shelf for a long time, only to finally be released in 1982, when the label had been sold to Fantasy Records and was only doing reissues. A few online reviews of the album tend to give it short shrift: the recording quality not all that great, the playing competent but uninspired. They couldn't be more wrong.

Not every album is *Kind of Blue*, nor would you expect that. Actually, *Kind of Blue* couldn't have been made at Prestige, with its unrehearsed, jam session philosophy. But Prestige gave us real candid snapshots of the time, and this session is the real thing. This is jazz in 1952, a piece of living history, jazz as it was, and played by working musicians in small clubs in the Midwest, music that came out of the legacy of the territorial bands of the '20s and '30s, the nighttime wail of America that John Clellon Holmes captured so vividly in *The Horn*, still the greatest jazz novel.

Jimmy Forrest had played with Ellington and would later play with Basie, but here he is on his home turf, with hometown musicians—and Miles Davis. Later that year he would write and record his one huge hit, destined to become an enduring rhythm and blues classic: "Night Train," based on a riff by Duke Ellington. Here he's playing bebop, and with

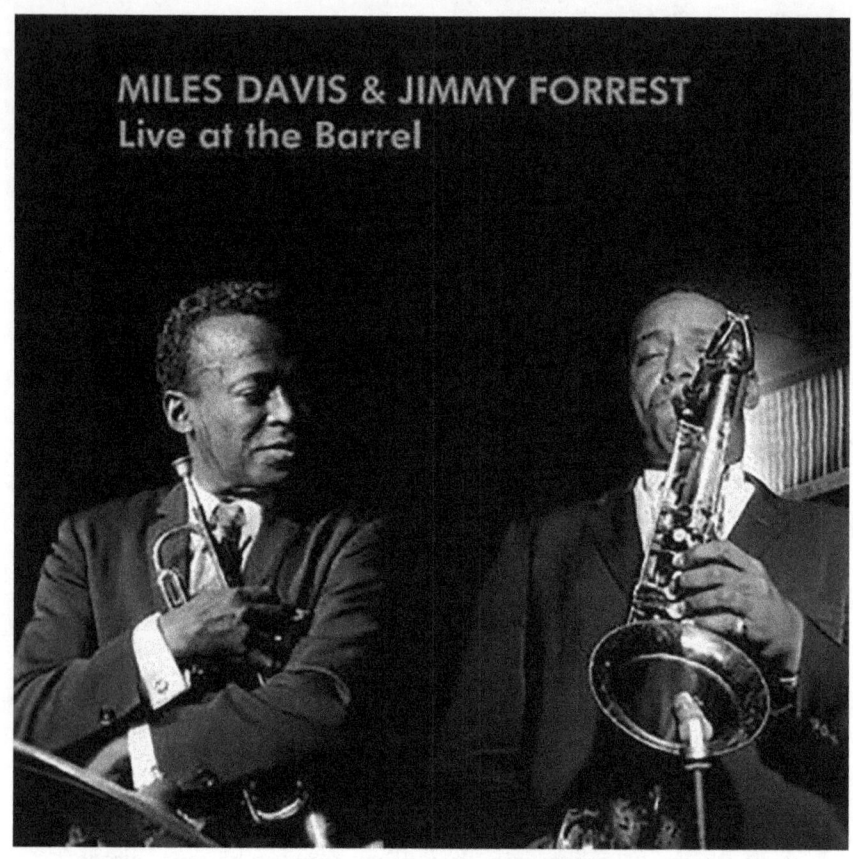

essentially the same guys with whom he would record "Night Train"—the worlds of bebop and rhythm and blues crossing in the American night. Playing easily, but intensely, Jimmy Forrest's gutbucket blues is balanced by Miles's lyricism and originality, not unlike the way Gene Ammons and Sonny Stitt balanced each other. And sometimes they switch over, Forrest getting lyrical and Miles getting down and dirty. Bebop and ballads; a honking rhythm and blues break by Forrest in the middle of J. J. Johnson's supercharged bebop composition "Wee Dot." They're playing in a club, for a club audience, not for a 78 rpm record for the jukeboxes, so they can stretch out: the songs run up to ten minutes. This was no big deal for a 1982 release, but it would have been remarkable if the album had actually been released in 1953.

Early in 1953, Prestige released a ten-inch LP called *Blue Period*, which gathered tunes from two sessions with Miles in 1951. "Blue Room," from January 17, featured Bennie Green, trombone; John Lewis, piano; Percy Heath, bass; Roy Haynes, drums; and "Out of the Blue" and "Bluing," from October 5, with Jackie McLean, alto sax; Sonny Rollins, tenor sax; Walter Bishop, piano; Tommy Potter, bass; Art Blakey, drums. The nonet sessions, while a commercial flop, had resonated with many musicians and at least a few critics, apparently including the anonymous reviewer for *Down Beat*. Davis was experimenting on the *Blue Period* sessions with the sound that was to crystallize in a few years as hard bop, but it wasn't bebop or the new sound that would gradually be identified as "cool," and *Down Beat* was having none of it: "*Blue Period* is the title of this LP, and it was certainly that for us, as we thought back to Miles' great Capitol sides and reflected how sadly that great promise, that exceptional talent, has been betrayed."

Weinstock has told interviewers that he would have loved to start off his new label by recording Charlie Parker and Dizzy Gillespie, but they were committed to other labels. He did finally succeed in getting Parker into the studio in spite of that. On January 30, 1953, Parker agreed to do a session with his onetime protégé, Miles Davis—a session that also included Davis's protégé, Sonny Rollins. It wasn't the smoothest of sessions. Davis recalls:

> It was like having two leaders at the session. Bird treated me like I was his son, or a member of his band. But this was my date and so I had to get him straight. . . . I got so angry with him that I told him off, told him that I had never done that to him on one of his recording sessions. . . . And do you know what that motherfucker said to me? He told me some shit like, "All right, Lily Pons . . . to produce beauty, we must suffer pain—from the oyster comes the pearl." He said that to me in that fucked-up, fake British accent. Then, the motherfucker fell asleep. . . . At this point, I was so fed up that I started packing up my horn to leave when Bird said to me . . . "Ah, come on Miles, let's play some music." And so we played some real good stuff after that.

A February 19, 1953, session may have been another of those Black-white tugs-of-war, as the front line featured Al Cohn, Zoot Sims, and Sonny Truitt, with the resulting album called *Miles Davis Plays the Compositions of Al Cohn*. If it was, Davis didn't dwell on it. In his autobiography, he says: "Bob Weinstock had gotten real upset over what happened on that last album with Bird, so he put together a group of more "respectable" musicians, at least in the studio: guys who wouldn't be getting high and acting the fool. But me and Zoot were the junkies in that band and we got off before we recorded that day. The date was all right in the end, because everybody played pretty well." Davis was content to win a few, lose a few, especially when the ones that he won turned out as problematic as the "Charlie Chan" session did (more about that fiasco later), and the scales seemed more to balance between junkie/respectable than Black/white. In any case, it's a fine album, a good representative of those Prestige years when Weinstock was putting Davis together with different groupings of musicians. Cohn was a first-rate composer, and one of the tunes, "Willie the Wailer," became the basis for Davis and Cannonball Adderley's "Freddie Freeloader" on *Kind of Blue*. However, *Down Beat* still wasn't buying it, and the reviewer still wanted Davis to go back to a style he had left behind: "Prestige has evidently endeavored here to recapture some of the glory that was Capitol's, and Miles', when he last recorded with his own organized band some four years ago. Alas, Al and the guys aren't equal to the task. These are fair swing arrangements with nothing startling to offer in new sounds or new harmonic directions."

A Prestige session on May 19, 1953, is one Davis remembers as successful, although he was still battling addiction: "The record date was with a quartet—me, John Lewis, Max Roach and Percy Heath. . . . I had a chance to stretch out my own playing for this date because I was the main soloist. Plus Charlie Mingus played piano on one tune. Everyone played well on this album." It's notable that this session utilized one half of what was soon to be known as the Modern Jazz Quartet.

Much of 1952 and 1953 was given over to Davis's battle, finally a victorious one, over heroin. He went out to his father's farm in Missouri and went cold turkey. In his autobiography, he describes a week of torture, and "then one day it was over, just like that. Over. Finally over. I felt better, good and pure. I walked outside into the clean, sweet air over to my father's house and when he saw me he had this big smile on his face and we just hugged each other and cried."

He was not quite ready to face New York yet, so he went back to Detroit, where there was an active music scene. There was also heroin, and he discovered that if getting clean had been hard, staying clean was harder. But the old compulsion was fading. He sardonically blames the poor quality of drugs in Detroit—"It was like Philly Joe used to say about some dope—'You could have bought a Hershey bar and saved your money'—because it was cut so much." But chiefly, he credits another influence from a world that always held considerable sway over him: the world of prizefighting:

> I really kicked my habit because of the example of Sugar Ray Robinson. I figured if he could be as disciplined as he was, then I could do it too. . . . He was . . . cleaner than a motherfucker. . . . Sugar Ray looked like a socialite when you would see him in the papers getting out of limousines with fine women on his arms, sharp as a tack. But . . . when he was in the ring, he was serious, all business.
>
> I decided that that was the way I was going to be, serious about taking care of my business and disciplined. It was time for me to go back to New York.

Chapter 8

Thelonious Monk

We've seen how Prestige Records got a pleasant jolt to its bank account from its first hit record, "Moody's Mood for Love." And we've seen that Weinstock did not choose to parlay that profit into going all in on King Pleasure as his next big star. But there was some capital to invest, and Weinstock made the right decision to use that money to increase his roster, signing up musicians who would play significant roles in writing the history of jazz in the 1950s. In 1952–53 these included Wardell Gray, Sonny Stitt, Billy Taylor, Teddy Charles, George Wallington, Art Farmer, Gigi Gryce, Sonny Rollins, the Modern Jazz Quartet . . . and Thelonious Monk.

Monk had spent the waning days of 1951 in prison. Police had arrested him and Bud Powell together. Powell had tried to get rid of a glassine envelope filled with heroin, but had succeeded only in tossing it in Monk's general direction, which meant that Monk was the one booked for possession with intent to sell. Before the charges were dropped, he had spent sixty days on Rikers Island. Alfred Lion had led the drive to raise funds for Monk's bail, and for a lawyer. Monk made one more record for Blue Note, and the label released its second of two ten-inch LP collections of Monk's 78s, titled *The Genius of Modern Music, Vol. 2.*

Bob Weinstock had been won over to the cause of progressive jazz by listening to a Blue Note 78 of Thelonious Monk, so it would seem only natural that the young entrepreneur would want to sign him. But this was not exactly a no-brainer, and certainly not without financial risk. The prospect had to appeal to Monk, who had an infant son and precious few sources of income. Weinstock was known for his enthusiastic marketing of his artists.

But if Monk was considered a genius by Alfred Lion and other jazz cognoscenti—and history has proven them right—the record-buying public had not yet caught up with that assessment. Out of fifty piano players in *Down Beat*'s 1951 jazz poll, Monk ranked . . . nowhere. He didn't make the list. In 1951, Bud Powell was still the giant among bebop pianists. What one might call the mainstream dominated the list, with Oscar Peterson, George Shearing, Errol Garner, and Art Tatum taking four of the top five spots; Lennie Tristano was the token avant-gardist. But the list ran down and down, with some pianists who are still highly regarded, some who are mostly forgotten, and Monk was nowhere to be seen. In 1952, he did a little better, coming into the list at number 41, trailing such jazz luminaries as Liberace at number 33. He was, however, tied with another artist on the brink of recognition: John Lewis.

Monk made his first recording for Prestige on October 15, 1952, with Art Blakey on drums and Gary Mapp on bass. Mapp, whose presence on this and one other Monk session represent his entire discography, was a Barbados native who had settled in Brooklyn, which is where he came to Monk's attention.

One of the risks of signing Thelonious Monk to a recording contract was the limited possibility of Monk's promoting the records. His jail sentence for heroin meant that he could not get a police-issued cabaret card, which meant that he could not play in any New York City club. But that prohibition did not extend to Brooklyn. Actually, it probably did, but no one cared; in 1952, except for the Dodgers, Brooklyn was considered the sticks, and the Manhattan police were not checking up on who played there. So Monk had the occasional gig in Brooklyn. It wasn't enough to enlarge his reputation or increase his potential record-buying audience, but it introduced him to Gary Mapp, whom he liked enough to use for two sessions.

The two 1952 sessions, October 15 and December 18, followed the traditional format of four songs to a session, each of them short enough to fit on one side of a 78, although the album, *Thelonious Monk Trio*, was released at the same time as the 78s. Both sessions featured one standard and three Monk original compositions: "Little Rootie Tootie," "Bye-Ya," and "Monk's Dream" in October; "Trinkle Tinkle," "Bemsha Swing," and "Reflections" in December. The recording was done at Beltone Studios at 1650 Broadway, around the corner from Prestige's offices at 50th Street and Broadway, with a slightly out of tune piano, which, as Robin Kelley says in his biography, *Thelonious Monk: The Life and Times of an American Original*, "no one seemed to notice, except Monk, who decided to milk the bad notes rather than avoid them."

Kelley also gives us the story behind some of Monk's titles, which were often as idiosyncratic as the tunes themselves. Why "Trinkle Tinkle"? Well, that may not have been the title at all. It's possible that Monk called it "Twinkle, Twinkle," and Ira Gitler, producing the session, wrote it down wrong, and Monk decided to stay with the misheard title. "Bemsha Swing," which doesn't seem to mean anything, may also have been a mistranscription, in this case from "Bimsha," which also doesn't mean anything—unless you happen to be from Barbados, which Gary Mapp was, and so was the tune's cocomposer, Denzil Best, a drummer and fine composer in his own right. ("Move," from the Miles Davis *Birth of the Cool* sessions, is his.) Kelley explains that " 'Bimsha,' to a Barbadian, is the phonetic pronunciation of 'Bimshire,' and Barbados's nickname was 'Little Bimshire.' " Bimsha, Bemsha, or Bimshire, Bob Weinstock didn't like the tune at first, but Ira Gitler did, and he persuaded Weinstock to leave it on the record. The title of "Bye-Ya" was originally offered as "Go" by Weinstock, who then decided that a Spanish title would be better; he asked for a translation of "Go," and misheard it as "Bye-Ya."

Monk would spend only three years with Prestige, but during that time he debuted many of his most enduring compositions. In addition to these cuts, there were "Let's Call This," "Think of One," "We See," and "Blue Monk" (probably his most covered tune next to "Round Midnight," and the tune that Monk himself recorded most often). It should be noted that in these years there was no great respect for Monk as a composer. Today, he is considered in the first rank of jazz composers, with most lists putting him second only to Duke Ellington. But such was not always the case. Robin Kelley quotes Barry Ulanov, reviewing the album *Thelonious Monk Trio* in *Metronome*: "[Monk is] as monotonous a composer as ever . . . rooting, tooting, trinkling, tinkling and rarely emerging from a boppist Impressionist morass." So some credit has to be given to Blue Note, Prestige, and, later, Riverside, the label Monk went to after Prestige, for sticking with him as a composer. And it should also be noted that Prestige did not take, or even share, the publishing rights to Monk's compositions; they remained with him.

Soprano saxophonist Steve Lacy recorded an album of Monk's compositions in 1956, one of the first albums ever devoted to the work of a single jazz composer. But he was very much in the vanguard. One number on Lacy's album is "Reflections," certainly a challenging tune—Gary Giddins has described it as "classic, paradoxical Monk, beautiful and memorable yet a minefield of odd intervals, each essential to its bricks-and-mortar structure"—but is often held up as one of Monk's most beautiful melodies. It has been recorded over 150 times. It has even had lyrics set to it by Jon

Hendricks, for a recording by Carmen McRae, which has been covered several times. But during the 1950s, in addition to Lacy's recording, it was recorded only by J. J. Johnson and Kai Winding, and Sonny Rollins recorded it with Monk for Blue Note, and that was it. The next recording of "Reflections" came twenty years later, by Roland Hanna and George Mraz. Chick Corea recorded it in 1982, and only then did it become a standard. "Think of One" was recorded for the 1954 album *Thelonious Monk Quintet—Blows for LP Featuring Sonny Rollins* and then untouched by an American jazz artist until Chick Corea in 1982 devoted one half of a double album to Monk's music. Since then it has been recorded more than 80 times.

By the end of 1953, it was clear that the LP was here to stay, and, more than that, it was clear that it was the best format for jazz. The first long-playing records had been classical to accommodate longer works like symphonies. But jazz had changed in the 1940s. At late-night jam sessions at Minton's Playhouse in Harlem, the nightclubs on 52nd Street in New York, and clubs like the Blue Bird Inn in Detroit, the new jazz musicians were developing complex ideas with solos building on one another, with extended improvisations that couldn't be contained in three minutes.

Monk returned to the studio on November 13, 1953, to record a new album for Prestige at the WOR studio at Broadway and 40th Street, which had a superior piano to the one at Beltone. He had Sonny Rollins on tenor sax for the session, and he had planned to use trumpeter Ray Copeland. But Copeland came down with the flu, and French horn player Julius Watkins was called in to substitute at the last minute.

Watkins was a classically trained musician, but his race had kept him out of the major symphony orchestras, and he had found a home in the jazz world, first as a trumpet player, and then with his favored French horn. He had been part of the Miles Davis nonet sessions and the Royal Roost gig (although not part of the group that recorded), and recorded with Kenny Clarke, and Milt Jackson. He had even played rhythm and blues on the French horn, backing up H-Bomb Ferguson.

Percy Heath was the bass player, and on drums, Monk chose an unknown, Willie Jones, one of his Brooklyn connections. Jones held his own, and he would later be tapped to record with groups led by Elmo Hope and Charles Mingus. He even replaced Max Roach in Mingus's group for one set at the New York club Basin Street East, a gig that was part of a live recording.

Monk had carte blanche to stretch out and play as long as the tune required it. This was to be an LP session, for an LP record. "Let's Call

This" came in at 5:08, "Think of One" at 5:47, and "Friday the Thirteenth" was 10:32, an entire side of a ten-inch album. And that wasn't just Monk luxuriating in his newfound freedom from the strictures of 78. Both Monk and Rollins had been late for the session, and Julius Watkins had to be quickly brought up to speed. As they started in on "Friday the Thirteenth" (improvised on the spot, and named for the bad-luck-omen day of the recording) they were running out of studio time, and there would be no way they could get another number in. As Robin Kelley recounts it:

> Because it was the last song of the day and Gitler needed more material to fill out an LP, he kept gesturing to the band to keep going. "There I was in the control booth, giving signs, holding up a cardboard sign telling them not to stop. It got to be pretty

comical." The song exceeds ten minutes. Still, both Rollins and Watkins turn in wonderful explorations on their instruments, but ultimately it is Willie Jones who saves the day. The dynamic interchange between Jones and the rest of the band, especially toward the end, confirmed Monk's choice.

The album's title, *The Thelonious Monk Quintet Blows for LP,* reflected this new concept in the creation of a jazz record. Later, when that novelty had worn off, the CD reissue included two Monk sessions and was simply called *Thelonious Monk with Sonny Rollins and Frank Foster.* In 1954, two of the tracks from this session, "Let's Call This" and "Think of One," were issued as two sides of another new format, the 45 rpm EP (for Extended Play). While jazz recordings that were thought to have jukebox possibilities continued to be released on 45, the EP never really caught on as a jazz sales medium. The record-purchasing world was dividing into two groups. Single records were popular music. The 78 rpm record quickly became a dinosaur, and the 45 became the vehicle of choice for that new music called rock and roll and that new demographic, the postwar teen market. LPs were for grownups, and jazz was music for grownups, especially young grownups, a group that would increasingly include college students.

Chapter 9

Enter Rudy Van Gelder and Recording More Monk

There's one figure who was as important in the history of recorded jazz as Monk, Miles, or anyone who ever picked up an instrument, although he played no instrument himself. His story begins with an avant-garde composer-pianist named Gil Mellé, who brought a demo to Alfred Lion and Blue Note. Lion was not interested, at least not right away, in Melle's music, but he had a burning question: *Where did you record this?* It had a sound like nothing Lion had ever heard.

The answer was Hackensack, New Jersey, in the home studio of an optometrist and part-time recording engineer named Rudy Van Gelder.

Rudy Van Gelder can be said to be the first person to take the craft of recording modern jazz seriously. He made it clear from the start that he was not a producer, he was a recording engineer. He didn't choose the musicians or select the tunes or run the rehearsals (well, this was Prestige, so there were no rehearsals). His job—a job he invented for himself—was to make musicians sound on record the way they sounded in the studio. He worked with the musicians to get the sound that they wanted. Van Gelder had begun engineering sessions for Blue Note the year before. By the end of the decade, he would be the go-to guy for every independent jazz label.

Van Gelder first became interested in sound recording at the age of seven, when he acquired a $2.98 home recording machine. From there, he began tinkering, improving, making his own recording devices. He went to school for optometry, and began his practice in 1942, at the age of eighteen. All through the '50s, as he was becoming the most acclaimed sound engineer in the business, he continued to support himself as an optometrist. But his heart was always with sound recording. By 1946, he was already recording local musicians, and when his parents were building a new house in Hackensack, New Jersey, he asked his father if they would include a living room that would double as a recording studio.

I'm trying to picture asking my father to do something like that. In the first place, I can hear him saying "Look, you're finally making something of yourself as an optometrist. It's a living. Stick to that." In the second place, a living room is a fairly important part of most people's houses, and it's generally built around entertaining, displaying tchotchkes, and generally being a space that the neighbors would admire. But as Van Gelder remembers it, in an interview with Marc Myers of JazzWax,

> When my father was having the blueprints done, I asked him if I could have a control room with a double glass window next to the living room. I wanted to perfect the techniques of contemporary music recording.
>
> **JW:** How many months of begging did it take?
>
> **RVG:** None. My father agreed immediately. He knew how passionate I was about the music and the process of recording. Passion mattered to both my father and mother.
>
> **JW:** What did you tell your father—or the architect?
>
> **RVG:** I asked that the living room be as large a space as possible, within the footprint of the house. My father's architect decided to accomplish this by making the living room ceiling higher than the rest of the house, which made for great acoustics.

Rudy Van Gelder's parents are the unsung heroes of jazz.

Exactly what Van Gelder did to capture the essence of a musician's sound was his secret, and pretty much remains his secret today. It's said that he would put dummy mikes up around his studio, so that no one ever knew exactly which mikes were live for a recording. He was the first to use a German-made Neumann condenser microphone, which had a sensitivity that enabled the capturing of subtleties of sound.

Enter Rudy Van Gelder and Recording More Monk | 57

Listening to Prestige:
James Moody in the Van Gelder Studio

James Moody's Moods

Recorded at Van Gelder Studio, Hackensack, NJ, January 8, 1954

*Dave Burns, trumpet; William Shepherd, trombone;
James Moody, tenor, alto sax; Pee Wee Moore, baritone sax;
Sadik Hakim, piano; John Lathan, bass; Joe Harris, drums;
Eddie Jefferson, vocal*

*Tracks recorded: I'm Gone; 100 Years from Today;
Keepin' Up with Jonesey; Workshop*

James Moody was back in America, ready to begin to make his mark as a leader, to begin a career that would last six decades and establish him as one of the giants of American music. He entered the studio with a septet composed mostly of bandmates from the Dizzy Gillespie big band, who were joined on one cut by Eddie Jefferson, who had written the vocalese interpretation of his solo on "I'm in the Mood for Love" that was to bring fame to both Moody and King Pleasure. But more than anything that happened in front of the mike, this session is notable, even historic, for what was happening on the other side of the mike: This was the first Prestige recording session to be engineered by Rudy Van Gelder.

Van Gelder's close-miking of individual instruments allowed him to create better separation between instruments, and to tailor the sound to the needs of each instrument. Beyond that, he used newer techniques of equalization and compression to get just the sound he wanted to hear. With the new developments in hi-fi sound equipment that were being pioneered in the 1950s, Van Gelder's signature sound added an enriching experience for listeners to Blue Note and Prestige records.

Van Gelder would record nearly all of Prestige's sessions from this point forward. Nat Hentoff commented, when reviewing one of Miles Davis's first ventures out to Hackensack, "Prestige has recently been recording at Rudy Van Gelder's in New Jersey and using better material in its pressing. Believe me, the difference is enjoyably noticeable."

When Van Gelder moved to the cathedral-like studio he built in Englewood Cliffs, New Jersey, in 1959, he finally had the studio of his dreams. He would continue working into the twenty-first century. He died in 2016 at the age of ninety-two, and in 2022 his studio was added to the National Registry of Historic Places.

> **Listening to Prestige:**
> **Thelonious Monk with Sonny Rollins and Frank Foster**
>
> *Recorded at Van Gelder Studio, Hackensack, NJ, May 11, 1954*
>
> *Ray Copeland, trumpet; Frank Foster, tenor sax; Thelonious Monk, piano; Curly Russell, bass; Art Blakey, drums*
>
> *Tracks recorded: We See; Smoke Gets in Your Eyes; Locomotive; Hackensack*
>
> Perhaps the only thing better than listening to Thelonious Monk is listening to Monk play with someone who really gets him, who is in perfect harmony with Monk's moods, Monk's ideas, and Monk's tempi. That's why it's such a moment of pure satisfaction to hear the tenor sax take his solo at around 2:20 of "We See," and realize that yes, yes, he's got it, and he gets Monk.
>
> And sometimes you listen to the music before you read the set notes, and then you go back to check the personnel, and the identity of Monk's soulmate both surprises and delights you.
>
> If there's any musician who is inextricably connected with one bandleader, it would be Frank Foster and Count Basie. Foster played with a variety of musicians who encompassed a variety of styles, but it's hard to think of him without thinking of Basie. He joined the Count in 1953, the year before this session with Monk, and his final bow as leader of the Count Basie Orchestra came in 1995. But listen to him here, especially on "We See," which may be my favorite, by a close margin, of four great cuts. Foster and Ray Copeland play the head in a jaunty fashion: swing filtered through Monk. Monk takes an extended solo, with some powerful assistance by Art Blakey and Curly Russell, and then close to two and a half minutes in, Foster hits with his solo, and there's no way to miss being struck by how right it is. Ray Copeland follows—and he's right, too—and then Foster again.

> I also should say something about Copeland. He was one of the unsung but in-demand sidemen of this era, and later a valued jazz educator before his early death in 1984. He had played with Monk before, and was supposed to be on the earlier Prestige date with Sonny Rollins and Julius Watkins.
>
> I love to hear Monk's originals—he's one of the greatest jazz composers—and I love to hear him play standards. "Smoke Gets in Your Eyes" has it all: great work with the melody, great ensemble work, completely unexpected and always appropriate piano work from Monk, beautiful solos by the others. "Locomotive" builds off a "Now's the Time"–reminiscent riff. "Hackensack" is a tribute to sound engineer Rudy Van Gelder's hometown; it has a blistering solo by Copeland, and a wonderfully creative solo by Blakey. Van Gelder comes through on this entire session, making every instrument clear and vivid (you really get a sense of how good Curly Russell is).
>
> But finally, the lasting impression from these four tunes is that, for all Monk's deserved reputation as an eccentric genius and iconoclast, he was one hell of a bandleader: these arrangements, the unison parts, the way Monk counterpoints the unison parts, the way he sets up the others for their solos . . . just listen.

Studying Thelonious Monk's career with Prestige is constantly having to remind ourselves that these albums, revered now as major works, important milestones in the legacy of one of one of America's greatest composers and a pianist of rare originality, were not highly regarded at the time. The May 11 session, released on a Prestige 10-inch LP as *Thelonious Monk Quintet*, was dismissed by Barry Ulanov in *Metronome* as "dull" and "monotonous." Its release, to no fanfare at all, was followed by Monk's trip to France. Even in Europe, famously hospitable to American jazz musicians, no one had heard of Monk, and no one knew quite what to make of his music, especially since the French musicians lined up to accompany him could not follow him at all. The trip was far from being a total loss, in that he acquired the friendship and patronage of the Baroness Pannonica de Koenigswarter. But it was not what he had hoped for.

Back in New York, Weinstock had not given up on him, and he was back in the Van Gelder studio in Hackensack on September 22, 1954, recording with a dream trio: Percy Heath and Art Blakey. The four tunes recorded that day included three Monk originals: "Work," "Nutty," and "Blue Monk." All three of these are significant compositions that have become jazz standards.

But that did not happen right away. "Blue Monk" quickly entered the repertoire of many jazz musicians, and it has been recorded well over three hundred times. With lyrics added by Abbey Lincoln in 1961, it became a standard for jazz singers as well. But it was the exception. "Work" has been recorded over fifty times, but it was virtually ignored for three decades. Steve Lacy, one of the first to recognize Monk's genius as a composer and the first to record a whole album of his music, included "Work" on his 1958 Prestige album. Japanese musicians Kazuo Yashiro and Sadao Watanabe recorded it in 1976, and then nothing at all until 1984, and that was a real outlier: not an American jazz musician, not a Japanese jazz musician, not a jazz musician at all, but two British rock guitarists, Chris Spedding and Peter Frampton. This was for a Monk tribute album, *That's the Way I Feel Now*, and it's an oddity—Thelonious Monk meets Link Wray—but it's pretty damn good. It actually took until the mid-'80s for people to really start looking into the Monk catalog. "Nutty" has also been recorded close to fifty times, but only three of them before 1984.

Down Beat gave the album four stars, and called it "Monk's best album to date," but they still were not won over by him as a composer, calling the three originals "intriguing but underdeveloped as usual."

Monk was back in the studio a month later. It was scheduled as a Sonny Rollins date, with Monk, bebop veteran Tommy Potter on bass, and Arthur Taylor, one of the musicians Rollins had grown up with in Harlem, on drums. They recorded three standards, "I Want to Be Happy," "The Way You Look Tonight," and "More Than You Know." A second sideman date, this one with Miles Davis, finished up the year on Christmas Eve, 1954, with Milt Jackson, Percy Heath, and Kenny Clarke: three fourths of the Modern Jazz Quartet. It was the only commercial recording that Monk and Davis ever made together, and it was not without its contentious moments. It had seemed like a good idea at the time. As Weinstock told Michael Jarrett:

> Everybody was down. Miles said, "Man, I need money. It's Christmas. My kid . . ." Monk called me on the phone: "I need money. My kid . . ." Then I got a call from Bags, who always had money, and he said, "I need some bread."

"We'll work something out," I said. So I called Miles: "Listen, why don't we have an all-star session? I want to use you, Monk, and Bags." Bags and Monk played good together.

He said, "I don't know."

"Don't worry," I said. "It's going to be good, and if it's no good, we won't issue it. Everybody just plays—simple stuff."

What could possibly go wrong?

Listening to Prestige: Davis and Monk

Bags Groove

Recorded at Van Gelder Studio, Hackensack, NJ, December 24, 1954

Miles Davis, trumpet; Milt Jackson, vibes; Thelonious Monk, piano; Percy Heath, bass; Kenny Clarke, drums

Tracks recorded: Bags' Groove (takes 1 & 2); Bemsha Swing; Swing Spring; The Man I Love (takes 1 & 2)

This is an all-star's all-star session, and one might wonder why they didn't do it more often, but the wonder seems to be, instead, how they got through it at all. In terms of personality clash, it's one of the great disasters in jazz history. In terms of music, it's magnificent.

The big story that came out of the session was Miles and Monk almost coming to blows. Or so some say. Miles says no. Actually, everyone says no, as far as actual blows being landed.

Monk says, "Miles'd got killed if he hit me." Miles agrees: Monk "was too big and strong for me to even be thinking about fighting." But there was an argument. You can hear part of it on take one of "The Man I Love," at which point Miles may have been a little fed up with Monk. Monk can be heard asking when he should start playing, and Miles breaks in, telling Rudy Van Gelder, "Hey Rudy, put this on the record, man—all of it!" So all of it is there. If Monk's question seems a little odd, it's because Miles had told him, earlier in the session, to lay out—to stop playing during Miles's solo—and Monk had not taken kindly to the suggestion.

But there were no fisticuffs. Ira Gitler, who was there for part of the session but did not produce it, writes, "Things were not serene when I left towards the dinner hour (the session had started somewhere between two and three in the afternoon). Later that night, at Minton's, I saw Kenny Clarke who answered my "How did it go?" with "Miles sure is a beautiful cat," which was his way of saying that despite the obstacles Miles had seen it through and produced something extraordinary and lasting." One of those obstacles is described by drummer Charli Persip in a video interview. Persip had been invited to the session by his mentor, Kenny Clarke, and as he tells it:

> I'm sitting there in heaven. Here I am in the same room with Thelonious Monk and Miles Davis. And Monk . . . there's one spot on one tune where Monk's solo—he started playing ding-da-ding-ding-ding-ding, ding-ding-ding, ding-da-ding-ding-ding—what happened was, he had a beer, and he knocked it over on the floor, and he was trying to get that beer up before Rudy Van Gelder would see it, because he knew there'd be hell to pay, so he's fumbling around down there trying to get the bottle to stop it from leaking on the rug, and at the same time he was still playing the solo! And after, to keep Rudy off of him—Rudy came in with a rag, and he was fussing and carrying on, but he wasn't really too upset, because it wasn't his equipment, it was just the rug. But Monk wanted to impose his will on Rudy, so every time Miles would start playing, he'd stand up and look stupid, just look off into space. . . . Everybody broke up, every time he did it.

Persip probably meant that Monk wanted to impose his will on Miles. Persip's description of what happened next is hard to understand, but basically Miles told Monk to cut it out, which is probably why, by the time they got to "The Man I Love," Miles told Rudy to leave everything in. And once again, one has to tip one's hat in gratitude to Mr. and Mrs. Van Gelder, who no doubt had to deal with the beer stains on their living room rug.

The session itself . . . what more can you say than that it's great? And, fortunately, take one of "Bags' Groove" was preserved, so we hear Monk's beer solo. And one could say that this shows you could get away with anything in bebop . . . but it's actually a wonderful solo: a little strange, but musical. And reaching up from the floor, scrambling around for his beer, Monk still swings. And appropriately enough, Bags finds the groove and adds some appropriate fills.

This is the only studio album Miles and Monk ever made together, and it may help to explain why the Columbia album *Miles and Monk at Newport* actually features the two cats leading two different groups, in two different years.

Davis's ad-libbed instruction to Van Gelder is, incidentally, an example of what was, as Lewis Porter points out, something of an innovation in the history of recorded music. No one had ever included little snippets of conversation between musicians at a session. Porter says:

> This way, instead of aiming for a polished gem, one could let the audience in on the process of recording. It appears to be Coltrane who says, "Can I have the beer opener?" after "Woody 'n You." The most famous one begins "If I Were a Bell," when Davis, apparently in response to Van Gelder's request for the title of the next piece, says "I'll play it and tell you what it is later." Weinstock recalls, "this started because of Rudy Van Gelder. I always used to edit with him, and we'd hear that and he'd say, 'Why don't you leave it in? It's historic hearing those guys say a few words.' You're supposed to be quiet for about 20 seconds after each take, in order to get a clean edit, but if someone talked we decided to leave it in."

If Monk came away from the session with a grudge, it might not have been against Davis. This was the second date he had been called upon to play as a sideman, with no scheduled albums as leader on the horizon. Further, as Kelley points out,

> Weinstock had no intention of including any of Monk's tunes on the date. He was the best known composer in the room, and the exclusion of his songs was insulting, especially in an all-star session. Composer's royalties were at stake and Monk needed the money. Ira Gitler was in the studio and . . . came to Monk's defense, persuading Weinstock to include at least one of his compositions on the playlist. Ironically, Monk suggested "Bemsha Swing," the song Weinstock resisted at one of Monk's recording sessions two years earlier.

Davis and the Modern Jazz Quartet were the label's rising stars. Monk was, as always, severely strapped for money. Prestige didn't pay much, but the recording dates were his only source of income, since the loss of the cabaret card meant no Manhattan club bookings. As meager a living as making records for Prestige might be, working as a sideman on someone else's record was even more so. Monk was ready to move on, and Orrin Keepnews and Bill Grauer of Riverside, fans of his music, were glad to have him. Monk owed Prestige $108.27 for an advance he had been given; Keepnews and Grauer advanced him the money to pay off his debt, and Monk moved on.

Monk spent six years with Riverside, during which time recognition began to accrue. In 1962, he signed with Columbia, moving up to a major label. In 1963, the *Down Beat* Readers Poll voted him into the *Down Beat* Hall of Fame, and in 1964 he appeared on the cover of *Time* magazine. In 1973, when Monk had essentially retired from the music scene, Columbia released an album called *Monk's Greatest Hits,* so at least some of his compositions were sufficiently recognized that Columbia saw fit to promote them in a "Greatest Hits" package. But musician/critic Michael Zwerin, writing the liner notes, seemed a little desperate to make Monk "relevant."

He begins with his daughter overhearing a Monk record he's put on the turntable. He explains to her who Monk is, and then: "After my little lecture, we listened for a while, quiet. Then Amy said, 'This might be a dumb thing to say, but he reminds me of Tim Hardin . . . or at least I get the same feeling from both of them. It's such dreamy music, so sexy' . . . I kissed her and told her it wasn't dumb at all and we spent the whole day listening to Tim Hardin and Thelonious Monk."

"So dreamy . . . so sexy," even if it's in the context of Tim Hardin, is a long way from "monotonous a composer as ever . . . rooting, tooting, trinkling, tinkling."

Chapter 10

The Modern Jazz Quartet

John Lewis first recorded for Prestige in 1949, as a member of J. J. Johnson's Boppers, along with Kenny Dorham, Sonny Rollins, Leonard Gaskin, and Max Roach, so he could certainly claim the distinction of card-carrying bebopper. The following year, he would be back in the Prestige studio with Zoot Sims, and again in 1951 with Miles Davis. His work with Charlie Parker included the memorable piano lick at the beginning of "Parker's Mood," which he would later reprise on King Pleasure's vocal rendition of the same tune on a Prestige recording. He would also work frequently with Dizzy Gillespie, so his credentials as a key figure in the creation and development of bebop are impeccable.

But even before the end of the decade that birthed bebop, Lewis was looking beyond it. He had been part of the group that gathered with Miles Davis in Gil Evans's West 55th Street basement apartment to work out the sound that Davis—with Lewis—brought to the Royal Roost on 52nd Street, and later recorded for Capitol in the historic *Birth of the Cool* sessions. That nonet was to spawn some of the most striking digressions from the musical genre pioneered by Parker and Gillespie: Davis's experiments with modal jazz would culminate in *Kind of Blue*; Gerry Mulligan brought the nonet's "cool" sound to the West Coast; and Gil Evans's orchestrations were realized through collaboration with Davis.

Lewis, who arranged "Move" and "Rouge" for the nonet, had his own ideas about a new direction for jazz. He was dissatisfied with the loose formula of head-solo-solo-head, or melodic theme–series of solo improvisations–restatement of theme. It allowed for great creativity, but maybe it wasn't challenging enough. And Lewis wondered if it was the best way to reach an audience. He told Nat Hentoff, in an interview for *Down Beat,* "If solos go on for chorus after chorus, it's hard enough for the musician to remember what he's constructing. It must be even more difficult for the listener. . . . The audience for jazz can be widened if we strengthen our work with structure. If there is more of a reason for what's going on, there'll be more overall sense, and, therefore, more interest for the listener."

Others in the jazz world were also becoming concerned that modern jazz was increasingly painting itself into a corner, appealing to an insular audience of urban hipsters, and Lewis certainly wasn't the only jazz musician to want to move jazz in new directions. The transmogrification of bebop into hard bop was an attempt to make the music a little less cerebral while retaining its modern sound. Some musicians, like Dave Brubeck, were reaching out to new audiences, booking themselves into college campuses.

Lewis drew inspiration from modern classical composers, but he was not the only one to have a keen ear for this music. Charlie Parker and Wardell Gray were admirers of Stravinsky. Dexter Gordon's Dale Turner, in *Round Midnight*, surprises his French host by citing Debussy as an influence. George Russell's 1953 book *Lydian Chromatic Concept of Tonal Organization* is clearly not the work of a guy who likes to kick back and jam to the blues; it laid the theoretical groundwork for the modal music that Miles Davis and others were to make later in the decade. But Lewis was a leader in adapting classical ideas, chiefly counterpoint and fugal structure, to jazz instrumentation—and more importantly, adapting them to a jazz sensibility.

Nonetheless, as the 1940s drew to a close and turned over into a new decade, Lewis was the center of Dizzy Gillespie's rhythm section, and it was Gillespie's rhythm section—Lewis, Milt Jackson on vibes, Ray Brown on bass (replaced by Percy Heath, another Gillespie regular, after the first recording session), Kenny Clarke on drums—that came together in August 1951 to record for Gillespie's short-lived Dee Gee label as the MJQ: The Milt Jackson Quartet. And it was the Milt Jackson Quartet that accompanied Charlie Parker at Birdland on November 1, 1952.

That same group—Lewis, Jackson, Heath and Clarke—would come together less than two months later, on December 22, 1952, to record for Prestige, as the Modern Jazz Quartet.

Bob Weinstock's Prestige record label was the first home to many of the giants of 1950s jazz, so perhaps it's not surprising that the Modern Jazz Quartet should be among that number, but in another way perhaps it is. Weinstock, after all, was the youthful entrepreneur whose romantic notion of jazz was formed at Minton's Playhouse and along 52nd Street, who believed in the spontaneity of the jam session and discouraged rehearsal. One might have imagined that John Lewis's concept of a classical fugue–inspired, carefully rehearsed jazz would have been seriously at odds with Weinstock's. And that may not have been so far off the truth. Weinstock was a fan of Jackson's loose, bluesy, improvisational style, and had been eager to bring him into the Prestige fold. He wasn't so crazy about Lewis, and he was in the middle of his mission to revive Miles Davis's career, by placing him with different combinations of the best musicians in town. It's entirely possible that he envisioned the same session-by-session evolution of Jackson. Jackson, however, insisted that Lewis be a part of the new group, which Weinstock, once he agreed to it, wanted to call the New Jazz Quartet.

If he was going to be signing an entire ensemble, why not make it the house band, and give it the name of his original—and still active—label? But the idea was rejected by the newly formed group, and their first ten-inch album, comprising the four tunes from the December session and four more from a session on June 25, 1953, was released in late 1953 as *The Modern Jazz Quartet*. The first session had two standards— "All the Things that You Are" by Jerome Kern, and "Rose of the Rio Grande" by Harry Warren—and two original compositions, "La Ronde" and "Vendôme." Both had French names, reflecting the European classical influence on Lewis's composition, but "La Ronde" had not always been so cosmopolitan. It had begun its life as "Two Bass Hit," composed by Lewis with Dizzy Gillespie for Gillespie's orchestra. Under either title, it's a good piece, and as "Two Bass Hit" it's become a jazz standard.

It was certainly a new kind of music, and it is possible that Weinstock didn't exactly know what to do with it. *The Modern Jazz Quartet* would shortly be rereleased as part of a twelve-inch LP called *Vendôme*, credited to the Modern Jazz Quartet/Milt Jackson Quartet. The big difference between the two groups was the absence of John Lewis in the second one. Horace Silver was at the piano, and the tunes had titles like "Opus de Funk" (written by Silver).

If Weinstock or anyone else had doubts about the Modern Jazz Quartet, they should surely have been erased by the group's next outing, December 3, 1954, now in Rudy Van Gelder's Hackensack studio. On that day they recorded three tunes: Ray Brown and Dizzy Gillespie's "One Bass Hit," a Lewis composition called "Milano," and the centerpiece of the day, Lewis's "Django," a tribute to the recently deceased European guitarist Django

Reinhardt and a composition of extraordinary beauty. They would go back to the Van Gelder Studio on January 9, 1955, to revisit "La Ronde," now moving even farther away from "Two Bass Hit" to become "La Ronde Suite," a four-part piece with each part built around a different member of the quartet.

"Django" was first released in 1955 on a ten-inch LP, *The Modern Jazz Quartet (Volume 2)*. By the end of that year, Prestige had entered the twelve-inch LP market, and "Django" became the title cut of an album that also included both Dizzy Gillespie's "One Bass Hit" and Lewis's "La Ronde Suite," plus his "The Queen's Fancy," "Delauney's Dilemma," and "Milano"; Vernon Duke's "Autumn In New York"; and George Gershwin's "But Not for Me."

Listening to Prestige:
The Modern Jazz Quartet

Recorded at Van Gelder Studio, Hackensack, NJ, January 9, 1955

Milt Jackson, vibes; John Lewis, piano; Percy Heath, bass; Kenny Clarke, drums

Track recorded: La Ronde Suite: Piano / Bass / Vibraharp / Drums

The MJQ was formed in part out of John Lewis's dissatisfaction with the head-solos-head format that had become ubiquitous in bebop, and this recording session, in its own unique way, is a break from that format, in that it's solo-solo-solo-solo.

Well, not exactly. But perhaps Lewis, in his own way, is simultaneously playing tribute to the classic bebop form and standing it on its ear. "La Ronde" in a shorter version was part of an earlier MJQ session. The newly Europeanized title (La Ronde is a fin de siècle play by the Viennese playwright Arthur Schnitzler) is in keeping with the European classical—and particularly Francophile—overlay that Lewis was putting on American bebop.

As "La Ronde," it makes more sense in its extended suite version. The Schnitzler play is a tag team series of sexual encounters, and "La Ronde Suite" is a sort of tag team, as well. It's in four sections, with each section featuring a different member of the group in an extended solo.

Kenny Clarke is the drummer for the "La Ronde Suite," and it was his last recording with the group; by their next session, in July, Connie Kay replaced him.

Most people think of Kay as the quintessential MJQ drummer, and with good reason. He was with them for forty years. He was a perfect ensemble drummer, in a group that emphasized the ensemble sound. Clarke was one of the innovators of bebop drumming, and like his fellow pioneers Max Roach and Art Blakey, he was much more of a soloist. "La Ronde Suite" would have been different without him.

Lewis was well on his way to achieving his goal of expanding the audience for jazz, and he had certainly captured the attention of the jazz audience. In 1953, the MJQ barely registered on the *Down Beat* poll for jazz combos. In 1954, they were second to the Dave Brubeck Quartet, and in 1955, they reigned supreme by a large margin. John Lewis had risen steadily in the composer category (until 1956 called "arranger"): not on the list at all in 1952, fourteenth in 1953, fourth in 1955, and, on the strength of "Django," first in 1956.

There were other factors that contributed to the expanding of the jazz audience in the 1950s. Dave Brubeck had started touring colleges in the early 1950s. He had released *Jazz at Oberlin* and *Jazz at College of the Pacific* on the Fantasy label in 1953, and the best-selling *Jazz Goes to College* on Columbia in 1954. Henry Mancini, with his wildly popular theme from the TV series *Peter Gunn* that began in 1958, contributed to a growing demand for jazz scores for movies and TV. Duke Ellington was commissioned in 1959 to write the score for *Anatomy of a Murder*, and Lewis himself, in the same year, for *Odds Against Tomorrow*. The Newport Jazz Festival, which began in 1954, brought a new audience, and a 1959 documentary film about the festival, *Jazz on a Summer's Day*, was an unexpected hit. *Playboy* magazine, the leading influencer of its day, debuted its jazz poll in 1957. (Brubeck was the winner for jazz combo, with the MJQ second.)

But the Modern Jazz Quartet certainly played their part. With John Lewis's classically inspired compositions, the group's tuxedo-clad stage presentation, and their expanding of venues from small jazz clubs to colleges and concert halls, they were a new force, and a highly marketable one. With this success came detractors. Joe Goldberg, in *Jazz Masters of the 50s*, while not denigrating the MJQ's musical contribution, also characterizes their success as "an example of an astute use of public relations unparalleled in jazz." Goldberg wrote his book in the early 1960s, when critics, audiences, and musicians alike were just beginning to look back at the 1950s, to take stock of the decade and realize how extraordinary it had been in the history of jazz, and to try to put it into perspective. It was also a time when the MJQ were flying high (they were still in the top three in *Down Beat*'s readers poll for combo, behind Brubeck and Oscar Peterson but ahead of Miles Davis and Cannonball Adderley) but were figures of controversy among jazz enthusiasts, and certainly among jazz critics. Goldberg doesn't exactly damn with faint praise, but he skirts the line: "Impeccably attired, with the bearing, manner and appearance of gentlemen in the employ of Schweppes beverages, its members play some of the most eminently respectable music ever to be called jazz. Their records are in the homes of suburbanites who might own nothing else more daring than the songbooks of Ella Fitzgerald. They have played places no jazzmen have ever played before, possibly some that no others will ever play."

The naysayers to the Modern Jazz Quartet had a hero: a hero in chains. Milt Jackson, they said, was a real jazz musician, a funky, bluesy, boppy improviser shackled by a chamber ensemble. Goldberg perhaps sums up this attitude best when he says "Jackson is regarded in several areas as being the musical salvation of the MJQ, and it is less certain that the MJQ has done as much for him." History might offer a different evaluation, as there are many great jazz instrumentalists, but the Modern Jazz Quartet occupies a special place in the annals of jazz, and far more people know of the ensemble than are familiar with the works and careers of any of its individual members.

Lewis answered the critics who said he was straying too far from what jazz was really about, in a 1956 interview with Oberlin College's Jim Neumann when the quartet gave a concert at the school: "Some things are almost completely written out, though things that are completely written out are no longer jazz, I feel. If the improvisation is gone, collective improvisation, then we don't have the thing that makes jazz." The MJQ would make one more recording for Prestige.

Listening to Prestige:
MJQ's Last Prestige Session

Concorde

Recorded at Van Gelder Studio, Hackensack, NJ, July 2, 1955

Milt Jackson, vibes; John Lewis, piano; Percy Heath, bass; Connie Kay, drums

Tracks recorded; Ralph's New Blues; All of You; I'll Remember April; Gershwin Medley: Soon / For You, For Me, Forevermore / Love Walked In / Our Love Is Here to Stay; Concorde; Softly as in a Morning Sunrise

This is the second MJQ album with Connie Kay, and the last for Prestige, before they decamped for their long and fruitful association with Atlantic.

Kenny Clarke had begun to feel a little claustrophobic within the strict confines of the MJQ. One of the pioneers, and one of the most prolific drummers of the bebop era, he was the original house drummer at Minton's, which means he played with everyone. As the modern jazz decade progressed, everyone wanted him, or Max Roach or Art Blakey, to play with them. Clarke might have been able to keep up this prodigious schedule and still make dates with the MJQ, but he was also had mixed feelings about living in America. By 1956, he was a full-time resident of France, where he could make more money and deal with less racism. He played many sessions with visiting American musicians, and led the Clarke-Boland Big Band with Belgian pianist Francy Boland.

Connie Kay had followed Kenny Clarke before he joined the Modern Jazz Quartet; he replaced Clarke as the house drummer at Minton's. Before that, as a teenager, he had worked at a club called Ann's Red Rose in his Bronx neighborhood, getting the gig a week after he had bought his first drum kit. The house drummer for the Red Rose had quit suddenly, and someone at the bar said, "Well, there's a drummer around the corner because I hear him practicing every night as I come home from work." So Kay played for comedians, singers, tap dancers, and chorus girls. He moved from there into the jazz world, playing behind every major figure at Minton's, and also in Lester Young's band for several years.

Kay was also putting his Ann's Red Rose experience to good use as the drummer for various rhythm and blues ensembles, including that of Frank (Floorshow) Culley, who had recorded "Cole Slaw" for Atlantic Records. Culley brought him in to Atlantic in early 1951 to record a demo for the Clovers, who had just signed with the label. The song was "Don't You Know I Love You," and the bass player didn't show up for the session, so Kay had to double his part on the bass drum. He got paid for the gig, and thought no more about until a couple of weeks later, when

> I'm driving my car and hear the tune and I say, "Wait a minute, that sounds like the tune we made a demo of." A week later I went to Atlantic and I went into Ahmet Ertegun's office and he said: "Man, I'm glad to see you. We've been trying to find you. I like the beat you used on that record." From that time on they kept calling me for record dates. When I couldn't make record dates, they'd postpone them.

Supposedly, the "concept album" began with Sergeant Pepper's Lonely Hearts Club Band. Concorde is a concept album in that the concept was that it would be an album. It was the third recording session scheduled by Prestige to produce a full twelve-inch LP's worth of music, with six selections, and over thirty-six minutes' worth of music. It's mostly standards. Perhaps in Lewis's mind, the group already had one foot out the door, so they were saving original material for Atlantic—although in fairness, the MJQ tended to be standard-friendly until later in its career, and their first Atlantic album only had three originals.

Concorde's originals are Jackson's "Ralph's New Blues" and Lewis's title track. I'd wondered if "Ralph's New Blues" was a tribute to Ralph Ellison—I'd sort of hoped it was—but appears to be for jazz critic Ralph J. Gleason, which is pretty good too. It's built on an irresistibly bluesy riff, and is the catchiest number on the record. "Concorde" is another Francophile nod from Lewis, and inspired the Eiffel Tower cover of the album, designed by Bob Parent. It has a richness of tone, a catchy melody, and an up-tempo swing. Lewis and Jackson know how to sustain a note for dramatic effect, and they know how to let loose a torrent of notes. But as always, the MJQ is a quartet, not a leader and sidemen, and you're always aware of the contribution each member is making to the sound.

Nesuhi Ertegun, at home in the concert halls that the Modern Jazz Quartet was gravitating toward, was probably more of a soulmate to John Lewis than Bob Weinstock ever could have been; and Atlantic, its coffers flush with the success of its small group swing sound as the teenage appetite for rock and roll spilled over to rhythm and blues, was able to offer more than Prestige would ever be able to pay. The MJQ moved on.

Chapter 11

Cover Art, and a Dual Role for Esmond Edwards

Not a lot of thought was given to the covers of the first Prestige LPs. Their initial offering, a repackaging of the Lennie Tristano and Lee Konitz 78s, had nothing on it but text. Subsequent covers featured snapshots of the featured performer by Bob Weinstock, with no particular thought given to design. Blue Note, meanwhile, had stolen a march on Prestige by commissioning a brilliant young artist named Paul Bacon, whose drawings had been featured in small jazz magazines, to design and create art for its album covers, and Weinstock could not have failed to notice their impact—or that talented artists could be commissioned cheaply.

The cover art for the Modern Jazz Quartet's first ten-inch recording was created by David X. Young. In two colors, orange and yellow, it had abstract shapes suggesting the keys of a piano, and special typography used as part of the design. It was the work of an artist of some considerable talent. The 1952 release of *New Directions*, by Teddy Charles, signaled a new direction. An artist named Leo Sharper created a Miro-esque abstraction in green and red that was sure to stand out on the record racks.

There were a few more basic snapshot covers, and then in early 1953 Weinstock commissioned David X. Young to do the cover of a Jimmy Raney LP.

Young had come to New York from Boston in the late 1940s and had quickly fallen in with the Greenwich Village crowd of artists and jazz musicians who hung out at places like Bradley's and the Cedar Tavern. His father, a saxophonist with the Bix Beiderbecke orchestra, had committed suicide when his son was only two days old, and David had been raised by his straitlaced, music-hating grandparents.

Young would shortly find a decrepit, roach-infested loft at 821 6th Avenue, in the middle of Manhattan's wholesale flower market district. That unlikely crash pad would become the legendary Jazz Loft, as the florists all closed up shop and there were no neighbors to bother in the evenings and nights—mornings and afternoons on the jazz musician's clock—and gradually every musician in the city found it to be the perfect spot to stop by and jam at all hours. Musician Hall Overton, who shared the space with Young, worked there with Thelonious Monk to score his compositions for orchestra, for a historic Town Hall concert. The legendary *Life* photographer W. Eugene Smith moved in after the dissolution of his marriage, and his photographs and audio tapes have been collected in a documentary, *The Jazz Loft According to W. Eugene Smith*.

Young created many covers for Prestige, setting a high standard for artistic excellence. Other artists who did covers for the label include:

- Gil Mellé, who was a musician as well as a graphic artist. He recorded for both Prestige and Blue Note, then went to Hollywood, where he became noted for the use of self-built electronic instruments for film scores (most famously his award-winning score for *The Andromeda Strain*). His Prestige covers include *Thelonious Monk* (PLP 7027), a black-and-white futuristic abstract drawing against a rough blue background.

- Tom Hannan, an abstract expressionist painter and jazz fan who found a second career creating jazz album covers for Prestige, Blue Note, Columbia, Bethlehem, Jubilee, Roulette, and other labels. His signature look featured abstract shapes and distinctive typography. A characteristic work is *Thelonious Monk—Sonny Rollins* (PLP 7075), a red-and-black abstraction with raw hand-lettered brush-and-ink calligraphy, or the photo of Rollins in silhouette for *Saxophone Colossus* (PLP 7079).

- Don Martin, who would go on to fame with *Mad* magazine as "*Mad*'s maddest artist." Martin may not have been the ideal interpreter of the spirit of modern jazz, but his covers were undeniably unique. *Trombone by Three* (J. J. Johnson, Kai

Winding, Benny Green) (PLP 7023) features three glowering, trombone-wielding ghouls. It's hard not to appreciate it, but one wonders if Johnson, Winding, and Green did.

- Bob Parent, noted jazz photographer whose photo of Charlie Parker with the Thelonious Monk Trio has been called the "greatest photo in jazz history" by *The New York Times* (one wonders if they remembered Art Kane's "A Great Day in Harlem"). Original prints of the photo now fetch over ten thousand dollars. Parent's moody photo of Miles Davis is the memorable cover image of *Dig* (PLP 7012).

- Photographer Reid Miles, one of the most influential jazz album cover designers, is considered the principal auteur of the Blue Note style, but he also did some work for Prestige, including *Conception* (PLP 7013, tracks by Lee Konitz, Stan Getz, Miles Davis, and Gerry Mulligan), a black-and-gray abstraction with shapes suggesting handcuffs. Miles reportedly hated jazz, and would never listen to the albums for which he designed memorable covers, relying on Alfred Lion or Bob Weinstock to give him a sense of the music in a few words.

- Richard "Prophet" Jennings, primarily a journalist for several African American publications, took up painting while convalescing from tuberculosis, and his paintings became the backdrop for musical performances by Sonny Rollins, Eric Dolphy, and others. His Dali-esque painting is the cover for Dolphy's *Out There* (PLP 8252).

In 1956, a young New Yorker and aspiring photographer named Esmond Edwards had a neighbor named Art Taylor who he had heard was some kind of a jazz drummer. He told Taylor he'd like to see a jazz session and take some pictures. Taylor invited him along to his next recording session. Young Edwards may have been expecting a romantic, Bohemian setting like the Jazz Loft, but what he found instead was a suburban living room that had been converted by the Van Gelder family into a recording studio for their son. But the music was great: It was Jackie McLean, making an album for Prestige. Edwards took his photos from the day down to the Prestige offices, and one of them became the cover of McLean's *Lights Out!* album.

Edwards became Prestige's photographer, present at all of Prestige's recording sessions (and farther afield: his cover for *When Farmer Met Gryce* shows the two musicians meeting on a country road). He began working part-time in the company's office. On May 31, 1957, he was scheduled to go out to the Van Gelder studio in New Jersey to photograph a John Coltrane session. At the last minute, Weinstock couldn't make it and asked Edwards to fill in. *Coltrane*, the great tenor saxophonist's debut as a leader with the label, was released with Weinstock credited as producer, but young Esmond Edwards was at the threshold of a new career. On June 20, 1958, Edwards was appointed head of "Artists and Repertoire," which meant head of production, and he got his first official production credit on an album. He would remain a prolific producer for Weinstock over the next decade, before moving on to Verve, Chess, and other labels. He would also continue his career as an important jazz photographer. And it's worth noting that he was one of the first African American producers in the New York jazz recording world. (A second photographer, Don Schlitten, would also graduate to a career as a producer for Prestige.)

Listening to Prestige: Eddie "Lockjaw" Davis

The Eddie "Lockjaw" Davis Cookbook

Recorded at Van Gelder Studio, Hackensack, NJ, June 20, 1958

Jerome Richardson, flute, tenor sax; Eddie "Lockjaw" Davis, tenor sax; Shirley Scott, organ; George Duvivier, bass; Arthur Edgehill, drums

Tracks recorded: The Chef; Have Horn, Will Blow; In the Kitchen; But Beautiful; Three Deuces

Eddie "Lockjaw" Davis connected with Shirley Scott in 1953, when he went looking for a jazz organist to round out his group. This wasn't exactly a common lineup at that time. Count Basie had recorded on organ with his big band, but the more usual formation, the one favored by Jimmy Smith, was a trio. Bill Doggett's recordings in the early '50s also were trio recordings. Perhaps Davis got the idea of the organ-saxophone combo that shook the world with "Honky Tonk" from Davis and Scott. It certainly turns out that Davis was onto something. This was a powerful sound for the nascent movement that would come to be known as soul jazz, and given an added richness by the presence of Jerome Richardson. The session was produced by Esmond Edwards, who had been listening to the new sounds out of Harlem.

"In the Kitchen," a two-sided 45 rpm single, became one of Davis and Scott's best-known recordings. The culinary theme of The Eddie "Lockjaw" Davis Cookbook would be continued over three albums, all of them produced by Edwards.

An interview with Edwards, appearing in *The Music Aficionado* blog, gives a vivid picture of a Prestige recording session:

> With Prestige we primarily worked on a limited budget, and things were, more or less, done in the studio: no rehearsal as a rule, it was the matter of getting compatible musicians together, and to some extent giving them a direction in advance. A lot of times things were ad-hoc. You get four or five guys in the studio and, "What are we going to do now?"
>
> I used to go to sessions as a photographer and watch how Bob functioned. He'd say, "Okay, let's try such and such a tune. Let's try a standard. Let's do a blues." Blues were kind of a stock-in-trade. "Let's do" what Bob would call "a funky ballad." That's the way things more or less went down.
>
> A lot of times I was a combination of traffic cop, psychologist, and "producer/director," trying to keep things moving. Waking a guy up when he was on the nod so he could start his solo. Everything.

One such artist was Gene Ammons, one of Prestige's most popular artists, whose heroin addiction cost him two lengthy prison sentences. Edwards noted: "Gene Ammons, he was our typical junkie. He would sit there with a lit cigarette in his mouth, nodding, and the ashes would be burning up his tie, and you'd swear he was in a trance. When it was time for him to play, he just came out of it and blew his butt off. Then he went back to dozing again."

Edwards gives valuable insights into other artists he worked with:

> You could tell [Coleman Hawkins] six months in advance you had a session, and he would not do anything towards preparing for it. I'd show up at the date with a briefcase full of sheet music and say, "Hawk, you want to try this? You want to try that?"
>
> Surprisingly, a lot of the tunes which I considered well-known standards, he wasn't that familiar with, but the guy, you'd stick the music in front of him. He'd run it down once, and it was like he wrote it the second performance.

Producing Eric Dolphy proved to be a particular challenge for both Edwards and Rudy Van Gelder. Edwards was aware of Dolphy's prodigious talent when he signed him, but not of his skill as a multi-instrumentalist:

> When he pulled out his bass clarinet, Rudy Van Gelder and I did a double take. It was phenomenal. That's some of my favorite playing of his, on the bass clarinet. I love that sound. [But] in the studio [Van Gelder] had rather strict parameters as to how he wanted to set up his microphones and so forth. Now, here's Eric doubling on an alto and a flute on a tune, and Rudy wanted to mike the alto primarily, and when Eric was to do his flute solo, he had to almost bend double to be close to where the mike was set up for the alto. He protested vehemently, and Rudy was adamant that he didn't want to move the mike. It was quite a crisis. I think Rudy prevailed.

Weinstock ultimately made Edwards vice president at Prestige, making him only the second African American to hold an executive position at a white-owned label (Quincy Jones had been the first, at Mercury).

Edwards left Prestige in 1962, to run Chess Records's jazz subsidiary Argo. He would later go on to head the jazz divisions at Verve, Columbia, and Impulse! He garnered two Grammy nominations in his career, for Ramsey Lewis's "The In Crowd" on Argo, and the original cast recording of *Your Arms Too Short to Box with God* on MCA. As a photographer, he is particularly noted for his portraits of John Coltrane.

Chapter 12

Sonny Rollins

Sonny Rollins was born and raised in New York city, in the Sugar Hill section of Harlem, a neighborhood that was a virtual Hall of Fame of American music (Duke Ellington and Rollins's idol Coleman Hawkins were just two of the residents), as well as a Who's Who of Black America (W. E. B. Dubois, Thurgood Marshall, and Roy Wilkins all lived there). He grew up absorbing music, going to the Apollo Theater and later to Minton's Playhouse, and using a fake mustache to sneak into the downtown clubs on 52nd Street. It was a time and a place where you could make music the center of your life. It was a breeding ground for young musicians, and the band that formed in the neighborhood, the Counts of Bop, included Rollins, Jackie McLean, Kenny Drew, Walter Bishop, and Art Taylor. Kids just a few years older, like Gil Coggins, were already being absorbed into the New York music scene.

Rollins graduated high school in 1948, knowing he was going to be a professional musician. He worked small jobs in the neighborhood, and he and his friends were starting to get noticed. One who noticed them was Bud Powell, only six years older than Rollins, already known as a major force in the new music, but also already battling the mental illness that would dog him the rest of his life. Newly released from Creedmoor State Hospital, Powell wasn't someone who could get them any work, but he mentored them. A paying gig in the Bronx (he got stiffed) put Rollins on the same bill with Miles Davis, who liked what he heard and told him he'd like to use him some day. He worked a few trio gigs with Roy Haynes, another Sugar Hill resident, and a few with Art Blakey.

But Rollins's real break came in 1949, when Babs Gonzalez tapped him to join his group. Gonzalez was by many accounts the original bebop vocalist, and by all accounts a hustler supreme; young Rollins could perhaps learn something about music from him, and certainly something about how to survive in the music business. And most importantly, Gonzalez had just signed a record deal. Capitol, a well-financed newcomer to the major label scene, had achieved some success in the jazz field with Stan Kenton and Nat "King" Cole, and they were starting to take an interest in this new bebop phenomenon, which was not all that new in 1949, but new to the major record labels. Capitol signed up Miles Davis, who disappointed them by making a series of 78 rpm records that weren't bebop but turned out to be gold a decade later when released as *Birth of the Cool*; Lennie Tristano, again not exactly a bebopper; Dave Lambert, an early vocalist on the progressive jazz scene; and composer-pianist Tadd Dameron, never a big star, but always respected by his peers, and the composer of such jazz standards as "Hot House," "Good Bait," "If You Could See Me Now" and "Our Delight."

Gonzalez assembled a nine-piece group made up of seasoned professionals, and, as Aidan Levy quotes in his extensive biography of Rollins, "a new cat from on my block uptown, 'Sonny Rollins' on tenor." Gonzalez recorded two numbers for Capitol on January 20, 1949. The 78 rpm record was well reviewed in the trade publications. He was a popular singer at the time, so he was called back for a second session on April 27, this time with a substantially different group that included Dexter Gordon, Fats Navarro, and Don Redman along with Rollins. J. J. Johnson had been the arranger for the first session, and in spite of having Redman—legendary arranger for Fletcher Henderson, Jimmy Dorsey, Count Basie and others, as well as leader of his own orchestra—Gonzalez kept Johnson as arranger for the second session.

So Rollins had his foot in the door as a recording artist, and continued touring with Gonzalez. And Johnson liked what he had heard on the Capitol sessions, so he brought Rollins in on his next recording session, for Savoy. A label that issued a lot of classic recordings in the jazz and rhythm and blues fields, Savoy was owned by Herman Lubinsky, a man not widely known for honesty. Teddy Reig, who produced J. J. Johnson's Boppers, described Lubinsky this way: "Lubinsky was a *gonif* and without a doubt the cheapest bastard on the planet." Lubinsky also had a very different philosophy of recording than did Bob Weinstock. Weinstock prized spontaneity, and he felt that the first take was likely to be the most spontaneous. He also prized saving money, so if the first take wasn't right, he would tape over it, so as not to waste tape. Lubinsky would call for numerous takes, and sometimes he would decide that a tune just wasn't working, and tell the musicians to forget it and go on to another. This was not because he was a perfectionist, or because he was profligate with money. He would keep all those alternate takes, all those unused tunes; for the cost of a little tape and a couple hours of studio time, he had a bunch of material he could use later on, without paying the musicians anything.

For Rollins, who was so new in the studio, so new to playing with musicians of this caliber and level of professionalism (John Lewis was on the date, as were bassist Gene Ramey and drummer Shadow Wilson), the opportunity to try it over and over must have been welcome. To Johnson and the others, the young tenor man was a joy to welcome into the fraternity. Levy quotes Johnson: "Sonny Rollins was a very outgoing, fun person. Sonny had his own way of playing, his own style of playing that really caught our fancy, and it was just great just to be involved in his . . . bursting onto the scene. And burst onto the scene he did." Johnson did more than bring Sonny into the recording studio; he used two of his compositions on the date, "Audubon" and "Goof Square."

Two weeks later, on May 25, Johnson assembled a new group of boppers, keeping only Rollins and Lewis, to record for a new label: Bob Weinstock's New Jazz. The rest of the group was Kenny Dorham, trumpet; Leonard Gaskin, bass; Max Roach, drums. *Down Beat* referred to them in a review as "six well-known boppers," so apparently Rollins was already one of the fraternity, but not one who made much of an impression on the reviewer: "Rollins . . . solos to no great effect." He would record next on August 9, 1949, with his neighbor and mentor Bud Powell. Then the upward trajectory of his career was slowed, as heroin really got its hooks into him.

Rollins left New York and his neighborhood, where drugs were too easily available. He ended up in Chicago, not a place one should seek out to get away from drugs, but he did play some music out there, notably with drummer Ike Day. Day, another victim of the heroin scourge, never recorded, but he was a legend in Chicago. His home base was an after-hours club, the Macomba Lounge, where two drum kits were set up side by side, and any drummer foolhardy enough to make the attempt could come and duel with him. Many tried, including Buddy Rich, but none emerged victorious. Rollins credits his time with Day as a key point in his development as a musician. Returning to New York, Rollins resumed playing here and there, getting a steady gig at club in Harlem, and building a reputation in the jazz community. Miles Davis came to hear him one night, and liked what he heard. He repeated his casual offer made that night in the Bronx, and this time it was more than casual; Davis asked him to join his group, and Rollins accepted. On January 17, 1951, he was back for another recording session with Bob Weinstock, this time for the newly rebranded Prestige label (discussed in chapter 5).

Weinstock, who had recorded Rollins a couple of years earlier with J. J. Johnson and Bud Powell but had not heard him since, had been reluctant to use him on this session. He had brought Davis back from his self-imposed exile in the Midwest, wanted proven talent for the session that would reestablish the trumpeter as a major figure on the jazz scene. Davis had told him that Rollins was ready, and now, as this session was winding up, wanted to showcase him even more: one number on which Rollins would be the leader. Lewis had to leave for another date, so Davis sat in on piano, and although it would not be released right away, Sonny Rollins, at twenty, had his first session as leader.

The next session, on October 5, 1951, was billed as "Miles Davis Sextet Featuring Sonny Rollins." Charlie Parker came along to offer moral support, and watched from the control room. This was that first LP session for Prestige, the one where Weinstock told Miles he could stretch out (see chapter 5). Jackie McLean, also on the date, was not ready—at least in Weinstock's opinion—for much extended improvisation, so the stretching out was left to Davis and Rollins. After the session, Weinstock offered Rollins a contract to record for Prestige.

Things were looking up for the young musician, but they were about to come crashing down. A few days later, Rollins, Drew, and a third musician from the neighborhood, all three of them strung out on heroin, decided it would be a good idea to go downtown and rob a store. Somehow Rollins was given a gun. As he would later tell Eric Nisenson, author of *Open Sky: Sonny Rollins and His World of Improvisation* (quoted in Levy): "I was sort of the dumb guy who was just going along. I was the big dope who took the gun. I didn't really know anything about guns. I have never fired a gun in my life." They got as far as getting out of the cab on 59th Street when a couple of policemen, suspicious of three young Black men getting out of a cab in a white part of town at one o'clock in the morning, stopped them and frisked them and found the gun on Rollins. They were bailed out, and Rollins was able to make his scheduled December 17 recording date, the first for the Sonny Rollins Quartet. Ultimately, charges were dismissed against Drew and Martinez; however, Rollins was charged with criminally carrying concealed a loaded pistol and criminally possessing a pistol without a license.

December was a busy month for Prestige. Weinstock had booked sessions with Joe Holiday; a gospel session with Dr. Alvin A. Child; a hectic December 20 date with the Cabineers, vocalist John Bennings, saxophonist Lem Davis, and gospel harmonizers the Dixieaires; H-Bomb Ferguson; the Charlie Mariano Boston All Stars (that one was recorded in Boston, so he wasn't scheduled to supervise it); and a group called Ralph Willis Country Boys, which wasn't country but rather vocalist Willis with blues stalwarts Sonny Terry and Brownie McGhee. Weinstock was starting to feel the strain; he was diagnosed with what was called in those days manic depression. Although Rollins was surely the most important of these projects, Weinstock had to beg off and leave it to Ira Gitler, inexperienced but the only other employee Prestige had at the time. Gitler was called in to supervise the session, which was not such a change from Weinstock, who was an amateur himself. As Orrin Keepnews of Riverside Records said,

> The fifties were a heyday for the formation of independent labels . . . they were the result of fans turning professional. This is what Blue Note was. It's what Prestige was. It's what Riverside was. In California, it's what Contemporary and Pacific Jazz were. The self-professionalizing of a bunch of enthusiasts. I used to say, if you own the company, there's nobody to tell you that you're not qualified to be a producer. That's how a lot of us started out. Nobody could tell us not to.

Rollins was probably the one who chose his old friend—and, unfortunately, partner in crime—Kenny Drew on piano. Drew, at twenty-three, was himself already a veteran. He had made his recording debut just two years earlier with Howard McGhee, but since then he had been in nearly constant demand. In 1950, he recorded with Sonny Stitt, Lester Young (multiple sessions), and Charlie Parker; in 1951, there were Oscar Pettiford, Miles Davis, and Paul Quinichette before the Rollins session. Active throughout the decade, he would leave the United States in 1961 and settle in Denmark, removing himself from the mainstream of the jazz world but continuing to make great music.

Percy Heath on bass and Art Blakey on drums were two seasoned veterans who could be counted on to give a solid underpinning to any session, and either Rollins (who had worked a lot with Blakey) or Weinstock might have chosen them. Certainly, there would have been general agreement. Sabu Martinez had been booked for the session, but he didn't make it.

Eight tunes were recorded, including three originals, one of which was "Mambo Bounce," a nod to the popular Latin dance rhythm, on which they had expected to be joined by Sabu. Another was an on-the-spot improvisation by Rollins and Drew, titled "Newk's Fadeaway" by Ira Gitler. The title was a reference to the nickname Rollins had picked up because of his resemblance to Brooklyn Dodger Don Newcombe, the possessor of a mystifying slow curve, but it was to prove unfortunately prophetic.

Rollins was still in his developmental stage as an artist, and a lot of people, Weinstock included, thought that he was not fully formed yet. Nonetheless, Joe Goldberg, writing in 1963, notes that "many of the factors that were to shape his unique style were already in evidence." But *Down Beat*'s reviewer, reviewing the "Mambo Bounce" single from the album, heard "just another record of just another tenor man playing just another blues." And when the record came out, Rollins, who had agreed to plead guilty to a misdemeanor charge of possession of a firearm in exchange for the dropping of the more serious felony charge, and had hoped for a suspended sentence, saw his nascent career fading away: He was given one to three years.

The jazz public had just started to take notice of Rollins. The ten-inch *Sonny Rollins Quartet* was released in 1952; in the year-end *Down Beat* Readers Poll—although he was still not getting particularly good reviews from *Down Beat*—Rollins cracked the list for the first time. He was thirty-seventh with eleven votes, which doesn't sound so great, but he was poised to move up. And when you consider he was tied for thirty-seventh with Don Byas, and one vote behind Gene Ammons, it wasn't bad company to be in. Rollins served ten months of his sentence. He was released on October 14, 1952. But getting back into the music world was not going to be easy.

Rollins came out of Rikers into a world—his world—that was still staggering under the scourge of heroin. Back then, there was a rumor on the street that heroin had been introduced into the ghetto by police and social workers who wanted to break up the street gangs. A white paper by Joseph D. McNamara of the libertarian Cato Institute doesn't go that far, but it says that "some analysts believed that the New York teenage fighting gangs causing great concern during the 1950's disintegrated when the members began to use heroin." Certainly New York in the 1950s, especially Harlem and Times Square, was in the grip of a heroin epidemic. According to an article in the online journal *Vital City*, "during the 1950s and 1960s, years when 4% to 5% of the U.S. population lived in the city, between 43% and 50% of the addicts listed in the Federal Bureau of Narcotics registry were city residents."

Certainly one reason for the prevalence of addiction among New York's jazz musicians was the influence of Charlie Parker. Parker knew what heroin had done to him, but perhaps his greatest regret in life was knowing that younger musicians, wanting to be like him in every way, had begun using heroin. The easy availability of drugs was probably the main contributing cause, but Parker was sadly not entirely wrong in blaming himself.

In 1952, Rollins made the *Down Beat* poll, and also the *Metronome* poll, tying for the twenty-fifth and last spot. So jazz fans were aware of him. The first Prestige session booked for him after his release came on January 30. Miles Davis had organized the date, and it was historic in more ways than that. It was the first and only time that Charlie Parker appeared on a Prestige recording, and it was the first and only time that Parker and Rollins ever recorded together.

It was also something of a debacle. Davis had returned from going cold turkey at his father's house in East St. Louis to be plunged back into the depths of addiction. Philly Joe Jones and Walter Bishop were both seriously addicted. And Rollins, who had come out of Rikers drug-free, had also been pulled back into the heroin orbit. Parker at this point in his life was weaning himself from heroin, but only by drinking large quantities of alcohol. Ira Gitler, who was supervising the session, had provided some alcoholic refreshments, only to see Parker down almost an entire bottle of gin.

Because of the importance of finally getting Parker (under the alias of "Charlie Chan," as he was contractually bound to Verve) on a Prestige record, Gitler had taken the extraordinary (for Prestige) step of scheduling a rehearsal. Parker was the only one who showed up for it. On the date of the recording itself, only Bishop and Heath showed up on time. The others all straggled in late, Davis more than an hour late.

The session was marred by sloppy play, and by Parker nodding off between solos. There was friction between Davis and Parker. Rollins recalled it to Levy, "Bird was really dressing him down like a father to a son. 'Why'd you do that? What's the matter with you, you can't have a band and come in late.' . . . This was the relationship they had even though Bird was doing it under Miles's name. . . . Bird was explaining to him how a leader was supposed to do it."

The session nearly crashed and burned when Gitler blew up at Davis and told him, "You ain't playing shit!" Miles responded by packing up his horn and getting ready to leave, and only Parker's intervention convinced him to stay.

With some difficulty, they recorded two complete numbers. But by then it was 5:30. The recording was taking place at WOR studios, where

Prestige did most of their recording in those days, but their regular sound engineer was not in that day. The backup sound engineer informed Gitler that he was booked until six, and he would be leaving at six on the dot. They were scheduled to record a Monk tune, "Well, You Needn't," but they couldn't get it together. After fifteen minutes, time was running out, and they were clearly never going to get it together, when Gitler called a Hail Mary. He told them to do a tune they all knew, Monk's "Round Midnight." They had time for one take, and they nailed it. The last notes were played as the clock was ticking down toward six.

Two other tunes were recorded during this session. There was a Davis composition, "Compulsion," and a tune improvised over a series of changes submitted by Jimmy Heath, who had been bumped off the session when Parker became available. Gitler titled it "The Serpent's Tooth," and credited it to Davis, as was not an unusual procedure when a number was essentially improvised in the studio. Heath, years later, reported that whenever he ran into Davis, he would say, "Hey, Miles, about 'Serpent's Tooth?'" and Miles would say, "Oh, shit, yeah," and give him a couple hundred dollars.

"Round Midnight" was kept, along with two takes of "The Serpent's Tooth" that Gitler deemed possibly good enough to use, and both takes made it onto the recording, *Collector's Items*, which included other material, and was not released until December 1956. By then, Parker was dead. Davis was already with Columbia, and had already released his first Columbia album, *'Round About Midnight*. The comparison was unavoidable. On the one hand, the glistening perfection of the Columbia version, with one of the most famous, and arguably one of the best, groups in jazz history, now known simply as The First Quintet. On the other, the Prestige recording, which came from one of the shoddiest, most drug-addled sessions ever put together by a ragtag group of jazz immortals. But somehow, the earlier "Round Midnight," recorded as the session's doomsday clock was approaching midnight, had caught lightning in a bottle. Gitler, in his liner notes, accurately describes Parker's solo as "full of the pain and disappointment he knew too well." Which is better? There is literally no comparison; they are night and day. Both amazing recordings, both artifacts of an era, both irreplaceable parts of the history of jazz.

One other thing came out of the January 30 session. Parker had not seen Rollins in some time, and Rollins was looking fairly together. Rollins lied to him, saying "Yeah, man, I'm straight now," and Parker was delighted. When he found out the truth, he was devastated, and he never spoke to Rollins again. For Rollins, it was a turning point. He told Art Taylor, for Taylor's book *Notes and Tones*:

I saw for the first time that he didn't dig my doing that. I realized I must be doing the wrong thing. Up until that time I had thought it was all fun and games and that it was okay to use drugs. I subsequently got myself off drugs, when he showed me that wasn't the way to go. Unfortunately, when I did get myself straight, I was anxious to let him see I had dug his message, but as life would have it, he passed away before I was able to meet him again.

In an interview with *Down Beat*, Rollins also recalled that moment:

On that record date, he really told me what to do as far as music and my life were concerned . . . he showed me the thing he wanted me to do and the thing he stood for. The purpose of his whole life was music and he showed me that music was the paramount thing and anything that interfered with it I should stay away from. Later on I was able to take advantage of his advice but he died before I had a chance to see him and tell him I had.

The turnaround would not happen right away. But that was a beginning.

Listening to Prestige: Sonny Rollins with the Modern Jazz Quartet

Recorded in New York, October 7, 1953

Sonny Rollins, tenor sax; Milt Jackson, vibes; John Lewis, piano; Percy Heath, bass; Kenny Clarke, drums

Tracks recorded: In a Sentimental Mood; The Stopper; Almost Like Being in Love; No Moe

The quartet was brought in for this session with Sonny Rollins, and although Rollins was the featured performer on the gig, the Modern Jazz Quartet was credited as such. A few years later, Atlantic would bring out *The Modern Jazz Quartet at Music Inn, Vol. 2*, with guest artist Sonny Rollins.

The Atlantic album has been in my collection since the '50s, but I'd never heard this earlier collaboration before. It's a fascinating one.

This is definitely a Sonny Rollins session, but it's definitely MJQ, too. This is probably the first time all four of them had worked as the MJQ with another artist, and it's an experiment worth listening to. These guys knew how to play together as a rhythm section, and they show that here. But they also knew who they were, and they show that here, too. And all five of them make a pretty convincing argument that bebop is not dead, as they take on two standards and two riff-based originals by Rollins in the head-solos-head format, with Rollins taking the lead and the others contributing tricky and enthusiastic improvisations in their turn. "The Stopper," one of the Rollins tunes, showcases all of this, as Milt Jackson plays behind Rollins, adding deft and unexpected notes in commentary on the saxophone solo that takes up a good two-thirds of the three-minute, jukebox-length number ("The Stopper" was released on 45). Jackson's part gets more and more pronounced as the tune progresses, until he finally takes over as the soloist—at which point Lewis performs the same function, building up his part under Jackson's until he finally bursts forth with a brief solo, after which Rollins returns.

It's worth remembering that before they were legends, the MJQ were working musicians playing the gigs that they got, unlike the Brubeck Quartet, who pretty much made it clear that they were legends to begin with. And working musicians like these are always worth listening to.

The four tunes from the session were released on 45 and 78 rpm singles, a 45 rpm EP, and eventually on LP in 1956 as Sonny Rollins with the Modern Jazz Quartet, Art Blakey and Kenny Drew.

It seems as though the critics of that era did not know what to make of the Rollins/MJQ combination. Nat Hentoff, in Down Beat, wrote that "Rollins blows acceptably on both sides," but could not resist adding that "there's just not much point in adding something to the MJQ just for the sake of adding." Joe Goldberg, writing in 1965, points out that Rollins "at the time was . . . a good, but unknown musician trying to make a living and a reputation in the fiercely competitive New York jazz world," suggesting that here he may have been seen as punching above his weight. Gunther Schuller, writing the liner notes for the 1958 Atlantic album The Modern Jazz Quartet at Music Inn, Guest Artist Sonny Rollins is lavish with praise, as befits liner notes, but at the same time can't seem to quite figure out what they're doing together: "Sonny was in one of his more whimsical and sardonic moods that night. Sonny's unwavering insistence on funny produces a very interesting byplay of reactions in the Quartet."

Today, all of these figures are legends, and any opportunity to hear them together is a privilege.

Listening to Prestige:
Rollins with Thelonious Monk

Recorded at WOR Studios, NYC, November 13, 1953

Julius Watkins, French horn; Sonny Rollins, tenor sax; Thelonious Monk, piano; Percy Heath, bass; Willie Jones, drums

Tracks recorded: Let's Call This; Think of One (Takes 1 & 2); Friday the Thirteenth

Looking back over the fall of 1953 at Prestige, I'm seeing a sort of mini-unit, starting with Sonny Rollins and a cerebral, groundbreaking pianist, John Lewis, and ending up with a cerebral, groundbreaking pianist of a very different mindset, Thelonious Monk. The Lewis collaboration resulted in the four tracks recorded by Rollins with the Modern Jazz Quartet in October 1953; the Monk tracks were recorded a month later.

Percy Heath from the MJQ was the bass player for this session, and Willie Jones the drummer. There are a bunch of Willie Joneses in jazz, two of whom are drummers, and none of whom are related. The drummer who's played with Horace Silver, Herbie Hancock, Arturo Sandoval, and others calls himself Willie Jones III, to distinguish himself from Monk's drummer, who was sometimes called Willie Jones Jr. Then there was Willie Jones the piano player, sometimes known as "the piano wrecker" because he would play an upright piano so hard it would vibrate, who recorded with Gene Ammons and Clark Terry, among others. Willie Jr. is playing his first recording gig here with Monk. He would have a short career but a good one, including playing on Charles Mingus's classic Pithecanthropus Erectus.

Julius Watkins was almost certainly the first significant French horn player in jazz, and there have been precious few since. Another of Detroit's seemingly endless stream of jazz greats, he heard a French horn when he was nine, fell in love with it, and the horn was life from there on. Jazz came later, as it became clear that there were not going to be openings for Black horn players in major symphony orchestras. Also, he wanted to solo, and that meant jazz. He does solo on this date with Monk, to particularly powerful effect on the ten-and-a-half minute "Friday the Thirteenth," and when he and Rollins play together, the tonal quality is wonderful, and very appropriate for Monk's music.

No 78s for these five- and ten-minute cuts. "Let's Call This" and "Think of One" were released on EP. The whole session was put on a ten-inch album called Thelonious Monk Blows for LP, and later included on twelve-inchers: Monk and Thelonious Monk and Sonny Rollins.

Ira Gitler produced half of this session, and when he pressed Monk for the title of his first new composition, the pianist said, "Let's call this . . ." and then, starting to think of a name, got distracted. For the second tune, Monk was even less interested in giving it a name. When Gitler asked him, "What's the title?" Monk tossed the problem back to him. "Think of one!" he said.

Listening to Prestige: Rollins with Art Farmer

Recorded at Van Gelder Studio, Hackensack, NJ, January 20, 1954

Art Farmer, trumpet; Sonny Rollins, tenor sax; Horace Silver, piano; Percy Heath, bass; Kenny Clarke, drums

Tracks recorded: Wisteria; Soft Shoe; Confab in Tempo; I'll Take Romance

There are the trumpet players who one listens to with reverence. The ones who changed the face of American music with their vision and their talent, including Louis Armstrong, Dizzy Gillespie, and Miles Davis. They would be pretty much on everyone's list. Then there are the trumpet players who seem to capture the essence of jazz music, the ones you listen to and say "Yes, that's what I love about jazz." A jazz fan will have her/his own list here, but a whole lot of those lists would include Bix Beiderbecke, Roy Eldridge, Clifford Brown—and Art Farmer.

All I can think, listening to this oddly forgotten session (released on a ten-inch and then buried until the 7600 reissue series in 1969, pretty much the end cycle for Prestige) is what a wonderful session this is. It's everything that makes me love jazz.

Art Farmer first made his name known when he played with Wardell Gray on the session that introduced "Farmer's Market." He led a septet for Prestige in the summer of 1953, then headed for Europe on the Lionel Hampton tour that produced a series of recordings. This was his first session back in the States as a leader. Sonny Rollins joins him, and Rollins is another of those everything that makes me love jazz guys.

Also on this date was pianist Horace Silver. If there's ever an artist whose name is synonymous with a jazz label, it's Silver and Blue Note. He had actually started with Blue Note in 1952, first with Lou

Donaldson and then as leader, and Blue Note kept him pretty busy, but during 1953–54 he also found time to record with Lester Young (released on the Italian Philology label and on Ambrosia), Sonny Stitt (Roost), Al Cohn (Savoy), both Art Farmer and Miles Davis on Prestige, and a few others. He had already started what became one of Blue Note's most famous groups, the Jazz Messengers, with Art Blakey. Blakey was to lead the group for years, but originally it was Horace Silver and the Jazz Messengers.

The session kicks off with "Wisteria," an achingly beautiful ballad composed by Farmer that has wonderful work by everyone, especially Horace Silver. "Soft Shoe," again by Farmer (there's a Gerry Mulligan composition called "Soft Shoe," but it's different) picks up the tempo, with the boppish ensemble riffing and inspired soloing that presages Farmer's work with Benny Golson in the Jazztet. For "Confab in Tempo," the tempo is confabbed by Kenny Clarke, followed by some great high-octane bebop, with Clarke pushing it all the way and coming back for a wild drum solo. "I'll Take Romance" was written by Ben Oakland (also known for the Ink Spots' great novelty "Java Jive"), with lyrics by Oscar Hammerstein. It's probably best known in the pop rendition by Eydie Gorme. There's a hipper version by June Christy, but Eydie did right by the song. Its cool passion and flowing lyricism make it a great choice for jazz improvisation, and it's been recorded by many. It's a good way to end the set.

This is the second session to be recorded in Rudy Van Gelder's studio. I wonder if it was difficult to cajole musicians into trekking out to Hackensack in the middle of January. It certainly wouldn't have been difficult to get them to go a second time, once they'd heard the results.

Rollins was active during the latter part of 1953 and into 1954. Prestige gave him cobilling on the MJQ and Monk sessions. He was a sideman as they brought Art Farmer in to take the leader role, for an album that has been curiously overlooked.

People were starting to listen to Rollins and pay attention. However, he was still on the lower rungs of the *Down Beat* poll in 1953, tied with Charlie Barnet and James Moody for twenty-seventh place. He had yet to convince the critics, particularly Nat Hentoff, who said in reviewing the Farmer album: "The session is uneven, and the recording lacks definition. . . . Sonny Rollins begins to be heard on 'Soft Shoe' and also has choruses on the last two. His conception is not on a level with Farmer's though his rhythmic sense is characteristically keen."

Not long after the Farmer session, Rollins took another step back. On the advice of his parole officer, he surrendered himself for a parole violation and was sentenced to Riker's again, ostensibly for treatment. But that did not happen. There was no treatment at Riker's, but there was one sympathetic soul: the prison chaplain, Father Jorjorian, who gave Rollins time and space to compose music. He left prison on June 8, 1954, with three new compositions, "Airegin," "Doxy," and "Oleo."

Rollins started playing again with Miles Davis, and was back in the Van Gelder studio in Hackensack on June 29 for a Prestige recording. Again, he was there as a sideman, but this would be, as Joe Goldberg said, "the breakthrough." The other musicians on the date were Horace Silver, Percy Heath, and Kenny Clarke; Heath and Clarke were two-thirds of the Modern Jazz Quartet, so Bob Weinstock billed them on the album as Miles Davis and the Modern Jazz Giants. Kenny Clarke, who was shortly to leave the MJQ for an extended *ex patria* in France, might have agreed with Weinstock on some level. According to Levy: "For Clarke, working with Miles during this period was in stark contrast to the meticulous preparation of the Modern Jazz Quartet: 'We'd all walk in the studio and then Miles would say, "What are we going to play?" And then right away something would come up in my stomach. It was such a thrill.'"

The session was in many ways a showcase for Rollins. They played one standard, "But Not for Me," and the rest of the day was devoted to Rollins's three Rikers compositions, although all of them were still works in progress, with much hurried scribbling in the studio. Silver improvised a bridge for "Oleo."

Hentoff, normally an astute critic, still did not get Rollins, writing, "Rollins to this ear is no particular asset to the session. . . . Sonny's tone is undistinguished and his conception almost never comes freshly alive. It's too bad Sonny's considerable personal force can't be concentrated into less cliche-like patterns. [The compositions] aren't exactly memorable, although Airegin has promise if developed."

The compositions have lasted longer than Hentoff might have guessed, becoming jazz standards. "Doxy" has been covered over 100 times, "Airegin" near 150, and "Oleo" over 200. Davis included both "Oleo" and "Airegin" in his farewell sessions for Prestige, with John Coltrane playing the tenor sax role.

Rollins had arrived, as far as the jazz world was concerned, and Weinstock was convinced. He hired him as leader with sessions on August 18 (with Kenny Dorham, Elmo Hope, Percy Heath, and Art Blakey), and again on October 25. He had wanted Hope for that session too, but the pianist was unavailable, and in a moment of last-minute desperation, he called on Thelonious Monk, and Monk was willing to step in and take the role of sideman to his young protégé.

Still, the reviews were not there. *Down Beat* was the jazz fan's consumer guide, and many record purchasers relied on it, saving their money for albums that got four or five stars from the magazine's critics. And Nat Hentoff was still their primary arbiter. *Moving Out*, the first album, with all compositions by Rollins, he dismissed as "unimaginative, however rhythmically powerful, and the overfamiliar lines of the 'originals' don't help either."

On his liner notes to the 1955 ten-inch release of *Sonny Rollins and Thelonious Monk*, Ira Gitler decided to challenge Hentoff head-on. He praised Rollins's "individual ideas and personality [that] have taken [Charlie Parker's] conception a bit farther," and named musicians who "have all concurred on his tremendous blowing." Then, after listing a string of prominent saxophonists who had, on a questionnaire by Leonard Feather for his forthcoming *Encyclopedia of Jazz*, named Rollins as one of their favorites, Gitler added, "The critics may be a bit slow . . . but musicians are quick to perceive those in their ranks who have something to say."

Hentoff fired back: "Ira Gitler's argumentative notes fail to convince me that Rollins possesses particularly 'individual ideas' or that his blowing is 'tremendous.' Rollins swings hard, and he plays with considerable warmth, but as has been stated here before, he lacks freshness of conception and his imagination is not individually distinctive enough to raise him to the top level of jazz improvisers." Perhaps Rollins might have secretly agreed with Hentoff. It was a year before he would record again for Prestige, a year spent away from New York. He moved to Chicago, a second hometown for him, where there was a vibrant and very democratic music scene, where he played blues clubs, strip clubs, avant-garde jazz clubs, and casual jam sessions. He had hoped Chicago would be a place where he could hide from the constant lure of heroin, but this did not prove to be the case. He and a fellow musician journeyed to Lexington, Kentucky, and the nationally known drug treatment center there. It did not have a great success rate, but Rollins defied the odds.

He returned to Chicago, where he lived with a family of gospel singers, and worked at odd jobs away from the music business. He also audited some music classes at the University of Chicago. In a 1956 *Down Beat* interview with Hentoff, who had finally come around to appreciating his music (Hentoff describes him as "the first major influence on a significant number of young tenors since the Stan Getz of the late forties and early fifties"), he discussed those classes and said, "I wanted to get a thorough foundation because I was very depressed about the records I'd made."

Rollins was working his day jobs, practicing at night. Much is made of Rollins's celebrated sabbatical from music from 1959 to 1961, when he practiced by himself under the Williamsburg Bridge between Brooklyn and Manhattan, but that was not the first time in his life that he put the music itself ahead of his music career. He told Hentoff, "Next year I may take some time off, go back to school, and stay away from the scene completely until I'm finished." He would make good on that three years later.

But he did venture out occasionally. When Max Roach and Clifford Brown came to Chicago, he went to hear them play, and was invited to sit in with them. There was an instant rapport between Rollins and Brown, who was just getting started when Rollins had heard him play in New York but was now recognized as one of the leading trumpeters of the time. He began playing with them regularly when Harold Land, who had been the tenor player with the group, decided to return to his hometown of Los Angeles. Rollins recalled, in the Hentoff interview: "On the last job we played together, all of a sudden we both heard it. We were phrasing, attacking, breathing together. That's a very difficult thing for two horns to make in unison playing. It's easier playing harmony. In unison, for one thing, the intonation of both has to be exactly the same. That's why I really think all groups that are together should stay together. It's the only way for them to achieve what they want to."

It should be noted that Brown was an important influence on Rollins in another way. The young trumpeter, who was to die in a car accident on June 26, 1956, had never touched drugs in his life. If Rollins had had any lingering suspicions that a drug-free life would impact his creativity, Brown was proof that this did not need to be the case. He would later tell an interviewer, "Clifford was a profound influence on my personal life. He showed me that it was possible to live a good, clean life and still be a good jazz musician." One recording exists of Brown and Rollins playing together: *Clifford Brown and Max Roach at Basin Street*, recorded in January and February 1956, and released on EmArcy.

Rollins was still under contract with Prestige, and now that he was playing again, and venturing back into New York — a different New York, that of middle-class family men Roach and Brown—he came back into the Van Gelder Studio in Hackensack on December 2, 1955. He might have been leery of Prestige, which had in the past been so tolerant of addicted musicians that it was known by some as "the junkie label," but that was starting to change, too. The Modern Jazz Quartet projected a very different image. And Weinstock, in a 1954 interview, had talked about how pleased he was that the heroin era in New York jazz was coming to an end.

Rollins brought Max Roach with him to the session, with the agreement of EmArcy, to whom Roach was contracted. Ray Bryant, at the beginning of an outstanding career, was on piano. He had first recorded for Prestige the previous August, with Miles Davis. At around this time, Miles Davis was putting together a new quintet, and wanted Rollins to join him. He told Rollins that Brown and Roach were a self-contained unit, and didn't really need him. But Rollins's commitment was to staying off drugs and away from his old life, and Brown and Roach offered that new path. The tenor sax position in Davis's new quintet went to a newcomer, John Coltrane.

Rollins's December 1955 session followed Prestige's philosophy—no rehearsals, one take—but that didn't mean Rollins was planning to take it easy, or make it easy on his sidemen. They started with "There's No Business Like Show Business," a tune that had entered Rollins's repertoire when playing for strippers on the Illinois/Indiana border. Max Roach announced the song's anthemic theme with no ordinary drum roll. Its syncopation set the tone: driving yet complex, which is what Rollins delivered. He belted the melody in a manner worthy of Ethel Merman, but this was certainly another branch of show business; in the hands of Rollins and his cohorts, it could surely be said that there really is no business like the bebop business. Ray Bryant, new to the scene but up to the task, would later tell an interviewer that he had never had to play so fast, before or since. In an interview quoted by Goldberg, Rollins explained his love for tunes that were off the beaten track (outside of a 1966 recording by Sadao Watanabe, I can find no other jazz recording of "There's No Business Like Show Business"): "Jazz is not limited, as people think it is . . . but so many guys keep playing the same few songs over and over again. There's so much music in the world that it's silly just to stick with a small part of it."

"Raincheck" is a Billy Strayhorn composition, and at the time was a fairly obscure one. Rollins was the first artist to record it since the Ellington orchestra had introduced it in 1942, although it has since become something of a jazz standard. "Paradox" is a Rollins original that has recently been picked up by other jazz musicians. "There Are Such Things" is popular with crooners, but this is the only recording by a major jazz musician. "It's All Right with Me" had just become a hit for Sammy Davis Jr., so jazz musicians were starting to pick up on it, but there had been few if any recordings when Rollins took it into the studio.

As Goldberg puts it, "There was no great audience awaiting" for the album *Work Time*. Rollins had not recorded in over a year, and his previous work had received middling reviews at best. Also, as Goldberg points out, "The Young-via-Getz tenor style was in great vogue, and Rollins [was] playing against the fashion." But this album, released in May 1956, even won over Nat Hentoff, who gave it four stars in *Down Beat*.

Before the release of *Work Time*, Rollins teamed up with Miles Davis for a March 16 date, recording three tunes to fill out the *Collectors Items* album. He made some recordings with Brown and Roach for EmArcy, and in return, the Mercury Records jazz subsidiary lent the two to Prestige for a March 22, 1956, date, notable for a Rollins composition that stretched the usual boundaries of jazz. When given the music for "Valse Hot," Max Roach realized he had never been asked to play jazz in three-four time before, and he spent the night before the recording date in his basement practicing. The tune has become a jazz standard, and Rollins has listed *Sonny Rollins Plus Four* as one of his personal favorite albums. Nat Hentoff gave it four and a half stars.

In the 1956 *Down Beat* readers poll, while Stan Getz still held down the top spot by a wide margin, and Lester Young was second, Sonny Rollins had vaulted to sixth place, right behind Coleman Hawkins. It was a busy time. Rollins was the new saxophone sensation, and he was in demand. He was touring and working steadily with Brown and Roach. Finding time to go into the studio to fulfill his Prestige contract was something he had to fit in.

Rollins managed to fit in a session on May 26, 1956, with Miles Davis's rhythm section of Red Garland, Paul Chambers, and Philly Joe Jones; John Coltrane came along for the ride and to lend moral support. He had gone to sleep in the car, but as the afternoon was winding down, he woke up, came into the studio, and was persuaded to join in on the last track of the day. They chose a popular blues composition by Kenny Clarke that had been around for a while under different names. Clarke had called it "Rue Chaptal" and "Royal Roost;" Art Blakey had recorded it with Hank Mobley as "Sportin' Crowd." By the time Rollins and Coltrane got through with it, there was only one title that fit. As "Tenor Madness," it became the title of the album, and as "Tenor Madness," it has become a jazz standard, a must for every young saxophonist to learn. It was the only time that these two heirs apparent to tenor saxophone royalty ever played together.

"Heir apparent" is an interesting phrase: An heir apparent is the next in line for succession to a throne or a title, and is next in line no matter what. This is distinguished from an heir presumptive, who is next in line until someone comes along with a better claim. So in jazz, one would have to say that all heirs are heirs presumptive: They are one cutting contest away from being displaced as next in line to the throne. For that matter, jazz royalty are kings presumptive.

But after "Tenor Madness," these two young men may well have sealed the deal as heirs apparent. Time would bear that out, as the game of thrones would end in a draw, with two reigning monarchs of the saxophone.

It took a lot to convince Nat Hentoff that an heir apparent, or even an heir presumptive, had arrived. He had finally accepted Rollins, but he gave the album only three and a half stars, saying that Coltrane "mars what should have been an interestingly balanced all-Rollins LP."

Two consecutive album titles that have become the most closely associated with Sonny Rollins throughout his long and productive life come from this period with Prestige, although in this busy time, he would hardly have thought of either of them as being that important. But *Tenor Madness*, with its Rollins-Coltrane duel, has become iconic, both the performance and the title. It fell to Ira Gitler to come up with a title for the next album, and to Gitler, there was only one choice. His title would be forever after linked with Rollins, and decades later, would be the title of a documentary by Robert Mugge: *Saxophone Colossus*.

It was recorded less than a month later, with Max Roach on drums, and two young men from Detroit filling out the rhythm section: Tommy Flanagan, piano, and Doug Watkins, bass. Watkins would stick around to become the house bassist for Prestige. Rollins's composition "Blue 7" particularly excited Weinstock. But the tune that would become a signature song for Rollins was the calypso remembered from his childhood, "St. Thomas."

Four days after the *Saxophone Colossus* session, Clifford Brown was dead, killed in a car crash that also claimed the life of the group's pianist, Richie Powell, and his young bride. It was the end of one of the most significant groups in jazz of that era. Although Rollins would continue to work with Roach, the magic of the Brown-Roach Quintet was gone, and it was time to move on.

It was time to move on in other ways, too. Rollins was nearing the end of his contract with Prestige. He would record in September with the newly structured Max Roach Quintet (Kenny Dorham taking the trumpet part, Ray Bryant on piano) for EmArcy, then on October 5, 1956, with mostly the same personnel, for Prestige as the Sonny Rollins Quintet with Kenny Dorham and Max Roach (and Wade Legge, piano; George Morrow, bass). The album was called *Rollins Plays for Bird*, and the centerpiece was a medley of tunes written by or associated with Charlie Parker. Rollins was looking for the new, but revisiting the old, continuing his association with Roach, reliving the mentorship of Parker. He would continue on the same path, as he rejoined Thelonious Monk for a series of recording dates between October and December, for Monk's Riverside label.

On December 7, Rollins brought a quartet into the studio. Roach and Morrow were with him, and the piano part went to his old friend Kenny Drew. The album, not to be released until 1958, was *Tour de Force*. That same December, he finished sixth on *Down Beat*'s tenor saxophone poll, behind Stan Getz, Lester Young, Zoot Sims, Bill Perkins, and Coleman Hawkins. And by the end of the year, Rollins, like others before him, had passed out of the Prestige orbit.

Chapter 13

Miles Davis Back and Ready to Work
The Contractual Marathon

Miles Davis called both Alfred Lion and Bob Weinstock to tell them he was back and drug free, and they both told him to come in. His exclusive contract with Prestige had not gone into effect yet, so he first went out to Hackensack on March 6, 1954, to record a session for Blue Note with Horace Silver, Percy Heath, and Art Blakey; then on March 15, he took the same quartet into Manhattan's Beltone Studios on 31st Street to record for Prestige. Silver was new to Davis, and his rootsy, bluesy style fit well with the new sound Davis was looking for. "He had that funky shit I liked a lot at that time," he recalls in his autobiography.

Davis's biographer Ian Carr quotes Horace Silver's memory of the date, on the recording of "Blue Haze": "We'd tried it and it didn't seem to work at all. Then Miles told Bob Weinstock to put out all the lights in the studio—so the only light we had was from the window of the control booth. Miles sat in a chair and pulled his cap right over his face—and he also took his shoes off. Then he beat it in at just the right tempo . . . and the whole thing happened perfectly." Davis has a slightly different memory of the moment: "When I asked them to turn out the lights in the studio, somebody said, 'If we turn out the lights we won't be able to see Art or Miles.' That shit was funny. They said that because Art Blakey and I are so dark."

More important, Davis was moving toward the sound he wanted. On April 3, they went back into the studio again, this time with Kenny

Clarke on drums. Miles said: "Because I wanted that brush stroke thing. When it came to playing soft brush strokes on the drums, nobody could do it better than Klook. I was using a mute on that date and I wanted a soft thing behind me, but a swing soft thing." Davis was using a cup mute on this session. He had not yet found the Harmon mute that he was to make famous. The quartet was augmented by Dave Schildkraut, an alto saxophonist whose playing was very similar to that of Charlie Parker. On the drive out to Hackensack, Weinstock said to Schildkraut, with a heavy overlay of sarcasm in his voice, "I hear you've been playing with Kenton." It was a put-down; Stan Kenton employed the very best musicians in his orchestra, but he was considered unhip, and Schildkraut took it as a snub. To prove to Weinstock that he could jam with the best of them, he declined any run-through on "Solar," which started out the session, and just went right into it. He would later tell author/saxophonist Allen Lowe that he thought he sounded a little out of sorts; Nat Hentoff, reviewing in *Down Beat*, seemed to feel the same way, saying that though Schildkraut is "an altoist of power and passion . . . his solo lines are not yet integrated into flowing, cohesive entities."

But the real breakthrough came later in the month, on April 29. Schildkraut was replaced by Lucky Thompson on tenor sax and J. J. Johnson was added on trombone, and Davis had the sound he had been hearing in his head: "I wanted that big sound that both of them could give me. You know, Lucky for that Ben Webster thing, but a bebop thing too. J. J. had that big sound and tone." He brought the sextet into engagements at Basin Street East and Birdland, so they came into the studio prepared.

The album was *Walkin'*, and it was a game changer, neither the first nor the last in Miles's career; most musicians, even the very good ones, don't change the direction of jazz even once. Miles agreed: "We knew when we finished that session that we had something good—even Bob Weinstock and Rudy were excited about what went down—but we didn't really feel the impact of that album till it was released later on in the year. That record was a motherfucker."

Even with the group tuning up in the clubs, that the album came off the way it did is a miracle—although any record that has the impact of *Walkin'* is a miracle, no matter what the circumstances. Davis had asked Lucky Thompson to bring in some arrangements, and Thompson had stayed up all the previous night writing them. Ultimately, none of them was used. As Silver describes it: "We tried them in the studio, but nothing came off. They didn't seem to work and neither Miles nor Bob Weinstock were happy. Eventually, they were abandoned and we busked a couple of head arrangements which turned out to be classics!"

Nat Hentoff gave *Walkin'* four stars in *Down Beat*. Joe Goldberg, describing Davis's 1954 output as "a series of brilliant recordings," puts *Walkin'* in context. Writing in 1965, after the genre had pretty much run its course, he said, "it is the best example of the 'hard bop' influence that was just beginning to pervade the work of the modernists."

Hard bop is generally described as funkier than bebop. Melodically and rhythmically simpler, easier to understand, and more danceable. Davis, in his autobiography, writing in 1989 and recalling what went into *Walkin'*, put it this way: "I wanted to take the music back to the fire and improvisations of bebop, that kind of thing Diz and Bird had started. But I also wanted to take the music forward into a more funky kind of blues, the kind of thing Horace would take us to. And with me and J. J. and Lucky on top of that shit, it had to go somewhere. And it did."

On June 29, Davis recorded with Sonny Rollins (see chapter 12). The session is also noteworthy in charting the development of the Davis sound, as it is the first recording on which he used a Harmon mute. It differs from other mutes in that while they partially block the flow of air through the bell of the trumpet, the Harmon completely blocks it. It can then be released with a rush of air and sound, creating a "wah-wah" effect. In Davis's hands, as Ian Carr explains,

> the mute [is] placed very close to the microphone, and the resulting sound is full and breathy in the lower register and thin and piercing in the upper. The two registers can therefore be played off against each other in a dramatic way, and this muted sound is much more expressive than, for example, that of the bland cup mute which Miles had been using earlier in the year. The Harmon mute can be used to express the most delicate nuances of feeling, and because its timbre is round and full and has a clear tongued edge, it is rhythmically very eloquent.

On December 24, Miles finished up the year with a session with Monk (see chapter 9). Davis, in his autobiography, downplays the idea that he had a dispute with Monk, saying only that he told Monk to lay out because "he never did know how to play behind a horn player," especially a trumpet player: "Trumpets don't have that many notes, so you really have to push that rhythm section and that wasn't Monk's thing."

Around this time, Davis had begun listening to Ahmad Jamal. Jamal was that anomaly, a modern jazz musician who worked steadily and was financially stable, and because of this, he was dismissed by many as a facile cocktail lounge pianist. But what Davis heard and appreciated was "his concept of space, his lightness of touch, his understatement."

The December session, whatever the truth about his conflict with Monk may have been, went a long way toward clarifying something in Davis's mind: "It was on the *Modern Jazz Giants* album that I started to understand how to create space by leaving the piano out and just letting everybody stroll. I would extend and use that concept more later; in 1954, going into 1955, it wasn't as clear in my mind as it would be later."

The year 1954 was a turning point for Davis. Even if, as he said in his autobiography, "the critics' heads were still somewhere else," it was hard for even the most acid-tongued critic to ignore *Walkin'*. Musicians were starting to "sit up and notice me again, more than ever before." He was getting some record sales from his Prestige albums. Capitol, testing the waters, brought out a ten-inch LP, also available as a two-record 45 rpm EP set, under the title *Miles Davis—Classics in Jazz*. It was an abbreviated version of the twelve-inch LP that would be released in 1957, with considerably more fanfare, as *Birth of the Cool*.

Bob Weinstock gave him three thousand to do his next album, more than he had ever gotten before. However, 1955 got off to a less promising start. Miles's ex-wife had him jailed for nonpayment of child support. (Weinstock kicked in to help bail him out.) Charlie Parker's death cast a pall over the whole jazz community. Davis did not record again until June 7.

The piano sound he had been looking for—and had not found with Monk—was still on his mind. He was still listening to Ahmad Jamal, and thinking about what he liked in Jamal's playing. There was no getting Jamal to join his group: the pianist was enjoying a financially successful career, playing and recording in Chicago. His friend the drummer Philly Joe Jones, with whom Davis had toured but not recorded, suggested a young pianist from Texas named Red Garland. The result was, in Davis's view, "a nice little album . . . and with Red playing with that Jamal feeling and touch, we got close to what I wanted to hear."

Ian Carr disagrees: "The bass is thin and barely audible, the piano is thin and tinny, and Miles's trumpet sound is rather pinched. [Davis] plays on the whole without fire or conviction, and he also drops several 'clinkers.' To complete the dismal picture, he sounds out of tune on almost every track, and this, added to the bad recording quality, prevents piano and trumpet from blending at all comfortably." But Nat Hentoff gave it five stars in *Down Beat*, saying "Miles is fine, and plays with so much heart and intelligently original conception that he's consistently cooking."

There was one more session, on July 9, with a completely different lineup: Britt Woodman, trombone; Teddy Charles, vibes; Charles Mingus, bass; and Elvin Jones, drums. Hentoff gave it another five stars, saying, "Miles is backed with taste and intelligence . . . [and] demonstrates again how lyrically he excels in this kind of context."

Among the people who were apparently still resistant to the idea that Davis had returned as a reliable performer and a world-class musician was George Wein. Wein booked the Newport Jazz Festival, and had not seen fit to add Davis to the program for 1955. Davis went to Newport anyway, and was added as a last-minute afterthought to a jam session featuring Zoot Sims, Gerry Mulligan, Monk, Percy Heath, and Connie Kay. Davis played a solo on "Round Midnight" that had everyone talking, including Columbia's jazz producer George Avakian. Avakian's message was simple: come to Columbia and I'll make you a star.

Avakian talked to Weinstock too, and Weinstock's message was also simple: Davis was contracted for five more albums, and it would not be cheap to buy him out of his contract.

Now they were talking Davis's language. "Man," he says in his autobiography, "I have to admit, this shit was starting to fascinate me. Those motherfuckers were talking about money, *real* money, so stuff was starting to look good. It was a good position, people talking good about you all over the place instead of badmouthing you." Avakian and Weinstock worked it out: Davis would finish up his five-album contract for Prestige. He could record for Columbia in the meantime, but Columbia could not release any of the recorded material until the Prestige contract had been honored in full.

Avakian, with all of Columbia's money and muscle behind him, had big plans for Davis, and an important part of that plan was creating what in these days is called a brand: an identifiable sound, and a cohesive group, with a distinctive sound, and distinctive names and faces to attach to that sound. It had been working for the Dave Brubeck Quartet; it was working for the Modern Jazz Quartet. Bob Weinstock had wanted Davis to play in different contexts, with different musicians. It had been a good idea at the time. It made for a series of interesting albums, and those early Prestige recordings are an invaluable part of the Miles Davis discography. Besides, with a pickup group, it meant that the musicians were playing for union scale.

Davis would have the money now to keep a cohesive, identifiable group together, and he had already started moving in that direction. He had a club date booked for the Café Bohemia, and the musicians he lined up for it were men that he wanted to keep playing with. He had Philly Joe Jones, who had worked together with him often on the road, when both were on drugs and Davis was incapable of holding a group together. Jones would go into a new town ahead of him, put a group of local musicians together, rehearse them a little, and then bring Davis in to join them. It didn't make for great music, but it allowed Davis and Jones to develop a close working relationship. Red Garland, the young Texas pianist who could absorb the ideas of Ahmad Jamal, had showed Davis he could deliver the sound and feeling that Davis was looking for. There was no hope of tying Percy Heath down to a group: he already had a group, the Modern Jazz Quartet. Jackie McLean had told Davis about a very young bass player who had just arrived in town from Detroit, that cradle of jazz talent. He had played with J. J. Johnson and Kai Winding, and with George Wallington. Everyone was talking about Paul Chambers, and when Davis finally heard him, "I *knew* he was a bad motherfucker."

The choice of tenor saxophone was easy: Sonny Rollins. Rollins did play on the Café Bohemia date. But when it came time to nail down the group that would stay together for a period of time, Rollins was nowhere to be found (it was later discovered he was in the drug rehab prison at Lexington, Kentucky). At around that time, Davis heard another up-and-coming young player, this one an alto saxophonist: Julian "Cannonball" Adderley. Davis loved his sound. But when the time came for Davis to make his decision about his new group, Adderley was also nowhere to be found. He had come from Florida, where he had been a schoolteacher, and he had decided to go back to his day job. Davis considered a few others, McLean being one of them, but no one who was right: "And then Philly Joe brought up John Coltrane. I already knew Trane [from a date Davis had played some years earlier at the Audubon Ballroom in Washington Heights, with Rollins]. But that night Sonny had just blown him away. . . . So I wasn't excited."

After a few rehearsals, Davis could tell how much Coltrane had progressed, but he still wasn't convinced. Davis expected musicians who played with him to find their slot and fill it, and Coltrane "liked to ask all these motherfucking questions" about what to play. And Coltrane apparently didn't like Davis's answers, or lack of answers. He left the group to play with Jimmy Smith in Philadelphia. But in the end, Coltrane decided he liked what Davis was doing musically better than Smith. And Davis had no choice but to take him back. He needed a tenor player right away for a five-city tour, ending up back in New York at the Café Bohemia, and Coltrane was the only one who knew all the tunes. By the end of the tour, Davis was convinced. "This guy was a bad motherfucker who was just the voice I needed on tenor to set off my voice."

They had the group for Columbia. But first, they had to make five records for Prestige. This could not have been a happy time for Davis. He had the pot of gold at the end of the rainbow in sight: real money. And he had the contract with Prestige, for peanuts. "When the word got around that I was leaving Bob," Davis wrote,

> a lot of guys thought that I was cold blooded to leave him like that after he had done all those records with me that nobody else would. But I had to look ahead, and start thinking about my future, and the way I saw it, I couldn't turn down the money that Columbia was offering. I mean I would have been a fool to do it. Plus it was all coming from the white man, so why should I have second thoughts about getting what I could at the time. I appreciated what Bob Weinstock and Prestige had done for me up until this time. But with all the money and opportunities Columbia was offering me, it was just time to move on.

Weinstock knew the realities of life in the record business, even if he didn't like it. As he told Michael Jarrett: "We were a farm team . . . I used to press my records at Columbia, at CBS, in their custom pressing division. They knew how well Miles was selling for me, and they knew how much to offer to get him away from me." Weinstock may not have done too badly out of this deal. He was never going to be able to come anywhere near matching what Columbia had to offer. But he was going to reap some benefits. The advance from Columbia (and Avakian's advice) meant that Davis was able to form a steady, cohesive group, and keep them together. The publicity machine already beginning to form around the new Miles Davis Quintet meant that Davis was able to jack up his price for club dates; the clubs that were vying to present the hottest act in jazz would have to meet those prices, so the quintet was playing regularly, getting tighter and tighter, learning each other's strengths. Garland and especially Chambers were young, relatively new on the scene, immensely talented—again, especially Chambers—and growing more self-assured, able to contribute more, with each live performance. And what was true for the two rhythm men was even more true for the young raw talent that was John Coltrane. Bob Weinstock was getting the hottest group in jazz, playing at the top of their form, with a massive PR campaign forming behind them, and someone else was paying for all of it.

Davis, of course, wanted to satisfy his obligation to Prestige as quickly as possible. And that led to a remarkable series of recording dates at Rudy Van Gelder's studio: the Contractual Marathon. The marathon started off slowly, on November 16, 1955. The group cut six tunes, which Davis remembers as "nice, but nothing like what we were going to do for them in our next sessions." Ira Gitler, just getting warmed up in finding ways to describe John Coltrane's playing, said in his liner notes, "Coltrane's style is a mixture of Dexter Gordon, Sonny Rollins and Sonny Stitt," and Nat Hentoff in his *Down Beat* review agreed, but with less enthusiasm, saying that "his general lack of individuality lowers the rating" from five stars to four.

Through all the acclaim for Davis and the excitement over his new group, that was the note of hesitancy that was struck in some quarters: was John Coltrane up to the task? Sonny Rollins, long Davis's favorite tenor sax player, was back in town, and many thought that Davis would make that move. And in fact, in March 1956, when Davis brought a group into the studio to record four tunes that would be added to the "Charlie Chan" session to fill out an album (*Collector's Items*), he did use Rollins, along with Tommy Flanagan, Paul Chambers, and Art Taylor.

On May 11, the Contractual Marathon began in earnest. The quintet recorded fourteen tracks that day (including two versions of "The Theme"). Here's Davis:

> I remember this session well because it was so long, and the playing was great. We did no second takes. We just recorded like we were playing a nightclub. That's the recording session where you can hear Trane saying on the record, "Can I have a beer opener?" [apparently Van Gelder hadn't learned his lesson from Monk's spilled beer], and asking Bob Weinstock, "How was that, Bob?" and "Why?" after Bob pulled my leg telling us we had to do a tune over again.

Two weeks later, on May 24, Coltrane recorded "Tenor Madness" with Sonny Rollins.

On one tune for the May 11 session, "Ahmad's Blues," both Davis and Coltrane sat out, and let the trio play. It was deliberate on Davis's part: an opportunity for the Red Garland Trio to audition for Prestige, and it was successful. On August 17, the trio made its first record.

On October 26, the Marathon wound up with twelve more tunes, including Rollins's "Oleo" and "Airegin."

While Davis was recording the Contractual Marathon sessions for Prestige, his contract didn't forbid him from recording for another label, but the other label would be forbidden to release any Davis product until the Prestige contract was satisfied. That restriction held only until he had finished the actual recording for Prestige, *not* until all those records were released (which took some years, as Prestige stretched them out). So to get ahead of the game and be ready as soon as they were legally allowed, Avakian brought Davis and his quintet into the studio on October 26, and for more extended sessions on June 5 and September 10, 1956. There were rehearsals, multiple takes, and some splicing, to achieve the perfect sound. The resulting record, *'Round About Midnight*, was released in March 1957, after the first Contractual Marathon release, *Miles*, came out on April 1956. *Cookin'* would come out in July 1957, and the rest would follow through 1961. Today, *'Round About Midnight* is hailed as one of Davis's masterpieces. And today, the Contractual Marathon albums have their passionate admirers (Chris May in *All About Jazz* said it "contains some of the most alive and moving music he ever recorded") but others find them more of a stepping stone to the work of *'Round About Midnight* and subsequent albums for Columbia.

At the time, while Ralph J. Gleason gave *'Round About Midnight* five stars in *Down Beat* ("modern jazz conceived and in the very best style") others found it too safe and middlebrow ("orthodox, middle-of-the-road conservative progressive jazz"—Ralph Berton, *Record Changer*) or pallid in comparison to *Cookin'* and its successors. (*Penguin Guide to Jazz* said it "somehow fails to cast quite the consistent spell which the Prestige recordings do.")

The lesson here is different times, different tastes. Today, in a world of million-dollar studios, multitracking, and digital editing, where the producer is royalty, perfection is the ideal. Back then, it was spontaneity.

Davis's valedictory to Prestige was given in his autobiography:

> You could be a great musician, an innovative and important artist, but nobody cared if you didn't make the white people who were in control some money. The real money was in getting to

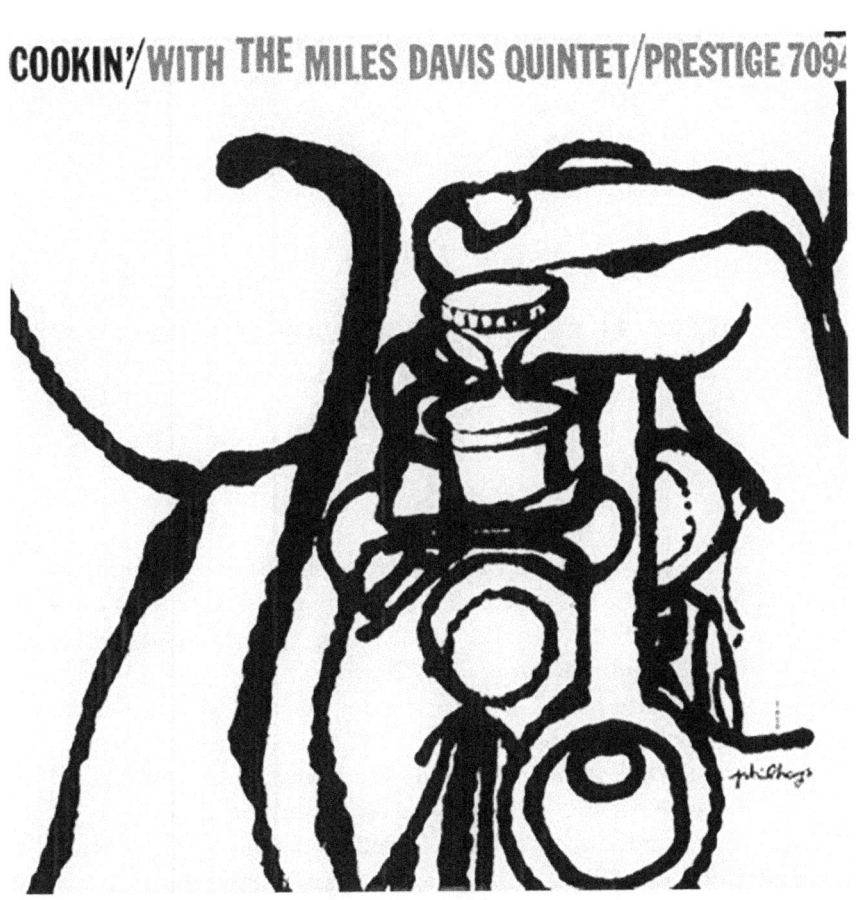

the mainstream of America, and Columbia Records served the mainstream of this country. Prestige didn't; it was making great records, but outside the mainstream.

. . . That was some great music we made at both of these [Contractual Marathon] sessions and I'm real proud of it today. But this ended my contract with Prestige. I was ready to move on.

Chapter 14

Changing Times and Technologies at Prestige

Lennie Tristano was Prestige's first artist, but he made only that one session, in 1949. Thelonious Monk was with the label from 1952 to 1954, making five ten-inch albums. The Modern Jazz Quartet recorded first for Prestige in 1952, and moved on after *Concorde* in 1955, their third album for the label (their fourth, if you count *Sonny Rollins with the Modern Jazz Quartet*). Sonny Rollins made his Prestige debut as a leader in January 1951 (if you count the one track on the Miles Davis session), or December 1951 (if you start with his first full-fledged outing as a leader). He made nine Prestige albums under his own name, including the one with the MJQ. By the time Miles Davis left the label in 1956, and moved on to Columbia and superstardom, Prestige had released seventeen albums under his name; there would be six more, including the Contractual Marathon sessions, in subsequent years.

These musicians moved on for various reasons: more money, a more harmonious relationship with the label executives, a sense that they'd done all they could at Prestige and it was time for a change. But all of them had gotten their start with the young entrepreneur who loved jazz and was willing to take a chance—admittedly at a low rate—on young talent, at a time when almost nobody else was. It was an extraordinary group. They constituted a Mount Rushmore of modern jazz.

They were also young men who, while they may have been grateful to Weinstock for giving them a start, were conscious of their own worth, and ready to expand their position in the world of music. Prestige had been a starter home for them. But like young people all over, they outgrew that starter home. Those years, especially the half decade 1951–56, could be said to be Prestige's Golden Age. It was an era that ended with a flourish, with Miles Davis's Contractual Marathon, which gave Weinstock enough material on the shelf to actually keep the gold going for several more years, with Miles's last Prestige album, *Steamin'*, appearing in 1961.

But if it had been a Golden Age, if it was the end of an era, Bob Weinstock would hardly have noticed. He was in the jazz business, the record business. Over that same half decade, he had recorded Stan Getz, Lee Konitz, Billy Taylor (ten albums), Ray Barreto, Kenny Burrell, Wardell Gray, Elmo Hope, James Moody (in Sweden and the USA), King Pleasure, Annie Ross, Sonny Stitt, Gene Ammons, Zoot Sims, Jimmy Raney, Eddie "Lockjaw" Davis, Al Haig, Gerry Mulligan, George Wallington, Red Rodney, J. J. Johnson, Kai Winding, Bennie Green, Urbie Green, Duke Jordan, Jo Jones, Teddy Charles, Joe Holiday, the Cabineers, H-Bomb Ferguson, Brownie McGhee, Bengt Hallberg, Lars Gullin, Hampton Hawes, Sam Most, Eddie Jefferson, Tadd Dameron, Art Farmer, Gigi Gryce, Al Cohn, Phil Woods, Jon Eardley, Freddie Redd, Jackie McLean, Earl Coleman, Gil Mellé, Hank Mobley, Donald Byrd, Barry Harris, Art Taylor, Philly Joe Jones, Red Garland, Herbie Mann, Blind Willie McTell, Barbara Lea, Mal Waldron, and Moondog. And more. Some had passed through and made one album; some had stayed around for a while; some were still under contract. He was in the business, and modern jazz was coming into its own as the music of choice for a sophisticated audience. It was not going to replace Elvis Presley; for that matter, it was not going to replace Guy Lombardo or Fred Waring and his Pennsylvanians. But it had a real audience, and if you were good, you could make a living at it.

There was a lot more music to be made, and more young stars to sign and record, and Weinstock, now joined by Esmond Edwards and young writer/occasional producer Ira Gitler, was just getting warmed up. Miles Davis had given him a parting gift: his rhythm section, led by the gifted pianist Red Garland. And another parting gift, wrapped up in a bow and placed at the top of the tree, a young horn player who would go on to rival Davis himself as an artist and as a jazz legend: John Coltrane.

In the early days of recording jazz, and up through the early days of the LP era, there was really no such thing as a producer. Record companies had someone, or a few people, in charge of artists and repertoire. In the studio there was someone—generally the same person, in a small operation—supervising the production. The work of the A&R man was done mostly before the session, talking to the guy who was going to lead it and discussing who else would be playing. As Weinstock told Michael Jarrett, "We'd always talk about the personnel, what we were going to do. A lot of times they'd have tunes. Other times, I'd have tunes. Our main emphasis was just to play."

Even that was more informal than it sounds. There would be general agreement on who was going to play on a session, but someone—especially true in those days of the heroin crisis—might not show up at the last minute. And since in those days there was no such thing as a concept album, and since for a Prestige session there was no rehearsal, the selection of material could be very much a last-minute thing. Rudy Van Gelder, who engineered most of Prestige's later sessions, once commented that one tune on almost every session should have been called "Five O'Clock Blues": it was near the end of the day, they needed one more cut, they didn't have anything else planned, so they just took a blues riff, jammed on it for five minutes, and called it whatever came to mind. Setting up the recording equipment, placing the mikes, or the single mike, might have been another part of the job, but Weinstock and other self-professionalized enthusiasts who ran the labels were mostly not particularly technically savvy, so a sound engineer handled that. When Weinstock first met Rudy Van Gelder, he asked him how he got his sound, and Van Gelder's only reply was: "I have my techniques. I don't discuss it. It's there on the records. If you hear it and you like it, fine."

When the LP came along, a handful of the A&R men who were also supervising the recording sessions—George Avakian at Columbia was probably the first, but Weinstock was close behind—realized that a jazz performance did not have to be limited to three minutes. This was a huge step forward. Up until this time, there had been two kinds of jazz: recorded jazz and actual jazz. The brilliant, game-changing solos of Coleman Hawkins on "Body and Soul" or Charlie Parker with Jay McShann on "Sepian Bounce" or Illinois Jacquet with Lionel Hampton on "Flying Home" were not what those musicians played at a jazz club or a Jazz at the Philharmonic concert or a dance, where the saxophone soloist would step forward to be cheered on by enthusiastic audiences and keep going: developing ideas further, or repeating phrases that were particular crowd favorites. When Leon Rene came to hear Joe Liggins play "The Honeydripper"—the tune that triggered the Texas Hop, the hot-dance craze on Central Avenue in Los Angeles—those dancers were not stopping after three minutes, and neither was Liggins. Rene had Liggins play two three-minute segments of "The Honeydripper," and put them on either side of a 78 rpm record, and it was a hit, but it still wasn't the live experience.

That was the way it had always been done on record, which is why Davis and Rollins were so surprised when, in Weinstock's words, "I said, 'Miles, we're going to stretch out.' He said, 'You mean we're just going to play?'" And it's why they had no trouble doing it. And it also meant the role of the A&R man was expanded. He was doing some actual producing, guiding how long he wanted the solos to be, signaling the soloist when it was time to stop, when it was time to stretch.

After hearing that they were just going to play, Davis suggested, "What about this young guy, Jackie McLean? He's pretty good, too, if we're going to stretch out." It was a suggestion Davis would probably not have made if they had been working with a three-minute limitation, with scant room for two soloists. And as it turned out, Weinstock as A&R man approved the addition of McLean, but Weinstock the producer decided that McLean was still too young and unformed to be given his head to that extent, and his stretch-out signals were given to Davis and Rollins.

It was an improvised part of the producer's job, but those self-professionalized enthusiasts were up to it. Weinstock told Jarrett:

> Next, I did either Zoot Sims with a quartet or Gerry Mulligan's Tentet [*Swingin' with Zoot Sims* and *Mulligan Plays Mulligan*, both recorded in 1951]. On the Gerry thing I had him stretch out. He played a long solo, and then he and [tenor saxophonist] Allen Eager would play. If I wanted them to play more, they'd look at me, and I'd nod my head, "yeah" or "no." Then they'd switch. I'd sort of "cut my throat," and he'd know to go out at the end of the chorus. One of the best Zoot albums ever made is called *Swingin' with Zoot Sims*, where [on "Zoot Swings the Blues"] he just kept going on and on and on.

And again, discussing a later Rollins session: "When I saw Sonny Rollins was playing his ass off, I'd give him a high sign. Other times, I'd show him the stopwatch and throw it on the couch. That meant, 'Play, man. Ignore the clock.'"

Another facet of the producer's job may have been a partial cause of a controversial bit of jazz history. The producer/A&R guy/session supervisor, in a small operation, was responsible for naming the album, finding someone to write the liner notes, and choosing what order the tunes would go on the album—or what tunes to leave off. He was also responsible for coming up with names for riff-based improvisations developed in the studio, such as "Newk's Fadeaway," and sometimes for assigning composer credit to a "Five O'Clock Blues"; the credit would typically go, in those cases, to the leader of the session. So it was that "Dig," a tune that Jackie McLean had brought to the session, was credited to Davis, the cause of a miniscandal in the modern jazz world. Davis, years later, was asked about it, and admitted freely that McLean had written the tune. But he was not planning to change the credit. McLean at one point asked a lawyer about suing, and was told there wasn't enough money involved to make it worthwhile.

When Esmond Edwards took over the main producer's job at Prestige, he extended the A&R responsibility. Weinstock had given a recorded voice to some of the greatest talents to come out of the 1940s, but he was not much for going out and scouting new talent. As his original class grew up, graduated, and moved on, it was time to find a new generation, new styles, new sounds. Edwards went out, went up to Harlem, kept his ears open, and listened.

Technology changed the producer's role, too. The LP record was made possible by the development of microgroove technology, allowing a ten- or twelve-inch record to hold fifteen or twenty minutes' worth of music on each side. But that was only part of it. The other technological advance was the use of magnetic tape, which provided better audio fidelity but also made it possible to record longer stretches of music. Tape also created new options for the producer. You could record from one reel-to-reel tape machine to another; Columbia's George Avakian, a pioneer in this new field, used that technique to create a recording of Louis Armstrong's trumpet accompanying his own vocals on *Louis Armstrong Plays W. C. Handy*. But that wasn't all.

Musicians are human. There's a classic story about disco-era producer Nile Rodgers, who was putting together a multitracked production with several rhythm tracks, each one electronically produced, and each one perfect. The sound engineer got frustrated with all this perfection, and programmed a tiny glitch, way down in the mix, almost impossible to hear. But Rodgers, as in the fairy tale about the princess and the pea, heard it, and hit the ceiling. "If I wanted mistakes," he shouted, "I would have hired a real drummer!"

Musicians make mistakes. Some of them are priceless, like Thelonious Monk's odd solo on the alternate take of "Bags Groove" from the Miles Davis December 1954 session. Some of them are barely noticeable as one is carried along by the excitement of the music. Some of them are forgivable, because, after all, musicians are human. But all of them became fixable, because one of the other advantages of tape was that you could cut it and splice it together. This meant that if someone flubbed a note and then corrected it, you could cut out the flubbed note. And if someone flubbed a whole sequence of notes, you could have the musician go back into the studio, redo that part, then cut out the flubbed part and splice in the new recording. It didn't even have to be a whole sequence of notes. If a single high note was a little flat, you could have the artist hit that note squarely, and splice it in.

This did not happen overnight. Don Schlitten, who got his start producing for Prestige, told Michael Jarrett:

> Recording was done primarily the same way as it had always been done. There was no mixing. You got a balance and captured the performance. Whatever you got, you got. In those days, some engineers working for small independent companies didn't even have the proper technique for splicing and editing tape. The only difference, when I started, was music went to tape instead of discs. Otherwise, things were the same. The idea was to get a proper balance and go for a take, make sure it wasn't too short or too long.

Columbia had the equipment, and the technique, and once again Avakian led the field. When he decided to record Duke Ellington at Newport, there was considerable trepidation on the part of the orchestra. A whole live concert, no second takes on anything? Ellington reassured them: "Don't worry about the performance. Billy Strayhorn and George have set up a studio for tomorrow morning, and we're going to go back to New York and make patches."

Not everyone was convinced of the legitimacy of splicing in notes. During a Buck Clayton session, Avakian told Jarrett, trombonist Urbie Green failed to hit two notes. Green was old school, and Avakian was too embarrassed to call him back in to redo them. He confided his problem to Clayton, who volunteered to come in and play the notes on the lower register of his trumpet. Apparently it worked; afterward, neither Clayton nor Avakian could recognize the two spliced-in notes. Years later, shortly before Clayton died, they ran into each other and Clayton asked, "George, did you ever find those two notes?" A friend of Avakian's queried him about editing a Dave Brubeck session, splicing in bits from different takes to fix imperfections. The friend, a writer, was dismayed with that sort of editorial interference with Brubeck's creation. Avakian invited him to ask Brubeck what he thought of the splices. He reported back, "Dave said, 'George saved my fucking ass.'"

Miles Davis famously said, "It's not the note you play that's the wrong note—it's the note you play afterwards that makes it right or wrong." Herbie Hancock, in an interview, recalled an example of that. They were playing "So What" onstage in a concert performance, and in the middle of the number, Hancock hit an egregiously wrong chord. He didn't know how he had done it, but he knew it had ruined the piece. He froze, put his head in his hands. And then he listened to what Davis was doing. He had hesitated for a second, and then he had taken his improvisation in a new direction, making the wrong chord right. But as it turned out, with Davis, as with every Columbia artist, there *were* wrong chords, and the way to make them right was the splice. Dizzy Gillespie, commenting on Davis's Columbia album *Bitches Brew*, said that it had been produced with a pair of scissors by producer Teo Macero.

Because of Weinstock's preference for the spontaneous jam session with few repeats, combined with his preference for saving money by taping over rejected versions, Prestige was not much for splicing. The razor blade was used when editing down an extended jam for 45 rpm release, but not much outside of that. This has led to criticism of the label by a younger generation, who criticized its careless, sloppy, rushed production. Times change, and values change. Weinstock was not alone in valuing spontaneity, but many today favor the Nile Rodgers approach.

Prestige, with its laissez-faire attitude—let them play, let the public hear what they played—is the quintessence of that era. Critics have charged that Bob Weinstock's approach was the result of his being too cheap to pay for rehearsal time, and there's some truth to that. But I don't believe it's the whole story. Weinstock started Prestige when he was nineteen years old—just a kid. Jazz as pure spontaneity is a fantasy. It was Jack Kerouac's fantasy when he set out to write poetry as "spontaneous bop prosody." And it was a kid's fantasy when young Bob started his own record label. Few kids get to live out their fantasies, and the world is probably the poorer for it. Bob Weinstock did, and recorded jazz is the richer for it.

Chapter 15

Other '50s-Era Prestige Recording Artists

As Prestige's stars wound down their careers with the label, new names were being added to the roster. Some were just passing through, while others would stay awhile. Some were signed to exclusive contracts with Prestige, not always happily. Almost all of them moved on.

Later, Weinstock would hire producers who would go out to the small clubs, not just in New York, to scout for new talent. But in these years, he mostly relied on word of mouth: established musicians bringing new raw talent to his attention, as Miles Davis did with Sonny Rollins and John Coltrane. Here are a few of the musicians who recorded for Prestige in the 1950s.

Jimmy Raney and Phil Woods

Guitarist Jimmy Raney joined Woody Herman's orchestra in 1948, and he recorded with Herman sideman Stan Getz for Savoy in 1949. He worked steadily but mostly anonymously with Artie Shaw, Buddy DeFranco, and others, along with continuing to work for Getz. He first came into the Prestige orbit when he was brought in for a December 1952 session with Teddy Charles, one of Weinstock's most reliable talent scouts. He must have also gotten the thumbs up from Getz, because when Prestige brought him back for his own date in the following April. Stan Getz (performing under the name of "Sven Coolson"; he was under contract to Norman Granz) was in the quintet. Pianist Hall Overton may have come to Raney through Teddy Charles.

Raney then left for a year of the expatriate life in Europe, but returned to New York in May 1954 to take up residency at the Blue Angel supper club and make a record for New Jazz, and then on August 11, 1954, to introduce a new alto saxophone player, Phil Woods. He appears to have been freelancing during this period as he recorded for ABC Paramount and other labels. A few more sessions for Prestige in 1954–55 were shelved and released on one LP in 1957, and that same year he co-led a session with Kenny Burrell, with an all-star ensemble that included Donald Byrd, Jackie McLean, and Mal Waldron. He maintained a good relationship with Prestige, appearing on albums by Barbara Lea (1957) and Dave Pike (1962).

Prestige proved the springboard for a long career for Raney, who recorded extensively in both America and Europe through the 1980s. When he died in 1995, he was described in a *New York Times* obituary as "one of the most gifted and influential postwar jazz guitarists."

Weinstock liked what he heard from Phil Woods on the Raney session, and signed the tenor sax man to an exclusive contract. He had him in the studio within a couple of months, on October 12, 1954, and then again on February 5, 1955, with a group of musicians who were mostly all making their recording debuts. Bassist Teddy Kotick, a bebop veteran who had recorded with Charlie Parker, was the exception. Pianist George Syran would have a steady if unspectacular career, in ensembles as varied as Cannonball Adderley and Lester Lanin. Drummer Nick Stabulas would find steady work, and many recording dates, before his untimely death in an auto accident in 1973. Trumpeter Jon Eardley made a strong first impression, and also played with Gerry Mulligan before moving to Europe.

Woods made the critics sit up and take notice as quickly as he had caught Weinstock's ear. Nat Hentoff said, "[Woods] and Frank Morgan are the two most exciting young altoists I've heard all year. Both have a passion, a strong beat, and ideas of their own." He would record regularly with Prestige for the next three years, to increasing acclaim—and increasing frustration. In a *Down Beat* interview with Nat Hentoff in January 1957, he complained:

> His contract is up in August, 1957.
> "I won't stay," he says. "I'm going to freelance and won't sign again with a record company unless I get a much better deal. I signed for three years with Prestige and lost my shirt. I'm not about to do it again. My contract for two LPs a year.

How can a man live on that with maybe three or four extra dates as a sideman thrown in? And with a few exceptions, they prevented me from making dates for other people. Well, I've made five LPs for them and have one more to do."

Weinstock, in an interview with Dom Cerulli the following June, had this to say about Woods and exclusivity contracts:

> When we sign an artist exclusively, it is not so much to keep him away from recording and to take away his earning power, but rather we assume responsibility for the artist. We try our best through the efforts of our organization and through outlay of funds to promote him . . .
>
> Phil Woods said he lost his shirt by being with Prestige and being tied up with a contract. He says we kept him from doing sideman dates. Well, I can't recall very many instances when he asked permission to do those dates, and if he did, we always allowed him to record.
>
> However, the few times we didn't let him record with other companies, it was because these companies would not let us use their artists, or the A&R man there planned a quartet or quintet date where Phil would have been playing more than the leader of the session.
>
> Then that record would be in competition with ours.
>
> When we heard him play on a Jimmy Raney session, he was unknown except to a few local musicians. We hired him and liked him. When we spoke about signing exclusively here, you never saw such an eager musician who wanted to sign a contract so fast.
>
> Where were all the companies who want him now at that time? As soon as the critics discovered him, those other companies all wanted to jump on the band wagon and record him. It happens every time because very few companies have the guts to sign unknowns, but they wait like vultures once the critics approve.

It's not hard to sympathize with both sides. Woods was young, and supremely talented. Everyone knew it. Prestige, as we know, was not exactly a money factory. At the same time, the big labels with the big money weren't handing it out to unknowns; it was labels like Prestige that took those chances.

Those Phil Woods recordings were money in the bank for Bob Weinstock, and they increased the value of his catalog when he eventually sold it to Fantasy Records. Woods would become even more bankable when he recorded a memorable solo on Billy Joel's "Just the Way You Are." A story is told of a young rock fan asking Woods if he was the guy who . . . Yes, he was, was the answer. "You're really good," the young fan gushed. "Have you ever recorded anything else?" "One or two things," was Woods's amused response. That Billy Joel recording brought a lot of new fans to Phil Woods, and increased the value of his Prestige catalog once more. There was considerably less long-term money in the bank (read: none) for the records of Jon Eardley, Gene Quill, or Jim Chapin, although they were all also good young players who Weinstock signed up.

An anonymous jazz musician, writing in *Down Beat* a couple of years earlier, anticipated some of Weinstock's arguments while debunking them:

> I would like finally to protest publicly—and I am not alone—about what I consider malpractice on the part of many record company owners and A&R men with regard to their use of jazz musicians. This malpractice, of course, has become even more widespread as modern jazz has grown more and more popular with the public and more modern jazz records are being made. Ironically, the musicians who are responsible for the growth of jazz interest across the country are the ones who suffer as that interest increases.
>
> I'm talking about the practice whereby record companies sign an artist for a minimum of eight sides a year on a five-year contract. The contract usually states that the company will not allow the musician to play as a sideman for any other group on another label. . . .
>
> The recording executives' viewpoint seems to be that if the name of a musician they've signed exclusively is spread out among a number of labels as a sideman, they'll have difficulty selling many copies of his albums on their own label.

But they're wrong. If a guy plays well on his dates as a sideman, he keeps adding listeners interested in his music, and the result will be that he'll sell more copies of his own album because he's been heard on other dates.

All of this is suggestive of a controversy in another facet of American life where talented youngsters were signed to exclusivity clauses by the owners of companies that represented their only access to recognition and renumeration in their field. Baseball's reserve clause was even more restrictive; a player was essentially bound for his entire career to the team that held his contract. If he was traded, the reserve clause went with him. And it meant that the player had little bargaining power. Slugger Ralph Kiner, after he had led the league in home runs, found his salary had been cut for the following season. Management's argument: "We finished last with you, we can finish last without you." Baseball's reserve clause was challenged in court and finally abolished in 1975, replaced by a system not unlike that of the independent music labels: a player is obligated to the team who signs him for a period of six years. Record labels today continue to issue essentially the same contracts to new artists. Billy Vera, a recording artist himself for many decades, comments, "It would be stupid for a company to spend all that money recording and publicizing an artist, only to have another company with relatively little investment reap the rewards."

Another difference between the baseball industry and the music industry: a baseball player leaves no back catalog of his accomplishments with his original team: Once he's gone, he's gone. Phil Woods, during the years 1955–57, when he was signed to Prestige, did appear on records for Savoy, Epic, Keynote, Coral, RCA Victor, Columbia, and Norgran.

Teddy Charles

Vibraphonist Teddy Charles had hooked up with Prestige early, as recording artist in 1951, and as Bob Weinstock's ambassador to the West Coast. Not exclusive with Prestige, he alternated sessions with Atlantic throughout this period, and gradually moved more into the role of freelance producer for several labels, notably Bethlehem. Not content with living one life to stir the romantic imagination, that of a jazz musician, he recreated himself in a second even more romantic existence, that of sailboat captain of a charter vessel in the Caribbean. His music was always considered bold and experimental, and was critically well received.

Gigi Gryce

Gigi Gryce first met Art Farmer in Sweden in 1953, when they were both part of Lionel Hampton's European tour. They recorded together in Paris, and each recognized a kindred spirit, so it was natural that Farmer would bring Gryce in for a Prestige recording date on May 19, 1954. The session included Horace Silver, piano; Percy Heath, bass; Kenny Clarke, drums. It was booked as the Art Farmer Quintet featuring Gigi Gryce, but of the four tunes recorded that day, three were by Gryce ("A Night at Tony's," "Blue Concept," "Deltitnu") and only one by Farmer ("Stupendous-Lee").

The pattern was repeated a year later, on May 26, 1955. Again, it was booked as the Art Farmer Quintet featuring Gigi Gryce. This time it was Freddie Redd, piano; Addison Farmer, bass; Art Taylor, drums. And again four tunes were recorded. One, "The Infant's Song," was written by Farmer, and the other three were all Gryce: "Capri," "Blue Lights," and a tune destined to be a jazz standard, "Social Call."

The first session was released in 1954 as a ten-inch LP, eponymously title *Art Farmer Quintet*. A follow-up ten-inch in 1955 was *Art Farmer Quintet Volume Two Featuring Gigi Gryce*. But when the two were combined as a single twelve-inch LP in 1957, with a striking photograph by Esmond Edwards on the cover (see chapter 11), it was *When Farmer Met Gryce*, and equal billing was given to the two young jazzmen on the cusp of stardom.

Gryce was heralded as a composer as well as an alto saxophonist. Stan Getz had recorded one of his tunes ("Hymn of the Orient") in 1952. Bob Weinstock, in arranging a session for vocalist Earl Coleman, brought the young altoist in to accompany him, explaining: "I felt Earl would need someone of a higher musical level to work with him. . . . Earl Coleman was a great singer, no question about it, but he needed some help, really. And I felt Gigi could give it to him." In addition to his all-around musical savvy, Gryce brought Coleman two original songs, both with lyrics by Jon Hendricks. One was "Reminiscing"; the other was the song that was to become Coleman's biggest hit and his signature: "Social Call."

Weinstock recognized that Gryce's real strength was as a composer. Referring to *Mal-1*, an album that paired Gryce with another brilliant composer, Mal Waldron, he said: "It was probably a fusion of two people who

were great jazz writers, Mal and Gigi. And there's one difference, though. Mal could really cook . . . and Gigi, unfortunately . . . wasn't right up near the top as a player." Bassist Bob Cranshaw, who worked with him, agreed: "Because he was such a great composer and writer, I think that overshadowed the playing because . . . that's how he got gratification. From watching the guys play his stuff."

Gryce's work with Prestige in the 1950s encompassed several sessions with Art Farmer, including a couple where he was just used as arranger, and the sessions with Earl Coleman and Mal Waldron. At the same time he was doing a lot of work with Donald Byrd for a number of labels, including the short-lived Signal, the label started by Prestige producer Don Schlitten. He returned in 1960 to make three albums for New Jazz.

But this bright star was destined to dim, and finally be extinguished, by the pressures brought to bear on a Black musician in the 1950s, especially one who would not accept the status quo. His attempt to change the face of the music business was at least as important as his work as a composer/musician, and it was his undoing.

In that era, the music business was controlled by a lot of unscrupulous men. It's well documented how they took advantage of naïve musical artists, many of them Black, at a time when the music of Black America was becoming the music of mainstream America. The gangster Hesh Rabkin, in *The Sopranos*, who cheerfully boasts of having made his fortune ripping off doowop groups in the '50s, is closely based on a real figure from that era, Mo Levy, who ran Roulette Records (Levy's career is documented in a fascinating book, *Godfather of the Music Business*, by Richard Carlin). One of the chief ways in which musical artists were cheated was the issue of publishing rights. Many young artists, whose dream was to make a record and get paid for it, signed a contract with a record company that paid them for the recording, and maybe even paid them royalties for the sales of that record, but gave the publishing rights to the song to the owner of the record company. So if, as so often happened with rhythm and blues hits, the song was rerecorded by a white artist, reaching a larger audience and getting much larger sales, the original songwriter got nothing more.

In the summer of 1955, Gryce started his own publishing company, Melotone, with the assistance of a young lawyer named William Kunstler. Kunstler, just getting started and not yet the fiery defender of civil rights, did little more than file the papers for Gryce, but his subsequent lawyer, Bruce Wright, who as a judge was a passionate advocate for the rights of the poor and minorities, was a much more active adviser. Wright later said of Gryce, in an interview with Noal Cohen for his biography of Gryce, *Rat Race Blues*, "One of the reasons he established these publishing companies was to become an honest broker in a field where musicians believed they were being cheated in large part. So he was stalwart, upright, and wanted everything to be kosher."

Gryce was a trailblazer. Horace Silver, who would also start his own publishing company, has said, "He was responsible for getting me into publishing." But he did more than inspire others. He actively set out to help others, either by helping them start their own companies (according to Silver, "whenever I had a problem, publishing-wise, I would always call Gigi . . . and he would try to straighten it out for me or explain what I should do about it"), or by enrolling them in Melotone or his other company, Totem. Among the many musicians who published with one of his companies were Benny Golson (who cofounded Melotone with him), Clifford Brown, Lou Donaldson, Bobby Timmons (both "Moanin'" and "Dis Here" were published with Melotone), Art Farmer, Hank Jones, and Ray Bryant. Coming as the civil rights movement was just gaining traction, it was a forceful statement of Black empowerment.

Bob Weinstock recalls:

> In the record business, most of the people that ran the companies . . . thought musicians were basically stupid and not businesslike . . . and they screwed them basically. They took the songs away. A lot of times they put their own names on them even if on the record it said the writer of the song was correct, the song contract was not in the writer's name . . . they would resent a person like Gigi Gryce that knew the publishing business and took care of business . . .
>
> I never cared whether Prestige Music Company got the publishing or the writer got it, or had their own publishing, because I always felt it's their right. . . . So when a Gigi Gryce came, more power to him that he should keep his songs in his own publishing company.

Miles Davis's recollection of Weinstock was a little different: "I had always appreciated what Bob Weinstock did for me before, back in the early days, [but] he wanted all my music publishing rights, which I didn't give him."

But if Gryce had no problem with Weinstock and Alfred Lion and a few others, there were enough people in the music business like the fictional Hesh Rabkin who were not going to allow anyone to interfere with their gravy train. Bruce Wright, in his memoir *Black Justice in a White World*, recalls: "Musicians left Melotone and Totem because they were told that having their music published by Gryce would prevent their ever having the opportunity to record the tunes." Some record labels simply ignored Gryce's invoices for publishing royalties, knowing that he could not afford the time and expense of legal action against them. Ultimately, Gryce had to close down Melotone and Totem. Disillusioned and bitter, he left the music business altogether. But, as musician Harold Ousley observed, "Now, almost every jazz musician, white or black, worth his salt, has his own publishing company. And that's due to the pioneering efforts of Gigi Gryce and the people like him."

Art Farmer

Art Farmer's early experience was on the West Coast, playing with rhythm and blues, swing, and bebop ensembles, including one recording date with Wardell Gray for a Prestige album (discussed in chapter 6). In 1953 he relocated to New York, where he quickly began making a name for himself around town, and was brought in by Prestige for a July 7 session with a sextet that included Quincy Jones as pianist and arranger. He then joined Lionel Hampton's European tour, making some records overseas with Jones, Gryce, and Clifford Brown, among others.

The Hampton tour wound up in early December, and by January 1954 Farmer was signed to Prestige and back in the studio leading a quintet with Sonny Rollins (see sidebar, chapter 12).

Listening to Prestige: Art Farmer Septet

Recorded at Van Gelder Studio, Hackensack, NJ, June 7, 1954

Art Farmer, trumpet; Jimmy Cleveland, trombone; Charlie Rouse, tenor sax; Danny Bank, baritone sax; Horace Silver, piano; Percy Heath, bass; Arthur Taylor, drums

Tracks recorded: Evening in Paris; Wildwood; Elephant Walk; Tiajuana

Art Farmer seemed to do very well with the midsized group, six to eight pieces. He was perhaps best known for the six-man Jazztet with Benny Golson in the late '50s and early '60s, and his work in the early '50s also tended toward that format. His early Wardell Gray session for Prestige in 1952 was a sextet, although only two of the group were front line players (the sixth was a percussionist). He led a septet in 1953 before joining the Lionel Hampton tour, and played with various midsized ensembles during the Hampton tour in Europe. His first two 1954 sessions were quintets, but he returned to the studio again with seven pieces for this one. The group included Horace Silver and Percy Heath, and maybe Kenny Clarke, according to the jazzdisco.com website, which has the set lists for every Prestige session. But they may be wrong. The label on the 45 says the drummer was Art Taylor, and the Art Taylor Wikipedia page credits him with this. Perhaps Clarke was booked but had to bail at the last minute.

These recordings were released on 45 and 78, and on a twelve-inch, 7000-series LP, as The Art Farmer Septet. It's the first Prestige session I've seen that didn't come out on a ten-inch LP first.

Farmer would record prolifically for Prestige between 1954 and 1958. As a sideman, he supported Gene Ammons (three times), Earl Coleman, Bennie Green, Gil Melle, and Mal Waldron. And during that same time period, as one of the most sought-after trumpeters in town, he freelanced for other labels on albums by a plethora of artists including Quincy Jones, Johnny Mathis, Oscar Pettiford, Kenny Burrell, Curtis Fuller, and Benny Golson—he would join forces with the latter two shortly after leaving Prestige to form the Jazztet. As a leader, he made another album with Gryce, and one with Hank Mobley.

Then there was a session on August 3, 1956, with a group of musicians contracted to Prestige and listed on the session log as a leaderless session by the Prestige All-Stars: Farmer and Donald Byrd on trumpet (Farmer doubling on flugelhorn); Jackie McLean, alto sax; Barry Harris, piano; Doug Watkins, bass; Art Taylor, drums.

One of the highlights of this session was a blistering fifteen-minute version of that well-known Miles Davis composition "Dig." Since one of the things that song was particularly well known for was that the actual composer was Jackie McLean (see chapter 5), it must have been a bittersweet session for McLean. He contributes a strong solo to this version, but Farmer and Byrd, with back-to-back solos, are most impressive. Also on the album are solo turns by just Farmer and the rhythm section (a warm, romantic "When Your Lover Has Gone"), then Byrd in the same quartet setting with a moody "Round Midnight."

By the time the album was released a few months later, the Prestige brain trust had figured out that they had not one but two of the brightest young trumpet stars around (they would both make the top ten in the 1957 *Down Beat* Readers' Poll), and the album was released as *Farmer/Byrd: 2 Trumpets*. A second Prestige All Stars session added Idrees Sulieman to the trumpet front line, and it was released as *3 Trumpets*.

It was also Art Farmer's last recording session for Prestige.

Donald Byrd

Trumpeter Donald Byrd came to New York from Detroit, and began recording as a sideman with various ensembles in 1955. He first drew the attention of Bob Weinstock in January 1956, when he recorded alongside Phil Woods in a quintet led by bebop veteran George Wallington. That same month, he was featured on another Prestige session led by Jackie McLean. He joined Art Blakey's Jazz Messengers, then returned to Prestige to play on a May session led by pianist Elmo Hope.

By then he was a regular on Weinstock's go-to list. There was a Phil Woods session in June; on July 13 he doubled up, recording with Jackie McLean and then with Gene Ammons; the following week he did it again, recording with McLean and Hank Mobley on the same day.

On August 3 there was the Prestige All Stars session that became the jointly headlined Farmer/Byrd *2 Trumpets*. On November 2 came another cobilling: the Phil Woods/Donald Byrd Quintet.

After that, through the end of 1956 and into 1957, came a series of Prestige All Stars dates. A December 28 session was first released as *All Night Long* by Donald Byrd, Jerome Richardson, Kenny Burrell, Hank Mobley, Mal Waldron, Doug Watkins, and Art Taylor, then later simply as *All Night Long* by Kenny Burrell. The follow-up All Stars session, on January 4, 1957, got the same treatment: *All Day Long* by Byrd; Frank Foster, tenor sax; Tommy Flanagan, piano; Burrell, Watkins, Taylor; then rereleased as *All Day Long* by Burrell.

March 5 saw another All Stars session with Burrell, this one with Jimmy Raney added, so Prestige released it as *2 Guitars*. Byrd would continue to record with the Prestige All Stars through the end of 1956 and into 1957, also sharing leader status on recordings with Farmer and Woods.

Byrd's career at Prestige ended in late 1957 and early 1958 with a series of sessions showcasing the label's new big star, John Coltrane. After that, he signed with Blue Note, and his career really took off. It seems that Prestige knew what they had, but were a little slow pulling the trigger on making him one of their headline attractions.

Mal Waldron

Another significant composer came to Prestige in 1956, and was to have a long association with the label. Pianist Mal Waldron had made a few records with rhythm and blues performers, then joined Charles Mingus's Jazz Composers Workshop. He played piano on Mingus's second Jazz Composers Workshop album, released by Atlantic as *Pithecanthropus Erectus*. Teddy Charles, a member of the Workshop, used Mingus on his influential Tentet album, which included one of Waldron's compositions, "Vibrations."

On July 13, 1956, Jackie McLean, who had worked with Waldron on the *Pithecanthropus Erectus* album, brought the pianist with him for a Prestige session, which included one Waldron tune, "Abstraction." Weinstock must have liked what he heard, because Waldron became a fixture. His first session as a leader came that November 9, with a group featuring Idrees Sulieman, trumpet; Gigi Gryce, alto sax; Euell, bass; Arthur Edgehill, drums. Considering Waldron's gifts as a composer, it's surprising that there are only two originals by him on the album (and one by the equally gifted composer Gigi Gryce). But there was certainly enough to show his worth as a piano player and as a leader. Prestige titled this album *Mal-1*, signaling a longer commitment to this new artist, which they were to keep, through *Mal-4*.

Waldron would become one of the most fascinating figures in '50s jazz; with his evocative, slightly sinister name, New York vibes (born in NYC), somewhat secretive personality (he switched from saxophone to piano because he didn't think he had the personality to be out front of a band), and his attitude (the London Jazz Collector says that you won't find a Waldron album cover without a cigarette dangling from his lips, which is an exaggeration, but you get the idea). Waldron was at the beginning of a long and distinguished career, though not one that would win him any *Playboy* jazz polls.

He began to make his mark as composer quickly. His compositions were featured on three sessions released as by "The Prestige All Stars." Waldron contributed "Pedal Eyes" and "Staggers" on a February 9, 1957, session with Gene Quill, Sahib Shihab, Hal Stein, Phil Woods, alto sax; Tommy Potter, bass; and Louis Hayes, drums. A bonus in listening to a Waldron composition is that Waldron is given a little more solo space, which is always a joy, but a particular joy when he's improvising on one of his own tunes. He approaches them with a keen, searching intelligence. "Staggers" found its way onto a number of different recordings, including one by Teddy Charles.

Seven days later, on November 16, he was back with the All Stars (now featuring Thad Jones, trumpet; Frank Wess, flute, tenor sax; Teddy Charles, vibes; Doug Watkins, bass; Elvin Jones, drum. The session showcased two of the best composers of this era: "Touche" and "Potpourri" were written by Waldron; "Blues Without Woe," "Dakar," and "Hello Frisco" are all by Teddy Charles, who also produced the session. A March 22, 1957, All Stars session featured Waldron's classic "Soul Eyes," with Idrees Sulieman, Webster Young, trumpet; John Coltrane, Bobby Jaspar, tenor sax; Kenny Burrell, guitar; Paul Chambers, bass; and Art Taylor, drums. The song is best known for the 1962 recording by Coltrane on Impulse, but it's become a standard, recorded by Stan Getz among others.

Listening to Prestige:
Mal Waldron Sextet

Mal/3 – Sounds

Recorded at Van Gelder Studio, Hackensack, NJ, January 31, 1958

Art Farmer, trumpet; Eric Dixon, flute; Caio Scott, cello; Mal Waldron, piano; Julian Euell, bass; Elvin Jones, drums; Elaine Waldron, voice #4, 5

Tracks recorded: Tension; Ollie's Caravan; The Cattin' Toddler; Portrait of a Young Mother; For Every Man There's Woman

It's hard to say how many compositions came from the imagination of Mal Waldron, but they certainly numbered in the hundreds. Any session that hired Waldron as pianist was more than likely to want one or more original compositions from him, and he wrote most of the material on the albums he recorded as leader. Waldron wasn't one to stay still. He had a wide range of passions and influences. He was still part of that generation that got its start in rhythm and blues. He was a lover of classical music, and recorded several pieces by classical and modernist composers. He worked with beboppers and the avant-garde, and he was Billie Holiday's accompanist during the last two years of her life. And he brought all of that experience, and his own restless genius, to bear on his work as a composer.

What is Waldron doing in this early 1958 session? It must be jazz, because it's got that swing. But listen to the beginning of "Tension." The number will move into jazz improvisation, with great solos by Art Farmer and Eric Dixon, but the opening section—I'm not even sure you'd call it a head—has a lot of the tonality and feeling that we associate with what I would call classical, oxy and moronic though I may be, and not just in what Waldron and Farmer and Dixon are doing; Jones also is very much a part of that stance.

"Ollie's Caravan" has a head that's very much in the bop tradition—and an arresting melody—but then it goes different places. Putting a caravan in the title can't help but make one think of Duke Ellington and Juan Tizol, but while Eric Dixon's flute solos have an Eastern tinge, they make one think of Yusef Lateef's experiments more than "Caravan." All these ingredients come together again in "The Cattin' Toddler": a striking drum intro by Jones, a catchy riff head, Eastern-tinged flute by Dixon, plus a wonderful extended solo by Farmer and the kind of work one expects of Waldron in improvising off one of his own compositions, which is to say, something completely unexpected.

> "Portrait of a Young Mother" provides a space for a wordless vocal by Waldron's wife Elaine, although the piece is by no means a song, or even primarily a vehicle for voice. At ten minutes long, it gives room for solos by everyone, including a wonderful pizzicato cello by Calo Scott.

Herbie Mann

Flautist Herbie Mann had made a couple of records for Bethlehem, then went off to Europe. He made a couple more for the Swedish label Metronome, which were picked up by Prestige, then returned to the United States and a Prestige contract. Mann was another one who slipped through Weinstock's fingers and went on to jazz preeminence, but his two Prestige albums, *Flute Flight* and *Flute Soufflé*, are among his best. Both were made with the Belgian musician Bobby Jaspar, with the two of them alternating on flute and tenor sax. They are some of the best work of Jaspar, a talented musician who died young.

Kenny Burrell

Guitarist Kenny Burrell graduated from Wayne State University and the jazz clubs of Detroit in 1955, and was immediately snapped up to tour with Oscar Peterson. He came to New York in 1956 with his reputation preceding him, and found work immediately. He began with three albums for Blue Note, one of which, *Midnight Blue*, was such a favorite of Alfred Lion's that it was buried with him. Over a career that has lasted seven decades, he has amassed a catalog of which Prestige represents only a small part, but that small part would represent a substantial career for most musicians.

He came to the label on December 28, 1956, as part of the Prestige All Stars session described above (see Donald Byrd), but the mesmerizing sound of the guitar combined with Jerome Richardson's flute made it a Kenny Burrell album, especially on his own composition, *All Night Long*, which became the title track. He would follow that up a week later, on January 4, 1957, with another All Stars session where he again became first among equals. His composition, "All Day Long," again became the title of an album that first had everyone's name (Frank Foster, Donald Byrd, Kenny Burrell, Tommy Flanagan, Doug Watkins, Art Taylor) on the front cover, then on a subsequent pressing just Burrell's.

Prestige kept Burrell busy in 1957. On February 1 he led a session featuring baritone saxophonist Cecil Payne (released as *Kenny Burrell*, rereleased in 1964 as *Blue Moods*). On May 10 he was listed as coleader with guitarist Barry Galbraith for a short session that was shelved and ultimately released in 1964 as part of an album on Prestige's budget label Status. He was also featured in on five more All Stars dates (one of them the Burrell/Jimmy Raney *2 Guitars* album), with another ensemble group called "The Cats" (with Idrees Sulieman and John Coltrane) and on sessions led by Gene Ammons and Red Garland. By the end of the year he had jumped from sixteenth to sixth in *Down Beat*'s poll of top guitarists.

Burrell was never exclusive with Prestige. In 1957 alone he also made records for Savoy, Blue Note, Vanguard, King, and a couple of smaller labels. After that breakout year he was very much nonexclusive, but he did continue to record for Prestige through 1965, tallying thirty-eight sessions altogether.

Listening to Prestige:
Kenny Burrell with John Coltrane

Recorded at Van Gelder Studio, Hackensack, NJ, March 7, 1958

John Coltrane, tenor sax; Tommy Flanagan, piano; Kenny Burrell, guitar; Paul Chambers, bass; Jimmy Cobb, drums

Tracks recorded: Lyresto; Why Was I Born?; Freight Trane; I Never Knew; Big Paul

Kenny Burrell and John Coltrane are an inspired pairing, but not unique to this session. They had been part of a Prestige All Stars date a year earlier. The two sessions had a couple of things in common beyond Burrell and Coltrane. For one, Tommy Flanagan was on piano. For another, both sessions were put on the shelf for a few years.

There were some significant differences. Here, Burrell and Coltrane were the only frontline instruments, where the other session had been a sextet. Paul Chambers was on bass instead of Doug Watkins, and on drums, an up-and-coming player making his Prestige debut.

Jimmy Cobb was no novice at this point. He had been on two Cannonball Adderley sessions for EmArcy. He had played with Earl Bostic, Dinah Washington, Billie Holiday, Pearl Bailey, Clark Terry, and Dizzy Gillespie. He had already joined Miles Davis's group, and would make his first recording with Miles, Porgy and Bess, later in the year. And by the time the Burrell/Coltrane session was released, in 1963, Cobb had progressed from hot new drummer to the Olympus of jazz greats, having appeared on the classic Kind of Blue album.

He's a welcome addition to the Prestige scene, and he makes his presence strongly felt from the first tune of the session, a Burrell composition, "Lyresto." He sets a groove right from the beginning, and comes in later for a dynamic solo.

Burrell and Coltrane really know how to play together, either in a quintet setting or just the two of them, on "Why Was I Born?" This is an unusual and haunting cut.

Tommy Flanagan contributes two originals, each a tribute to a bandmate ("Freight Trane" and "Big Paul"), and his customary precise and original piano playing. "Freight Trane" has had a few covers, some of them unlikely, like the U.S. Navy Commodores Jazz Ensemble.

One wonders if this album ever got the distribution and acclaim that it deserves. It was held back till 1963, and then released on New Jazz. It must have gotten some sort of a push, since "Freight Trane" was also released as a two-sided 45. The album was titled Kenny Burrell and John Coltrane. A much later rerelease on Prestige was called The Kenny Burrell Quintet with John Coltrane, which is also just a little curious. It came out in 1968, a year after Coltrane's death, and one would have thought his name would get top billing at that point. Goes to show that Burrell was also held in really high esteem, or else that Bob Weinstock was running out of steam (he would get out of the business four years later) and not making carefully crafted marketing decisions.

Ray Barreto

Percussionist Ray Barreto was almost as much in demand at Prestige, recording around two dozen albums for the label, all as a sideman (including four of Burrell's albums). Born and raised in New York, he was adept at swing and bop as well as Latin rhythms, which meant that his presence on a recording made a huge difference, adding that Latin touch to the straight-ahead jazz, and a jazz feeling to Latin dance music. From the mid-1960s on, he led his own groups, becoming one of the leading Latin music bandleaders, and one of the originators of salsa.

Jimmy Forrest

Jimmy Forrest could play anything, from swing to bebop to rhythm and blues, as he proved on the Prestige session that put him together with two other saxophonists of different schools, Oliver Nelson and King Curtis. He had reached number one on the rhythm and blues charts with his 1952 recording of "Night Train," the same year that Miles Davis sat in with his St. Louis group for a live recording that was released by Prestige (see chapter 7). "Night Train" bought him a contract with Prestige as they made their move into soul jazz, and he made his debut as leader on August 9, 1960, with a group that also introduced the formidable talent of organist Larry Young (see chapter 21). Altogether, he would make five albums as leader for the label between 1960 and 1962, with a few more as sideman.

Doug Watkins

Bassist Doug Watkins is a name not as familiar as the others here. He only made two records as leader, and he died in 1962, in an auto accident. But he was the backbone of Prestige's rhythm section in the late 1950s, appearing on thirty records. He came to New York from Detroit's jazz cauldron, found work with Art Blakey's Jazz Messengers, then left because of dissatisfaction with the drug use in the group. His first Prestige recording came on January 27, 1956, backing up Jackie McLean and Donald Byrd; his last was on January 27, 1961, backing up Gene Ammons.

Dorothy Ashby

Dorothy Ashby played the harp, an instrument not immediately associated with jazz. However, she came from one of the most demanding and inspiring schools of music in midcentury America: the streets and nightclubs of Detroit, where the only criteria for acceptance were dedication and excellence. Ashby made two albums for Prestige, both with Frank Wess, both hard-swinging mainstream jazz, and she was much in demand as a sidewoman in a number of contexts.

**Listening to Prestige:
Dorothy Ashby**

In a Minor Groove

Recorded at Van Gelder Studio, Hackensack, NJ, September 19, 1958

Frank Wess, flute; Dorothy Ashby, harp; Herman Wright, bass;
Roy Haynes, drum

Bohemia After Dark

Tracks recorded: Yesterdays; Rascality; Autumn in Rome;
It's a Minor Thing; Taboo; Alone Together;
You'd Be So Nice to Come Home To

There's a moment during "Bohemia After Dark" when Dorothy Ashby and Herman Wright are doing a harp-bass dialogue, and then it's Wright and Frank Wess doing a flute-bass dialogue, and you're not quite sure when the crossover occurred. That's how well these musicians play together.

This is the second and last Ashby recording session for Prestige. She would pack a lot of music into it, and she would pack a lot of music, art, writing, and performance into her short fifty-eight years on this earth. She was from the jazz hotbed of Detroit, and she would continue to make Detroit her home, although she toured and recorded widely. For five years in the 1960s, she and her husband, John Ashby, had a jazz radio show in Detroit, where they "talked about the new jazz releases, about the problems of jazz, and about the performers" (from an interview with her and Cannonball Adderley). She reviewed jazz records for the *Detroit Free Press*.

And she and her husband founded a theater company in Detroit, the Ashby Players. John wrote the scripts and Dorothy the songs, music, and lyrics. She even performed in at least one of the plays. Unfortunately, none of this work has been released to the public, although it's said to exist on reel-to-reel tapes.

But plenty of her other work survives. She recorded eleven albums as leader of her own group, including one with Terry Pollard, another Detroit woman who broke through jazz's glass ceiling. And she wasn't just a specialty act, either—"Hey, let's build an album around this chick who plays the harp." She was in serious demand as sidewoman, recording with jazz groups (Bobbi Humphrey, Wade Marcus, Stanley Turrentine, Sonny Criss, Gene Harris, Freddie Hubbard) and vocalists (Bill Withers, Minnie Riperton, Stevie Wonder, Billy Preston, Bobby Womack). She recorded with Japanese new age musician Osamu Kitajima. She's been sampled by hip-hop artists.

And if the harp wasn't enough, she brought another unusual sound into jazz: the koto, a Japanese multistringed instrument that she played on *The Rubaiyat of Dorothy Ashby*, a remarkable album released in 1970 on Cadet, the Chess Records subsidiary, an album that also featured an electric harp, and Ashby's vocals.

Ashby was active up until shortly before her death in 1986, but she had some interesting things to say about the era we're looking at now, also in the joint interview with Adderley: "I speak often of the decade of 1950–1960 as being the best for the Black jazzman. The economy of the country was in pretty fair shape. The United States was becoming aware of jazz's role in international goodwill. The jazz festivals were born, giving jazz some of its greatest and most diverse audiences. Jazz was used in the films, like *Odds Against Tomorrow, No Sun in Venice*, and Miles' *The Elevator to the Hangman*." Another nail in the coffin of the myth of the 1930s being the golden era of jazz's popularity.

This album features standards, and two compositions by Ashby, "It's a Minor Thing" and "Rascality." One sort of expects a minor thing to be moody and subdued, but this one is rowdy, rambunctious, and bursting at the seams. "Rascality" is a hell of a piece of music. It's hard to say what makes one jazz tune into a widely recorded standard, while another doesn't make it beyond its first recording session. Oscar Pettiford's "Bohemia After Dark," which Ashby and Co. start off the day with, is one such standard. "Rascality" is not, perhaps because nobody thinks a melody written by a harpist can translate into other instrumentations. Ashby discussed that in an interview with jazz historian Sally Placksin:

> Even arrangers admit that often they don't know how to write what they'd like to write. What they would be willing to write for harp often doesn't work, because they're writing from a pianistic point of view, or maybe another instrumental point of view, and that doesn't work on a harp, because you can only change two pedals at a time, and various other technicalities. . . . The harp has complexities that a person has to be able to work out in their head while they're spontaneously creating jazz on it.

The only other version of "Rascality" that I've been able to find is one by contemporary jazz harpist Destiny Muhammad, in a concert tribute to Dorothy Ashby. But a great tune is a great tune, and jazz musicians have made a mistake by not picking up on this one.

Detroiter Herman Wright, who often worked with Ashby, contributes, as does drummer Roy Haynes, who is always one to make his presence felt, and who ain't gonna play no chamber music. There's a terrific interplay between Haynes and Wess at the beginning of "Taboo," which is a tune that's hard to play without slipping into the clichés of exotica. There's no slippage here.

The album was released on New Jazz as *In a Minor Groove*, and much later (1969) on Prestige as *Dorothy Ashby Plays for Beautiful People*.

Moondog

An outlier in the Prestige catalog for this time period, but no less important, is Moondog, the Viking-garbed blind street musician who was a colorful fixture outside New York's Carnegie Hall for many years. More people knew him as a New York character than as a serious composer. But he did make a few records, including three for Prestige, before leaving for Europe in 1974, where he would finally find acclaim for his music.

Listening to Prestige: Moondog

Recorded in New York City, 1956

Moondog, oo, trimba, yukh, tuji, piano, recorder, voice

Tracks recorded: Caribea; Lullaby; Tree Trail; Death, When You Come to Me; Big Cat; Frog Bog; To a Sea Horse; Dance Rehearsal; Surf Session; Trees against the Sky; Tap Dance; Oo Debut; Drum Suite; Street Scene

Disc jockey Alan Freed took his radio name from an early 78 rpm recording called "Moondog Symphony," one of Moondog's first. It was a curious choice in every way. It was a symphony of percussion: drums, maracas, claves, gourds, hollow log, Chinese block, and cymbals, all played by Moondog. And there wasn't much in the way of multitracking for a self-made 78 in 1949, so he invented his own system, working back and forth between two tape recorders. It was curious that Freed found it at all. The record sold only a few hundred copies. It was perhaps even more curious that he liked it, and used it as the theme song for a radio show playing Black rhythm and blues for white teenagers. When he brought his radio show to New York, Freed was taken to court by Moondog, and had to stop using the name. Moondog himself later said that the courts would most likely have ruled against a Viking-accoutered street person, had not Benny Goodman and Arturo Toscanini testified to his importance as a composer.

It's hard to say why Prestige recorded him. There don't seem to exist any interviews with Weinstock where he discusses this particular choice, but actually there's more of Moondog on Prestige than anywhere else, and these recordings capture an important part of his oeuvre.

The music amazed me. I'm a fan of the avant-garde composers of the mid- and late twentieth century: Terry Riley, LaMonte Young, Pauline Oliveros, Gavin Bryars. And Moondog is one of the finest avant-garde composers I have ever heard. As other avant-gardists have done, and as was certainly appropriate for a street musician, he used a lot of ambient sound. There's the Queen Elizabeth in the harbor, its "deep-throated whistle" blending with, and extended by, Moondog's bamboo pipe. There's the horn of a tugboat, as eerily melodic as the songs of the humpbacked whale that would become popular a generation or so later, blended into an almost but not exactly orchestral blend of instruments. And the sounds move away from the street, too.

Moondog was married for a second time in 1952, to a Japanese American woman named Suzuko Whiteing, so he wasn't entirely homeless, though he still lived, by choice, mostly on the streets. "Lullabye" combines the cries of their six-week-old baby with Suzuko singing (or chanting) a lullaby in what I guess is Japanese, and music by a sextet composed in something like a pentatonic Japanese scale.

Moondog experimented with a wide variety of instruments, many of his own invention. He was particularly drawn to the oo, a triangular-shaped twenty-five-string harp struck with a clava. He also created a variety of percussion instruments, and percussion played an important part in his compositions. His music was always rhythmic, but rhythmic in his own way, with the slithery snaketime rhythms. On "Oo Debut," a short piece (as were most of his compositions), he simultaneously played the oo and the trimba, a triangular drum that is still used by musicians today.

The first of these sessions was released by Prestige as Moondog, then More Moondog and The Story of Moondog. More Moondog was largely recorded by Tony Schwartz, who was known as a sound archivist, and whose collections of street sounds were released by Folkways. One would have thought of Folkways as a more likely home for Moondog, but his work was much admired by modern jazz icons like Charlie Parker and Charles Mingus, and Prestige is the richer for it. The first album sold respectably, enough for Moondog to buy property upstate near Owego, which became his retreat from the city. Probably its sales were due to its novelty value, as there isn't much of a market for serious avant-garde music. The second two did not do so well.

Chapter 16

Miles's Sidemen and John Coltrane

In June 1957, Bob Weinstock discussed his eight-year-old label with *Down Beat*'s Dom Cerulli. Listing Sonny Rollins, Teddy Charles, Art Farmer, Milt Jackson, Phil Woods, and Billy Taylor as relative unknowns who had come to prominence with Prestige, he announced his plans to continue in the same vein. Prestige released four albums a month but recorded more than that; there were over sixty recording sessions in 1957 alone. "But that's because we are trying to record the modern jazz scene as completely as possible," he told Cerulli, "especially the newcomers. There are so many coming along now, we feel we have to record them. These musicians must be recorded in their formative stages."

Cerulli cites, as evidence of Prestige's "offbeat, unmajor-like manner," the fact that "the musicians themselves act as talent scouts and A&R men." This was certainly the case. As he got more and more immersed in the business of running a record label, and as the 52nd Street jazz scene that had originally pulled him to record the music withered away, Weinstock was not going out to clubs scouting for talent. But he would pick up on it when it came to him: when Phil Woods would walk in the door to record with Jimmy Raney, or Doug Watkins would be the bass player on a Jackie McLean date. But probably his most significant "talent scout" was the biggest star on his label: Miles Davis.

Davis had signed with Columbia. The members of his band had not. They have gone into jazz legend as the First Great Quintet, but they were hired musicians who could be fired just as quickly, which is exactly what happened to John Coltrane and Philly Joe Jones when a newly clean Davis could no longer deal with their drug addiction, although he did hire them both back. So Davis became talent scout and A&R man for Weinstock, showcasing his rhythm section of Red Garland, Paul Chambers, and Jones by giving them one number, "Ahmad's Blues," to themselves during the Contractual Marathon session of May 11, 1956.

Weinstock was suitably impressed. He signed Garland to a contract, but held off on Coltrane. The latter seems like a no-brainer from the perspective of history, but Coltrane was a virtual unknown when he was hired by Davis, and he was still a virtual unknown when Davis moved to Columbia. The albums that were to come out of the Contractual Marathon sessions, and enter jazz immortality, were yet to be released. As 1956 rolled into 1957, the record-buying public did not know who John Coltrane was. The *Down Beat* poll for 1956 did not mention Coltrane at all—and it took only fifteen votes to make the list. That would change rapidly. The next year, Coltrane was eleventh on the list, and in 1958 he was third behind perennial winner Stan Getz and Sonny Rollins. But he was no sure thing when he made his first recordings without Davis.

When Red Garland began with Davis, Garland was thirty-three, and a much more polished player, but he was still virtually unrecorded. He had recorded one tune nine years earlier, with Eddie "Lockjaw" Davis, which eventually showed up on a low-budget compilation LP called *Tenors Wild and Mild*. In 1953 he was in a pickup group accompanying Charlie Parker on a radio broadcast from Boston's Storyville jazz club. An aircheck from the session was released on Blue Note in 1985.

But his composition "Ahmad's Blues" had been enough to convince Weinstock, and the Red Garland Trio, with Art Taylor on drums in place of Jones, began recording for Prestige right away. There would be one more Contractual Marathon session on October 26, but by then Garland's group had already made their Prestige debut, going into the studio on August 17 to record a set of mostly standards, from the Great American Songbook that Davis had tapped for the Marathon sessions. They would come back on December 14 to record four more standards, including "If I Were a Bell," which Garland had done with Davis at the last Marathon. Their first album, *A Garland of Red*, was released before the end of the year, preempting *Cookin'*, the opening salvo from the Marathon sessions, which came out in July 1957.

Listening to Prestige:
Red Garland

A Garland of Red

Recorded at Van Gelder Studio, Hackensack, NJ, August 17, 1956

Red Garland, piano; Paul Chambers, bass; Art Taylor, drums

Tracks recorded: A Foggy Day; My Romance;
What Is This Thing Called Love; Makin' Whoopee;
September in the Rain; Little Girl Blue; Blue Red; Constellation

The trio plays eight songs, six of them standards from the Great American Songbook. It's always interesting to hear jazz versions of these standards for any number of reasons, but certainly one is the fresh focus they give to the songs themselves. Lester Young said that whenever he played a standard, he always had the words in his mind, and certainly a listener is going to be mindful of a familiar lyric. (Well, most listeners. I had a friend who told me she loved the blues, but she never listened to the words. I said, "That's like loving Rubens but not noticing the nudes." She said, "I do that too.")

Garland begins the set with "A Foggy Day," and it's not Fred Astaire's softly melancholy fog. Garland, with his hard-charging block chords, has his fog lights on, and he's not letting a little clammy low visibility stop him, or even slow him down. "Makin' Whoopee" is a gleeful expression of arch cynicism, but Garland slows it down to an almost stately pace, and you have to listen to it for a bit before you start noticing that the dry archness is there, but subtly. "September in the Rain" starts with an extended walking bass, which leads to a very brief piano solo, which leads to a bowed bass solo, and if you don't believe a bowed bass can walk, listen to this one. As a result, the head sort of isn't there. and we're really just walkin' in the rain.

The bowed bass solo is a frequent and welcome participant throughout this session. But if you really want to hear a bass solo, listen to "Blue Red," which opens with two and a half minutes of bass, walking, jumping, and standing still; it's a tour de force. When Garland comes in, you know that this is a blues played by someone from Texas, who knows how to play the blues. The number also includes a Garland tour de force: a repeated figure (repeated sixteen times) of the sort that one associates more with the saxophone than the piano, and more with rhythm and blues than modern jazz, but since I refuse to recognize any clear line of demarcation between rhythm and blues and modern jazz, why not?

The other non-Songbook tune is a Charlie Parker composition, and it's another interesting departure. Garland's style is generally noted for block chords of the sort that I associate with Thelonious Monk, but on "Constellation" he turns to a nimble style more reminiscent of Bud Powell (whom Garland named as his chief influence). We also hear boppish overdrive on a bowed bass solo, and some nifty soloing by Art Taylor.

The session was appropriately album-length, and was released as *A Garland of Red*. "Blue Red" also came out as a two-sided 45; the original track, at nearly eight minutes, is a little long for even two sides of a single, so I wonder if they cut the bass intro. "Makin' Whoopee" also came out on 45, but a few years later, as the B-side of Garland's cover of Count Basie's theme music for the TV show M Squad.

John Coltrane would become the caviar of this era, but Garland was just as certainly the label's bread and butter. Between 1956 and 1962 he made thirty-nine albums for Prestige, most of them as leader. The piano trio is a solid staple of any jazz label. Errol Garner's 1955 *Concert by the Sea* is one of the best-selling albums of all time. One of the best markets for American jazz is Japan, and according to Mark Feldman, of the successful independent label Reservoir, a good piano trio album is almost guaranteed to make a profit in Japan alone. And Garland consistently delivered. He recorded standards, blues, and originals, mostly with the trio, occasionally solo. He worked with Chambers and Taylor through 1958, and with different combinations after that, although Taylor was still frequently the drummer. Garland took his Miles Davis rhythm section out to the West Coast in 1957 to record an album called *Art Pepper Meets the Rhythm Section*. His rhythm section (Chambers and Jones) played on the Rollins/Coltrane "Tenor Madness" session. He recorded with Curtis Fuller, Phil Woods, and Donald Byrd (three sessions with Byrd and Coltrane). He added Ray Barreto for a couple of sessions. He worked with Coleman Hawkins for the Prestige subsidiary Swingville, and with Eddie "Lockjaw" Davis and Arnett Cobb for another subsidiary, Moodsville.

In 1963, the Beatles hit America, and Garland saw a new era opening up, and he did not envision his music as its soundtrack. He went back to

Texas and semiretirement, returning to New York in the late 1970s to make several records for small labels before his death in 1984.

The quintet that Miles Davis put together for George Avakian but previewed for Bob Weinstock really was an odd conglomeration of musicians. Philly Joe Jones was a veteran who had often worked with Davis but had not recorded with him before. Garland was respected by musicians but a complete unknown; no one would ever have heard him on record. Paul Chambers had made a few records, including a couple on Prestige (with King Pleasure, Bennie Green). He was considered the hot new young bassist, and he was only twenty years old.

Davis's selection of John Coltrane to round out the quintet has been discussed in chapter 13. Not everyone was as convinced as Davis that this was a good choice. Davis, recalling those days, has said, "People used to tell me to fire him. They said he wasn't playing anything." Nat Hentoff, reviewing the first Marathon Session LP, found Coltrane derivative and unoriginal, sounding too much like Dexter Gordon, Sonny Stitt, and Rollins. British critic Edgar Jackson noted that he "[tries] to say too much at once, thereby tending to befog his meaning and lessen his impact." (Ira Gitler, describing the same tendency but more positively impressed by it, called it "sheets of sound," a phrase that would stick with Coltrane for quite a while.) Even Coltrane himself was not sure. He told French journalist Jean-Claude Dargenpierre (quoted in Porter): "The standards were so high, and I felt like I wasn't really contributing like I should." He expanded on this in a 1961 interview with British journalist Kitty Grime:

> When I first joined Miles in 1955 . . . I thought I was lacking in general musicianship. I had all kinds of technical problems . . . and I hadn't the necessary harmonic understanding. I am quite ashamed of those early records I made with Miles. Why he picked me, I don't know. Maybe he saw something in my playing that he hoped would grow. I had this desire, which I think we all have, to be as original as I could, and as honest as I could be. But there were so many musical conclusions I hadn't arrived at, that I felt inadequate.

Coltrane was also continuing to struggle with heroin addiction, to the point where Davis had to fire him and Philly Joe Jones, also an addict, from the quintet. It was a crucial period in his development. He faced up to his addiction and finally conquered it. And he went to work with Thelonious

Monk, a very different experience from working with Davis. He explained one salient difference to an interviewer: "Monk is the exact opposite of Miles—he talks about music all the time, and he wants so much for you to understand that if, by chance, you ask him something, he'll spend hours, if necessary, to explain it to you."

Coltrane joined Monk's quintet at the Five Spot, but they didn't get much down on record. A June 25–26 date, recorded for Riverside, was notable in that Coleman Hawkins was also present. A concert at Town Hall in November was recorded but never released until the tapes were rediscovered in 2005 and brought out by Blue Note.

Still without a contract, Coltrane recorded for Prestige as part of a shifting group presented by the label as the Prestige All Stars. The first, on March 22, featured Idrees Sulieman, Webster Young, trumpet; Coltrane, Bobby Jaspar, tenor sax; Mal Waldron, piano; Kenny Burrell, guitar; Paul Chambers, bass; Art Taylor, drums. On April 20, it was Coltrane, tenor sax; Pepper Adams, Cecil Payne, baritone sax; Mal Waldron, piano; Doug Watkins, bass; Art Taylor, drums. On May 17, Coltrane and Paul Quinichette were billed as coleaders, with Mal Waldron, piano; Julian Euell, bass; Ed Thigpen, drums.

Coltrane was also talking to Blue Note at this time, and they were willing to offer him a one-record deal, but nothing long-term. But Prestige had heard enough, and Weinstock was willing to make a commitment. Just at that point, Coltrane recorded one track on a Monk session for Riverside, and Orrin Keepnews was sufficiently impressed to offer him a contract, but he had already signed with Prestige. He was still a gamble for any label, and very much of an unknown quantity. The first Contractual Marathon album, *Cookin'*, would not be released until July, and his first Prestige All Stars album not till the end of the year. In May 1957 Coltrane signed a contract to make three records, and on May 31 he was in the studio for the first of those. He would have liked to bring Monk on board for one of those albums, but Monk was having nothing more to do with his former label.

Coltrane's first session as leader used Johnnie Splawn, a friend from Philadelphia who would never appear on record again, on trumpet, and Sahib Shihab on baritone sax. Garland and Chambers, along with Albert "Tootie" Heath, were the rhythm section. The album was released as *Coltrane*. It included two original compositions, "Straight Street" and "Chronic Blues." Unlike many of the compositions from the bebop era, which were written on an armature of chords from an earlier song, Coltrane's melodies were completely original. Coltrane was intensely focused on making his own music. Lewis Porter points out:

> He almost never indulged in musical humor or in quoting entire phrases that would be familiar to listeners . . . a quote brings in a reference to a world outside one's solo . . . it may be funny, or it may suggest a homage to another artist, or it may simply establish a common background with the audience or other musicians. Coltrane's music, more and more, seems to be about here and now, about what he and his group were playing at that moment. Quotations had no place in that world.

Coltrane received a guarded review from Don Gold in *Down Beat*, who gave the album three stars, and said "Although Coltrane plays with a good deal of authority, I do not feel that his work on this specific LP is excitingly impressive." Others were more enthusiastic, though they tended to focus on one aspect: Coltrane's powerful playing. Nat Hentoff, in *HiFi Stereo Review*, said, "He plays with fierce, propulsive urgency, possessing a tone and attack that is bluntly direct." Similarly, *Miami News* reviewer William G. Moeser said, "John Coltrane wails on his tenor horn with a disturbing urgency." There was a general feeling that, as Charles A. Robertson put it in *Audio*, "He plays like a man on his way."

On August 16, Coltrane recorded three tunes with a pianoless trio (Earl May, bass; Art Taylor, drums; "the piano player didn't show up"), but none of these would be released until after he had left the label.

During the next three weeks, he would be in Rudy Van Gelder's studio three more times—first an August 3 date with the Red Garland trio, then September 1 as a sideman to Sonny Clark. Finally, on September 15, he led a sextet for the session that would become *Blue Train*. The sextet had Lee Morgan, trumpet; Curtis Fuller, trombone; Kenny Drew, piano; Paul Chambers, bass; Philly Joe Jones, drums. The consensus was that Blue Note had stolen a march on Prestige, because *Blue Train* was hailed as the most significant of Coltrane's early albums, the one that established him as a tenor saxophonist of the first rank—a consensus that continues to the present day. A list of Coltrane's albums ranked from worst to best on the website rateyourmusic.com places *Traneing In*, the Prestige August album, at number 26, *Blue Train* at number eight. However, the consensus is not universal. Joe Goldberg, writing in 1958, said:

The title piece on *Blue Train* is an exceptional blues, loaded with menace, perhaps the best Coltrane has ever recorded. . . . Unfortunately, on the rest of the record, his material seems casually put together, and the other musicians are of no great assistance. . . . *Traneing In* is another matter. Here he is surrounded exclusively with sympathetic musicians [Garland, Chambers, Taylor]. . . . The result is a thoughtful, cohesive album which represents Coltrane's most consistent recorded work to date.

**Listening to Prestige:
John Coltrane with the Red Garland Trio**

Recorded: Van Gelder Studio, Hackensack, NJ, August 23, 1957

John Coltrane, tenor sax; Red Garland, piano;
Paul Chambers, bass; Arthur Taylor, drums

Tracks recorded: You Leave Me Breathless; Bass Blues;
Soft Lights and Sweet Music; Traneing In; Slow Dance

This was the moment that changed my life. It was late winter or early spring of 1958. I was a freshman at Bard College, and I was living in the Barracks. The Barracks were really exactly that; wooden structures put up temporarily after the war and never replaced, according to a 1954 article in the *Harvard Crimson*.

I liked the Barracks. I probably would have liked them less if I were an actual World War II vet, but I wasn't. I was a kid away from home. Not for the first time, but these were not the boarding school dormitories that I'd hated. They were ramshackle and casual and casually named, and they were my first home away from home, and I could come in whenever I wanted to, including, this particular night, sometime after midnight.

I would have been just barely eighteen, the legal drinking age in those days (maybe younger), and would have been drinking, something I'd just learned to do. For sure, I was passionately in love with rhythm and blues. I was of the first rock and roll generation, raised on the Hound from WKBW in Buffalo and, when I could get him (WINS's signal didn't travel well to upstate), Alan Freed, and when, even more rarely (WOV's signal was even more unlikely), I could get Jocko, your ace from outer space. Rock and roll made me passionate about music, and I learned quickly that I wanted the real thing. I wanted what Alan Freed and Jocko played, the original records, the Chords' version of "Sh-Boom" and not the Crew-Cuts; LaVern Baker and not Georgia Gibbs singing "Tweedle Dee" (finding out about Red Garland's version came later). I discovered that the names in tiny letters below the titles of songs meant the person or persons who had written them, and "Lieber-Stoller" became my new heroes. And I discovered that, with the exception of Elvis and a few others (most of whom recorded on Sun Records), the music I loved was made by Black people.

I grew up in a Bohemian environment of artists and political leftists, so as a teenager I discovered the folk music of the '50s, and a new writing role model to put alongside Lieber and Stoller: Lead Belly. And then the blues singers who had crossed over to that audience of leftists and other folk music enthusiasts: Big Bill Broonzy, Josh White, Sonny Terry, and Brownie McGhee.

Then somehow—I can't remember how, and I can't even imagine how, a white teenager in upstate New York—I discovered that there was a whole different kind of music out there, that was being made by Black people and listened to by Black people, and it was called rhythm and blues. Some of the rhythm and blues artists, like Larry Williams and Smiley Lewis, got some airplay on the hipper rock and roll stations.

Some, like Magic Sam and Lightnin' Hopkins and even Muddy Waters, you just had to find. Some like Roy Brown and Arthur "Big Boy" Crudup were covered by Elvis.

So in that spring of 1958, away at college, I was already passionate about music as only a seeker can be. My kind of music: rhythm and blues, and the R&B artists like Little Richard who had made their mark in rock and roll. I didn't know anything about jazz. I had one Louis Armstrong record, Satch Plays Fats. I knew that jazz fans thought they were better than rock and roll fans, and maybe they were; if you were a rock and roller and traveled in intellectual bohemian circles, you always felt a little self-conscious. And neither the jazzers, nor the rock and rollers, nor my parents' Bohemian friends knew much about rhythm and blues.

But sometimes you could find it on all-night radio, and that's what I was doing in those wee hours of the morning in my dorm room in the Barracks. Twisting the dial of my AM radio, looking for some far-off station that might be playing Varetta Dillard or Joe Turner or the Harptones. And then I stopped. I didn't touch the dial of the radio again. And I couldn't even look away. I stopped and stood in the middle of the room and stared at the radio. I was suddenly and instantly under the spell of a music I had never heard before.

I remember everything about that moment in time. The station was CKLW in Detroit and Windsor, Ontario, and the disc jockey was Speed Anderson. Except I seem to remember it wrong. Ezra "Speed" Anderson was a late-night jazz DJ in Boston. Maybe I might still be right. For a short time his program was syndicated nationally. Anyway, the place was the Barracks, Bard College, Annandale-on-Hudson, New York. The disc jockey was Speed Anderson. And the music was John Coltrane and the Red Garland Trio. I was struck by lightning as sure as Michael Corleone in Sicily in The Godfather, Part II. Speed Anderson went on to become the most beloved hot dog vendor in Boston; John Coltrane went on to become one of the greatest jazzmen of his generation. And I went on to love jazz for the rest of my life.

The album, which I bought as soon as I could find it, was John Coltrane with the Red Garland Trio (titled Traneing In on later releases). It had that red-on-black Abstract Expressionist cover. It was my first jazz record. I was not hip enough, or experienced enough, to listen to the complex and subtle interactions of the instruments. Certainly not over a little dorm room AM radio. It was Coltrane that got to me, and still does. To me, the five tracks, even though only two of the tunes were written by Coltrane, have always felt like an extended suite, to be listened to all the way through. So I'm listening and responding in the order they appear on the record, not, as I usually do in these blog entries, in the order they were recorded in the studio.

The suite begins with Red Garland, doing a nearly five-minute intro/solo on "Traneing In," the longest individual cut, after which Coltrane enters, and as great as the other musicians are, it's his voice that you hear the rest of the way. Funny . . . I said this album has always felt to me like a suite, and the next track, "Slow Dance," actually was part of a suite: Manhattan Monodrama, written by contemporary composer Alonzo Levister for a group that included Teddy Charles. It was released on Charles Mingus's Debut label. "Slow Dance" actually is kinda slow, but the climactic piece on the album, "Soft Lights and Sweet Music," is anything but soft and sweet. It's an Irving Berlin tune, and though I often imagine the great American composers of popular song listening to modern jazz interpretations and approving, I'm not sure Coltrane's approach is exactly what Berlin had in mind. The tune, as recorded by singers like Lee Wiley and Barbara Lea, and swingers like Benny Goodman, is more sprightly than dreamy, but as Ira Gitler noted in his liner notes, this is more like the soft headlamp of an express train roaring down the track.

Unlike much of Coltrane's work for Prestige, this recording wasn't held back for a more opportune time. It was released in early 1958, in time for Speed Anderson to play it and for a young rhythm and blues–loving college freshman to have his life changed irrevocably.

This was a period of prodigious activity for Prestige. There were fifty recording sessions in 1956, forty in 1958; sandwiched in between those years was 1957, with an astounding seventy-two sessions. So John Coltrane got a lot of work. "I wouldn't do it now," Coltrane would say in the early 1960s, looking back on those years. It meant a series of much-needed paydays. For Coltrane, it was also a lot of opportunity to develop his craft, and for the label, a considerable Coltrane catalog.

Coltrane's next album session as the leader came on February 7, 1958, yielding the album *Soultrane* that was released in October 1958. By this time, he had solidly established himself as one of the most important new voices in jazz, and as an innovator who would only continue to develop. Dom Cerulli, giving him a five-star review in *Down Beat*, says with some prescience, considering the directions that Coltrane would take his music in the succeeding decade: "In this very, very good LP, John Coltrane gives a picture of himself which is true in several dimensions. . . . What I do admire in him is that he is always going for something beyond him, and that he never falls back on an easy or accepted way of doing what he wants to do." Weinstock, who produced the session, recalls the last tune they recorded that day, Irving Berlin's "Russian Lullabye," traditionally taken at a gentle, lullaby-appropriate tempo, but turned by Coltrane into a high-voltage tour de force. When the group had finished, Weinstock asked, "John, what was that?" and Coltrane deadpanned, "Like it says. 'Rushin' Lullabye."

Ira Gitler, in the liner notes to *Soultrane*, first coined the phrase "sheets of sound," which came to be the standard definition of Coltrane's 1950s sound. Coltrane himself, in a 1960 *Down* Beat interview with Don DeMichael, described how he developed this technique:

> Actually, I was beginning to apply the three-on-one chord approach, and at that time the tendency was to play the entire scale of each chord. Therefore, they were usually played fast and sometimes sounded like glisses.
>
> I found there were a certain number of chord progressions to play in a given time, and sometimes what I played didn't work out in eighth notes, 16th notes, or triplets. I had to put the notes in uneven groups like fives and sevens in order to get them all in.
>
> I could stack up chords, say on a C7, I sometimes superimposed an Eb7 up to an F#7, down to an F. That way I could play three chords on one. But on the other hand, if I wanted to, I could play melodically . . .

Coltrane, John Coltrane with the Red Garland Trio, and *Soultrane* were the three albums Coltrane was contracted for with Prestige. He then moved on to Atlantic, for a much more lucrative contract, and a new stage in his career. But a lot more music came out of those busy years, and Prestige would be releasing Coltrane albums for years to come, beginning with *Lush Life*, released in 1961. It included "I Hear a Rhapsody," which had come from the May 31, 1957, session but had been left off the *Coltrane* album; the tunes from the August 16 pianoless trio session; and a January 10, 1958, session with Donald Byrd (and Garland, Chambers, and Louis Hayes), which produced the title track for the album.

Coltrane had recorded with Garland, Chambers, and Taylor on March 26, 1958; four tunes from that session were released in 1961 as *Settin' the*

Pace. This, and subsequent Prestige releases, were bound to be compared to the more advanced work of *Giant Steps* and later *My Favorite Things, A Love Supreme*, and the rest of Coltrane's later catalog on Atlantic and Impulse! As Coltrane morphed from a titan of jazz to a near-mythic cult figure, his worshippers of succeeding generations focused on those later albums, and one finds younger fans and even younger critics treating the Prestige work with a gentle contempt that, incredibly, sometimes spreads even to *Giant Steps*. The later Prestige releases are marked in the Wikipedia entries with a harshly disapproving tone: "As Coltrane's profile increased during the 1960s, Prestige released recordings without Coltrane's input or approval." Generally speaking, if an artist goes into the studio and records a bunch of songs for a label, and it has paid for them, the artist expects (or hopes) that those songs will eventually be released on record, CD, or streaming service, and it is not customary for the label to contact the artist with, "Hey, you remember that record you made back in 1958? Do you mind if we release it?"

Even then, in 1961 and for the next couple of years, it was clear that Coltrane's music had progressed considerably from the tracks Prestige was releasing. But that did not mean that these releases were met with universal disapproval. The 1950s were an era of peak popularity for jazz, and many listeners who were not prepared for the gauntlets thrown down by Ornette Coleman, Pharoah Sanders, and Albert Ayler were more than ready to welcome an earlier sound. *Billboard's* review of *Settin' the Pace* praises it as coming from "one of Coltrane's most productive periods."

Standard Coltrane, released in 1962, is part of a session from July 11, 1958. Jimmy Cobb joins Garland and Chambers in the rhythm section, and the quintet is filled out by Wilbur Harden on trumpet and flugelhorn. Harden was one of the first musicians to bring the flugelhorn into a jazz context. He had come east with Yusef Lateef from Detroit, and recorded with Lateef for the Prestige/New Jazz and Savoy labels. A promising newcomer, his career was cut short by illness. He did not record after 1960, and died in 1969.

The July 11 session also furnished material for two later album releases, *Stardust* and *Bahia*. It provided the title song for *Stardust* (1963), along with "Love Thy Neighbor." The remaining two tunes on the album came from a December 28, 1958, session, with Art Taylor back on drums and another promising young trumpet player, this one on the brink of a glorious career. Freddie Hubbard had made only one previous recording, with Wes Montgomery for the Pacific Jazz label. He would go on to become one of the most important jazz voices of his generation. *Dakar*, also released in

1963, is the product of a session from April 20, 1957: before Coltrane had signed with Prestige, but he was getting work on the label as a sideman. Billed on the session log as a Prestige All Stars session, it featured baritone saxophonists Cecil Payne and Pepper Adams (Garland, Doug Watkins, Taylor), and became one side of a long-playing record in the short-lived 16 2/3 rpm format, titled *Baritones and French Horns*.

There were two releases in 1964. *The Believer* includes tracks from a December 20, 1957, session in which Coltrane played sideman to seventeen-year-old tuba prodigy Ray Draper (Gil Coggins, Spanky deBrest, Larry Ritchie); the Donald Byrd session from January 20, 1958; and the December 26 session. *Black Pearls* is from May 23, 1958. It's another session with Donald Byrd, and one whole side of the LP is devoted to a composition called "Sweet Sapphire Blues," credited to Bob Weinstock. Was Weinstock its composer? Well, sort of. With time to fill on the album, and mindful of Rudy Van Gelder's "Five O'Clock Blues" that always seemed to do the trick, he suggested a slow blues. Okay, said Coltrane, we'll do a slow blues. You write it. When Weinstock protested he didn't know how to write music, Coltrane played him a blues lick and said, "Should it go like this?" He kept going that way, tossing out licks, having Weinstock give a thumbs up or thumbs down to each one, until they had assembled a few, and Coltrane, Byrd, and Garland improvised eighteen minutes around them. When it was done, Coltrane said, "Okay, you wrote it," and Weinstock's name is on it as composer.

In 1965, five years after Coltrane had left the label, when his current album was *A Love Supreme* for Impulse!, Prestige finally released their last two albums of Coltrane material. *Bahia* is two tunes from July 11, and two from December 26; the appropriately titled *The Last Trane* had material from August 16, 1957, and January 10 and March 26, 1958.

Chapter 17

Mose Allison and Yusef Lateef

Two important new artists first recorded with Prestige in 1957: Mose Allison and Yusef Lateef. Allison and Lateef, in very different ways, both were outside of the New York bebop-centered jazz that Bob Weinstock had founded Prestige to present. They showed that Weinstock realized jazz was moving on, and it was time to move with it. He produced both of these artists, but a change was on the horizon there too. 1958 was the first year that Weinstock began to use other producers, and before long he was to get out of the recording studio altogether, concentrating on running the business, leaving the production to others.

Mose Allison's earliest musical influences were the blues he heard on the radio and the jukeboxes of the Mississippi Delta where he was born, in 1927, on his grandfather's farm. He started picking out tunes on the piano when he was five. In high school he started listening to jazz, and for a piano prodigy in the early 1940s, that meant Nat "King" Cole, an inescapable and powerful influence. A year at Ole Miss was followed by a stint in the postwar army in 1946, then a return to college at Louisiana State University in Baton Rouge, where he majored in literature and philosophy. It was that gumbo of influences that he brought to New York in 1956. A singer he had worked with in Texas, Marilyn Moore, was the ex-wife of Al Cohn, and she recommended the young piano player to her ex. Cohn hired him and used him on an LP recorded for Coral, a subsidiary of Decca, considered a major label in the 1950s. Coral, however, had mostly discontinued its jazz line by the mid-1950s, so there wasn't much promotion for the album. However, it did get Allison more work, and brought him to the attention of Stan Getz, who hired him, as did Gerry Mulligan. Allison was also composing prolifically, but none of the name musicians he played with recorded any of his compositions. He would recall later that when Getz took a break and let his backing trio play, he would get a chance to play some of his own works then.

A recognized figure in the jazz world of the 1940s and early 1950s who befriended Allison was George Wallington. Allison became a sort of protégé of Wallington's, and the older pianist took one of his tunes, "In Salah," into a recording session he had scheduled with Prestige. Wallington had two brilliant young horn players, Phil Woods and Donald Byrd, on the session with him, along with a veteran bassist, Teddy Kotick, and another relative newcomer, Nick Stabulas, on drums. (Stabulas would later work on two of Allison's Prestige sessions.) It must have been a thrill for Allison to hear these masterful musicians playing his tune, but a bigger thrill was yet to come. Perhaps the tune caught Weinstock's ear, and perhaps Wallington said something to his boss about the talented young piano player who had written it. At any rate, one week later—on March 7, 1957—Allison was in the Van Gelders' living room with a trio, to make his debut album.

Wallington's version of "In Salah" was a driving hard-bop romp, with burning solos by Byrd and Woods, and a nice drum solo by Stabulas. Wallington would put the Allison catalog to a further hard-bop test (it passed with flying colors), when he made another record a month later for a smaller label, with J. R. Monterose on tenor sax. They played "In Salah" and two other Allison compositions: "Promised Land," which, like "In Salah," is part of Allison's first album, *Back Country Suite*, and "Rural Route," which Allison seems never to have recorded. So Weinstock may well have been expecting a hard-bop session from his new pianist; if he was, he was in for a surprise.

Back Country Suite bears about the same relationship to the hard bop of its era that, just over a decade later, the Band's first album was to have to rock of its era. Like *Music from Big Pink*, it seemed to come from a different but hard-to-pinpoint time, certainly from a different place. And like *Music from Big Pink*, its down-home simplicity was balanced by a sophistication of a different order from Allison's contemporaries. This was Allison being Allison. His work with Al Cohn and Zoot Sims had proved that he could play bebop, and he could play hard bop. But for his first—and for all he knew, last album for an important New York label—he was going to play his own music.

Weinstock, as we know, was most comfortable with the music he was comfortable with, and that was the music that ended in "bop." But as we also know, he was a very hands-off producer. He had let John Lewis do it his way with the Milt Jackson quartet, even though he secretly would have preferred to have Horace Silver on piano. But it may well have made his palms itch with the desire to step in and change things when he was confronted by a young guy with no reputation and no track record, similarly going his own way, which included a couple of vocals, and one cut on which Allison played the trumpet.

There's one more thing we know about Bob Weinstock: He was a savvy businessman. He took great pride, in later life, in recalling that Prestige had always operated in the black (he may have been overlooking a few rocky moments, but he was close enough). He read the reviews of the Modern Jazz Quartet, read the publicity the guys in tuxedos were getting, and after that had no desire to change them (although he did also record Jackson with Silver). Would this newcomer strike gold in the same way? Time would tell. And it wasn't going to be a lot of time. Weinstock brought *Back Country Suite* out quickly; it was released before Wallington's album, because on the liner notes for that one, Ira Gitler says " 'In Salah' is a Mose Allison original which was originally recorded by the pianist-composer on Prestige 7091."

Back Country Suite found its audience, and it found critical acclaim. *Down Beat*, slow to warm up to John Coltrane, responded immediately to Allison. Dom Cerulli wrote the review: "This is an important record. Not so much because of the suite, which in itself is charming, fresh, and rooted in the blues, but also because Allison is a talent which bears watching. If his subsequent writing has the individuality of approach and the same earthy quality as in this excursion, jazz will have added another exciting voice to its roster of spokesmen. This deserves hearing."

The suite, ten short tone poems with titles like "New Ground," "Train," "Warm Night," and "Highway 49," creates a picture of the Delta of his boyhood and youth with melodies that are direct, recognizable, and bluesy, but with the subtle overtones of a Flannery O'Connor or Harper Lee—bringing together the two somehow not contradictory sides of Mose Allison—the country boy from Tippo, Mississippi, and the literature and philosophy major from LSU. And perhaps a third strand should be mentioned: Allison has always acknowledged a debt to Hungarian composer Béla Bartók, and that he drew inspiration from the way Bartók created a modernist reimagining of Hungarian folk melodies.

Prestige released one 45 rpm single from the session. One side was two pieces from the suite, "New Ground-Warm Night." The other, from the B-side of the album, was one of the two vocals Allison had included: a cover of 1953 Specialty Records recording by Mercy Dee Walton, "One Room Country Shack" (Ira Gitler, not familiar with rhythm and blues or the Specialty catalog, says in the liner notes, "Mose says the original record is by a blues singer named Mercy Dee.") The other vocal, simply called "Blues," is part of the suite, and at one minute and twenty-eight seconds was deemed too short for a single (although a couple of years later "Stay," by Maurice Williams and the Zodiacs, clocked in at 1:36 and went to number 1 on the charts). It was, however, an instant crowd pleaser, requested at all of Allison's live appearances, and a decade later, as "Young Man Blues," a huge pop hit for the Who. Had Weinstock guessed how popular a singer Allison was going to be, and how minianthemic the blues about a young man who ain't nothing in the world these days was going to become, he might have tried to convince Allison to make it a little longer. But in its minute and a half, it was just about perfect.

The rediscovery of the blues as an important cornerstone of American music was not going to happen until the 1960s, and white interpreters of the blues like John Hammond Jr., Dave Van Ronk, or Spider John Koerner were not yet on the horizon. The only white people who were singing the blues in 1957 had names like Elvis Presley, Carl Perkins, and Jerry Lee Lewis, and they were role models for no one in the jazz business.

Weinstock may not have figured out, right away, that he had the next hit vocal stylist on his hands in the form of a white guy who sang the blues; but he certainly figured out that *Back Country Suite* was a winner, and he had Allison back in the studio in November to do more of the same. *Local Color* had original Allison tunes on one side, played in his bluesy-rootsy-bebop style, and mostly the work of other composers on the B-side. There was one trumpet cut on the B-side, and one vocal on each side: an Allison original on the A-side, a rhythm and blues cover on the B. The cover was "Lost Mind," by Percy Mayfield, a Specialty recording artist known as "the poet of the blues." (Specialty label owner Art Rupe said of Mayfield, "If he'd had the proper encouragement, he could have been another Langston Hughes.") The original was "Parchman Farm," Allison's chain gang blues. Loosely adapted from a blues by Bukka White, it was released on 45: twice, once in 1957 and again in 1964, when he rerecorded it with some new lyrics as "New Parchman Farm."

If Allison's second album was following a formula, it was a new one, and with only one other example of it, it could certainly not be called overused. To the jazz fans who had bought *Back Country Suite*, everything on Allison's new album was welcome: the interconnected, bebop-flavored, down-home-drenched melodies; the little taste of trumpet; the two vocals, one an Allison original and one a rhythm and blues gem . . . well, a lot of his fans would have been glad to welcome another vocal or two. *Down Beat*'s Don Gold, praising the "fascinating glimpses into his Mississippi past," also commended Allison for "his two-handed approach to the instrument, his regard for melodic structure, and his understanding of the history of jazz piano." Gold gave the album four and a half stars.

Allison was on his way to becoming a cult figure, but the cult was still a small one. He made his first appearance on the *Down Beat* year-end polls in 1958, ranking twentieth among pianists, fifteenth among male singers, and with no votes in the composer category. But his Prestige albums, his obituary in the *New York Times* points out, were not commercial successes. They definitely had a devoted following, and enough critical acclaim, to make Allison an artist worth sticking with, but from the *Times*'s historical perspective, they could hardly be regarded as best sellers.

And here again, one probably has to consider the long term. Allison says he never saw a royalty check from Prestige. But when Weinstock sold his label and its catalog to Fantasy, it's a good bet that Allison's records, as opposed to, say, Earl Coleman's, were a strong plus in assessing the value of the package.

Young Man Mose was recorded in January 1958 and released that same year. It had one trumpet track and three vocals. His own compositions took a back seat to an offbeat collection of standards, with the trumpet cut, "Stroll," being the only original. Allison was back in the studio in April for a session that would be released as *Ramblin' with Mose,* but not until 1962. It featured four original tunes and only one vocal, an omission that Joe Goldberg discussed in his liner notes:

> Once before, when I spoke to Mose about an album of his, he said, "I sing, I write, and I play. I have my own little medicine show going." But at the same time, it must be said that Mose sometimes seems to resent his ability to sing. As has happened before, with other people in other fields, the thing that you do most easily and casually, perhaps for that very reason, receives great praise. And it is praise which the person involved sometimes wishes were reserved for aspects of his work that are more important to him.

If one can make an arbitrary distinction, Mose was primarily a musician, not a singer.

But in another interview, with the *Berkshire Eagle*'s Seth Rogovoy in 2001, he said, "The classic jazz men who sang were my early heroes, people like Louis Armstrong, Fats Waller, Nat King Cole and Louis Jordan. They all played well and sang. Jack Teagarden was another one. They all had singing styles and were all great instrumentalists, so I figured, what the hell, why not me?"

There was one more 1958 session, on August 15, which produced *Creek Bank,* also released in 1958. This was like *Back Country Suite* and

Local Color in that the instrumentals were a roughly even divide between originals and standards, and there were two vocals, one original and one a rhythm and blues classic, Willie Dixon's "The Seventh Son." *Autumn Song*, in 1959, followed essentially the same pattern: some original instrumental compositions, some standards. There were three vocals, none of them Allison originals. He did two blues associated with the Chicago/Chess Records style of rhythm and blues: Sonny Boy Williamson's "Eyesight to the Blind" and Jimmy Rogers's "That's All Right." The third vocal was Duke Ellington's "Do Nothing Till You Hear from Me."

In a 1958 interview for *Down Beat*, Allison had said, "In the South, I'm considered an advanced bebop type. In New York, I'm considered a country blues-folk type. Actually, I don't think I'm either. Maybe I'm a little of both." Perhaps nowhere is this more clearly demonstrated than in the vocal selections on *Autumn Song*. The two blues, but particularly "Eyesight to the Blind," are filtered through Allison's New York sophistication, and the piano break, as naturally as though this was something everyone did, swings from down home blues into bebop. The Ellington tune has no shortage of sophistication, so there it's Allison's southern vernacular style that makes his interpretation unique.

After that, Allison moved to the greener pastures of Columbia, where he made his first album in December 1959 and January 1960. *The Transfiguration of Hiram Brown* followed almost exactly the pattern set by *Back Country Suite:* a suite on the A-side (including one vocal), and standards (including two vocals) on the flip side. Even with the greater distribution and bigger publicity department at Columbia, it was still not a commercial success.

It's worth mentioning that in 1957–58, the commercial blues that was being released on labels like Chess and Specialty, and countless smaller labels, had no listening public outside of the Black communities. If you were a rock and roll fan, you knew Chuck Berry and Ray Charles, but if you were a jazz fan, the fact that Chuck Berry had appeared in the Newport Jazz Festival feature film *Jazz on a Summer's Day* was a bit of an embarrassment. If you listened to New York jazz disc jockey Symphony Sid, you probably agreed with his curt dismissal of callers who requested Ray Charles: "We don't play rock and roll." And even if you were a rock and roll fan, your knowledge of the catalogs of Atlantic, Chess, and Specialty did not go much deeper than Ray Charles, Chuck Berry, and Little Richard. And even for these artists, none of Ray Charles's now-immortal Atlantic singles like "I Got a Woman" cracked the *Billboard* top 100; he did not have a top ten single until "What'd I Say." Little Richard's records were regularly outsold by Pat Boone's pallid covers.

Willie Dixon is now a legendary figure, and his "Seventh Son" has been recorded more than seventy times, but when Allison found and recorded it, there was only the Chess recording by Willie Mabon. Well into the next decade, white audiences would discover Chicago blues through the fandom of the Rolling Stones and other blues-loving British rockers. Percy Mayfield has achieved some recognition largely because of "Please Send Me Someone to Love," and there have been some twenty covers of his "Lost Mind," but again, Allison was the first to cover it. And to this day, no other vocal cover of "Baby Let Me Hold Your Hand" exists. Allison's knowledge of the recorded blues of his era went deep.

During this period, Allison continued working as a jazz pianist with Al Cohn and Zoot Sims, and sometimes with Stan Getz. He was a talented jazz musician, and could certainly have established himself in a solid niche with George Wallington, Al Haig, and Hank Jones, all highly regarded within the jazz community, not widely recognized outside of it. But as the center of his own little medicine show, he was unique.

What seems remarkable, in retrospect, is how long it took for the jazz world, and perhaps for Allison himself, to recognize this. Perhaps it was reticence on Allison's part, as suggested in Goldberg's liner notes to *Ramblin' with Mose*. But, by the time the album actually saw daylight, in 1962, the horse was out of the barn. He was now sixth in *Down Beat*'s list of best vocalists, trailing only Frank Sinatra, Ray Charles, Oscar Brown Jr., Joe Williams, and Mel Tormé. Although his piano skills had not diminished, his fan identification as a pianist had shrunk. He was not mentioned at all on the piano poll.

Although Allison had left Prestige, Prestige had not finished playing its part in the Mose Allison story. In 1963, the label released a compilation album, *Mose Allison Sings*, gathering together all the vocals from his various Prestige albums. It became his best seller, and from there on, on Columbia, Atlantic, Elektra, Verve, and Blue Note, he was primarily presented as a singer, and more and more, he became known for his original songs. By the mid-1960s, with the advent of Bob Dylan and others who followed in his wake, a new category of performer arrived on center stage: the singer-songwriter. Most of these were folksingers or folk-rock singers, with guitars, but Allison certainly secured his place in their ranks. His songs have been recorded by the Who, Bonnie Raitt, Elvis Costello, the Yardbirds, the Clash, and Van Morrison.

So should Allison have recognized where his main gift lay, and taken the shortest route to the top right away? It's a good thing that he didn't.

The Prestige albums show the range of his unique talent, and *Back Country Suite* remains, by general acclaim, his best album.

Yusef Lateef is, among his fellow Detroiters, a late arrival on the New York scene, and not because he represented a younger generation. He was thirty-seven when he first came to New York in the spring of 1957 to record for Savoy and Verve, and then to make this session for Prestige. And he wouldn't actually move east for good until 1960.

Lateef had not been entirely homebound. He'd started playing professionally at eighteen, touring with swing bands and eventually with Dizzy Gillespie, but by 1950 concerns for his wife's health brought him off the road and home to Detroit, where he became an important figure, not only for his musicianship but also his cultural leadership. He was a founder and vice president of the New Music Society, an organization that reached out to younger jazz musicians and gave them a place to grow and develop. The year 1950 was when he converted to Islam.

His late arrival on the New York scene is part of the reason why, although he'd been an active musician for over twenty years by the time the decade turned, he is more associated with the jazz of the '60s than of the '50s. The rest of that reason is his free-flying creativity, which seems like a '60s thing but was part of Lateef's creative personality even back in Detroit. Pianist Terry Pollard recalled to authors Lars Bjorn and Jim Gallert in their book *Before Motown: A History of Jazz in Detroit* that "he sometimes had me blow into a pop bottle. He'd fill it with water . . . to get different sounds, to make the song sound like Yusef wanted it to be. And so I ended up blowing into these pop bottles. I didn't know how, and I would get dizzy every night."

While he was still in Detroit, Lateef began to experiment with Middle Eastern music, turned on to it by a fellow assembly line worker at the Chrysler plant. He realized, "I had to widen my canvas of expression. I spent many hours in the library . . . studying the music of other cultures. I met a man [at Chrysler] from Syria and he asked me if I knew about the rabat." That led him to seek out other traditional Middle Eastern instruments. In his memoir *The Gentle Giant* he wrote, "While visiting the Eastern Market, one of Detroit's landmark shopping districts with a variety of ethnic items, I used to go to the Syrian spice store and I discovered instruments such as the argol, a double reed, bamboo flute." That began a further exploration into the possibilities of music played on instruments outside the standard repertoire of the jazz musician: "I also began making my own flutes, like the pneumatic bamboo flute, and the earthboard, an instrument my son Rashid made, which was constructed on a board with bailing wire."

Lateef stayed longer in Detroit because of family obligations, loyalty to the city's arts mission, and his studies at Wayne State University with Dr. Robert Lawson, who introduced him to the European classical composers. His first high school music teacher had suggested that he play the oboe. That didn't quite happen, but, as Lateef says, a seed had been planted, and he began studying the oboe with Ronald Oldmark of the Detroit Symphony Orchestra. When he started studying with Oldmark, he had begun his recording career but was still living in Detroit and commuting with his band to New York just for recording sessions. Realizing that he might be continuing a recording career for some time, he resolved not to get caught in a rut, repeating himself. So he took up the oboe, and spent a lot of time in the library studying the instruments and musical styles of Africa, India, Japan, and China.

Lateef did not set out to take New York by storm, as so many of his fellow Detroiters had. He had begun a full-time job leading a band at Klein's Show Bar, and Dirk Schaeffer, a New York journalist who heard him one night, was sufficiently impressed to sing his praises to New York record producer Ozzie Cadena of Savoy Records (Cadena would later move to Prestige). It must have been quite a sales pitch, because Cadena, without ever having heard Lateef, got in touch with him and invited him to New York to make a record:

> It was an opportunity I had been waiting for. . . . After we finished our performance that Sunday night, we jumped into two cars and took off for Hackensack, New Jersey, to record at Rudy Van Gelder's studio, which at that time, I think, was located in the living room at his mother's house.
>
> This was in April 1957. Cadena was among the best producers I've ever worked with. He had put us under contract based on Mr. Schaeffer's word and the first time he had really ever heard the band was the recording session. The only thing that might have puzzled him was the assortment of odd instruments we brought to the session. But once he heard how well they were played and sounded he was pleased.

Lateef brought all of this knowledge, and all the instruments he was experimenting with, to his New York recording sessions. He had not signed exclusively with Savoy, so he was free to record for Prestige as well. His first Prestige session was October 11, 1957, and as he recalls in his memoir, "It was so enjoyable working with Bob Weinstock. . . . He allowed me to be very creative and imaginative." The eleven tunes he recorded that day were enough for two albums, *The Sounds of Yusef* and *Other Sounds*.

> ## Listening to Prestige:
> ## Yusef Lateef
>
> *Recorded at Van Gelder Studio, Hackensack, NJ, October 11, 1957*
>
> *Wilbur Harden, flugelhorn, balloon; Yusef Lateef, tenor sax, flute, argol, tambourine; Hugh Lawson, piano, Turkish finger cymbals, Seven Up bottle, balloon, bells; Ernie Farrow, bass, rabat; Oliver Jackson, drums, Chinese gong, earth-board*
>
> *Tracks recorded: Playful Flute; Taboo; Ecaps; All Alone; Anastasia; Love and Humor; Buckingham; Lambert's Point; Meditation; Mahaba; Minor Mood; Take the A Train*
>
> This October session with its twelve tunes was an impressive feat for five guys and their instruments packed into a station wagon and barreling in from Detroit. It was impressive for the sheer amount of work and how good it was, and really impressive for its range.
>
> "Playful Flute," the first tune laid down, was composed by brass player Wilbur Harden, but it embodies Lateef's love of Middle Eastern music, learned in the library, from his fellow Chrysler worker, and certainly also from his pilgrimages to Mecca. It incorporates the flute and the argol, or arghul, a two-tubed woodwind instrument that dates back to ancient Egypt.
>
> "Taboo" is one of those tunes that's always used when a movie soundtrack wants something Latin and exotic. Either that or Margarita Lecuona's only other hit, "Babalu," or one of the compositions of her cousin Ernesto, like "The Breeze and I" or "Malaguena." To refresh my memory, I listened to versions by Les Baxter (boring) and Cuban bandleader Jack Costanzo (not boring). But no one brings to it quite what Lateef does. From Oliver Jackson's arresting drum intro to Lateef's flute work, he turns what's generally an ersatz exotic into a genuine exotic, which is no small feat. "Taboo" is a tune that could easily be dismissed as kitsch. Not so here. And it's interesting to consider how it might have been chosen.

This was a quintet that Lateef held together for five years, working a regular five-night-a-week gig in a very hip jazz town. Five nights a week for five years means you work out a lot of material, and sometimes you're just goofing around: "Hey, let's take a tune that's straight from Squaresville, and see how we can mess around with it." And if you're Yusef Lateef, and you're playing what some have described as "world music before there was world music," even goofing around can lead to new discoveries. "Anastasia" might have been another one of those tunes. From an Oscar-nominated movie soundtrack by Alfred Newman, it had become a pop hit for Pat Boone, and you can't go much deeper into Squaresville than that. Here, Lateef does the really unexpected by staying quite faithful to the melody but giving it a bit of a Middle Eastern twist, and a moody cast: making it new.

Lateef's own compositions for this date are as eclectic as his covers. "Ecaps," in spite of its spacey title, is pretty much rooted on earth, with bop-influenced flute and tenor playing, and a very nice boppish piano solo by Hugh Lawson. Others range from boppish to proto–world music.

And then there's "Love and Humor": Most of the odd instruments listed in the session notes come into play here, including the balloons handed to Wilbur Harden and Hugh Lawson, for that unmistakable sound of two balloons being rubbed together, and Lawson is given Terry Pollard's 7-Up bottles. I couldn't help but think, as all of these unusual sounds wove their way into the mix, what kind of a challenge this session must have been for Rudy Van Gelder. The mood may be (sort of) Middle Eastern, with Lateef playing flute and argol, but the instrumentation is worthy of Spike Jones, who also knew something about love and humor. Lateef's humor is a little more subtle, and this is a very special cut, moving some distance away from jazz as we knew it, expanding our musical vocabulary. Lateef had used some of these instruments and sound effects on his earlier Savoy albums, but nothing quite like this.

I wonder if Bob Weinstock had entirely been expecting "Love and Humor." But he didn't shy away from it. It went onto his first Lateef release, The Sounds of Yusef, along with "Playful Flute," "Buckingham," "Meditation," and "Take the 'A' Train," and not only that, it was released as a 45 b/w "Meditation." "Taboo," "All Alone," "Lambert's Joint," "Mahabs," "Minor Mood," and "Anastasia" all went onto the New Jazz album Other Sounds, released in 1959. "Ecaps" was held off until the 1960 New Jazz Cry! Tender, the rest of which came from a later and much different session.

During 1958 and early 1959, Lateef recorded a few more albums for Argo and Savoy, and by the time he returned to Prestige on October 16, 1959, Esmond Edwards was in the producer's chair. The album was *Cry! Tender*, and by this time, critics were starting to wonder where Lateef fit under the umbrella of jazz, or if he fit there at all. (This would not have bothered Lateef, who hated the word "jazz.") Barbara Gardner, giving the album four stars in *Down Beat*, said:

> There must be some delineation as to where jazz begins or ends, yet this record flows fluidly across such markers, infusing the native jazz with a pervading essence of distant lands . . .
>
> It would seem incorrect to me to maintain that the album is a jazz offering in its entirety. Lateef must be considered as one of the important present-era jazzmen both as a performer and a composer; however, his work is more a welding of jazz with Eastern musical concepts yielding a provocative modern American music.

Lateef also appeared on a 1960 Prestige album by fellow Detroiter Doug Watkins, *Soulnik*. Watkins had been on frequent call as a bassist for Prestige in the latter half of the 1950s. He had made one previous album as a leader, for Transition Records. For *Soulnik*, he played cello (Herman Wright was on bass). The cello and Lateef's oboe gave the album a unique sound that unfortunately was not to be repeated. Watkins died in a car crash in 1962.

On September 5, 1961, Lateef recorded for Esmond Edwards and Prestige with a quartet that included two Detroiters, bebop pianist Barry Harris, considered a mentor to most of the young musicians who came out of Detroit, and Ernie Farrow, again doubling on bass and rabab. Lex Humphries was the drummer. Lateef played tenor sax, oboe, and flute—including on one piece, "Plum Blossom," the Chinese globular flute, an ancient instrument that played a lower register than one normally associates with the flute. The resulting album, *Eastern Sounds*, was released on Prestige/Moodsville, a subsidiary that Weinstock had set up perhaps in answer to Jackie Gleason's best-selling mood music albums, but that nonetheless presented real jazz musicians playing real jazz. It did have two pieces that might have seemed geared toward the Jackie Gleason crowd, the love themes from two blockbuster movies, *The Robe* and *Spartacus*. Played by a highly eclectic jazz quartet, they were not exactly the lush orchestral themes from their respective movie soundtracks. But if their inclusion on a Lateef album was a surprise, an even bigger surprise was in store: "Love Theme from *Spartacus*," released on 45, became a hit, the only hit single of Lateef's career.

Into Something, recorded on December 29, 1961, and released on New Jazz, was Lateef's last Prestige session. Barry Harris returned on piano. Detroit-born bass player Herman Wright was on board, and the drummer was a young recent arrival from Detroit, Elvin Jones. It was a top-flight quartet, and the repertoire, as always with Lateef, was eclectic, including an old chestnut perhaps more likely to be associated with a Dixieland band, "When You're Smiling." Lateef chose it because it reminded him of his father, who had loved it.

Lateef's prolific career lasted well into the twenty-first century, with numerous recordings on Impulse! and Atlantic. In 1991 he launched his own label, YAL Records, which released over thirty of his albums. His final date, a live recording with Ahmad Jamal in Paris, came just months before his death in 2013. But like Mose Allison, and indeed a number of artists who began their careers with the label, a Prestige album remains his most popular: *Eastern Sounds*, with the intoxicating "Love Theme from *Spartacus*."

Chapter 18

A New Era

Soul Jazz

The year 1959 was the tenth anniversary of Prestige. It could be said that it marked the first year of a completely new era, of a clean break with the bebop sound that had inspired Bob Weinstock to start his own label in the first place, a break that was clean enough that Weinstock virtually retired from the studio, devoting himself to the business end of things. He would attribute this to the increasing demand on his time as the business grew, but he may also have begun to feel a disconnect from the music. Mose Allison and especially Yusef Lateef were a marked departure from the past (although Weinstock produced both of them). And there was a new sound knocking at the door, although Weinstock was not as quick to answer that knock as he might have been. As he told Dan Gould,

> Jimmy Smith came knocking on my door, with a big tape recorder, said "I want you to hear something," He knew who I was, but I didn't know him. I said "It sounds good, but I don't see doing an organ"—that's what I knew.

DG: When Smith took off, did you regret the opportunity you missed?

BW: Well, like Billie Holiday said, No regrets. But when Jimmy Smith was selling big, I tell you what I did do (laughs)—I had the next ten organists signed to contracts.

Soul jazz was a new sound, and it was to be one of the defining sounds of the 1960s. While it didn't have much in common with bebop, it was a natural progression from the variant on bebop that came to be known as hard bop, and that many ascribed to the influence of Miles Davis's middecade recordings for Prestige: a music that, while accepting the intellectual underpinnings of 1940s bebop, emphasized the visceral aspects of the music. Jimmy Smith had flung that door wide open, and had found a new voice with which to express the most gut-felt impulses of jazz.

The voice of the 1930s had been the clarinet, with Benny Goodman and Artie Shaw defining the sound. Bebop in the 1940s had coalesced around the quintet, with Charlie Parker's alto sax and Dizzy Gillespie's trumpet as the lead instruments. As jazz moved into the 1950s the trumpet assumed a position of centrality, with Fats Navarro and Clifford Brown, bright lights too soon extinguished, with Chet Baker, Art Farmer, Maynard Ferguson, and especially as Miles Davis came more and more to assume a position of centrality.

No one was thinking about the organ as the voice of jazz. Then suddenly, with the ascent of Jimmy Smith, everyone was. Between 1956 and 1963, Smith recorded twenty-three albums for Blue Note. And Weinstock isn't exaggerating by much when he says that after he saw Smith's success on the rival label, he snagged the next ten organists. Blue Note seemed content to let Smith carry their organ banner, so Prestige scooped up Shirley Scott, Jack McDuff, Richard "Groove" Holmes, Johnny "Hammond" Smith (later known as Johnny Hammond), Larry Young, Don Patterson, Trudy Pitts, and Charles Earland during the decade, as the two labels established themselves at the epicenter of the soul jazz sound. Prestige was not at all reticent about its role, as throughout 1959 full page ads in *Down Beat* proclaimed that "Despite opposition of critics . . . Prestige gave birth to soul jazz!"

Along with the organ, there was a new prominence for the instrument that had always been at the center, and at the same time on the periphery of the jazz experience: the tenor saxophone. Rescued by Coleman Hawkins from its status as novelty instrument at best, the tenor arrived in the modern jazz era on the wings of Lester Young and Ben Webster, and was the instrument of choice of Stan Getz, Sonny Rollins, and John Coltrane. But it was also the driving instrument of the disrespected step-cousin of jazz: the small-group swing musicians who made the dance music of the era that was dismissed by purists as rhythm and blues, and later as rock and roll.

Bob Weinstock knew the jazz clubs on 52nd Street, now only a memory, and he knew the downtown clubs like the Village Vanguard and the

Half Note. But it was his new music supervisor, Esmond Edwards, who was equipped to pick up on the new sound that was soon to become known as soul jazz. Edwards realized that the music that had been dismissed as rhythm and blues would fit right in with the new sound that was gaining such popularity with the rise of Blue Note's Jimmy Smith. Edwards went to the Apollo, and to the Harlem clubs: Smalls Paradise, the Baby Grand, Count Basie's. It was at the Apollo that Edwards first heard a tenor sax player named Willis "Gator Tail" Jackson, who had been closely associated with the small group swing sound of the '40s and '50s. Weinstock had always been a fan of rhythm and blues, and he quickly realized that the new soul jazz sound was very closely akin to the widely popular but critically scorned genre, and that there were a lot of forgotten virtuosos who would fit right into this new sound. As a member of his trio, Jackson brought with him an organist who was to become one of the biggest jazz stars of the 1960s.

By the time Willis Jackson signed with Prestige in 1959, at the age of twenty-seven, he had already packed a lot of playing into his life. As a teenager, he turned down offers from Lionel Hampton and Andy Kirk to finish college, which is something to add to your stereotype of what a tenor sax wild man is like. After graduating from Florida A&M, he joined Cootie Williams in time to play the tenor solo on Williams's jukebox hit "Gator Tail," which functioned in his career in much the same way "Flying Home" had done for Illinois Jacquet and Arnett Cobb, plus it gave him the nickname he would carry for the rest of his life.

After Williams, he led his own popular groups, and worked with Ruth Brown at Atlantic. He had played on her megahit "5-10-15 Hours," and they would spend part of the decade as husband and wife. But as the 1950s wound down, the honking, dynamic tenor sax that had been a staple of the rhythm and blues of the '40s and '50s was waning in popularity, just as the new sound of soul jazz was waking up. Fortunately, Prestige figured out that if you were looking for a guy who could play down and dirty and could also play modern, there was a treasure trove of guys who had been doing it for a while, including at least one who had heard the siren song of the tenor sax/organ combo. Gator's career was rejuvenated, and Prestige got not one but three of its stars of the coming decade: Jackson himself, guitarist Bill Jennings, and organist Jack McDuff.

McDuff had joined Jackson's band as a bassist, and it was the Gator who convinced him to switch to organ, an instrument he took to the way the Smith Brothers took to cough drops. Bill Jennings never amassed the kind of discography that Jack McDuff did. He was one of those "musicians'

musicians," largely overlooked during his career, reclaimed—and claimed—by guitarists who followed him. B. B. King called him "a daring player, both rhythmically and technically . . . because he would start a groove to going, and then whatever it takes to keep that groove going, he would do it."

Rounding out the group was bass player Tommy Potter, one of mainstays of the early bebop era, but pretty close to the end of his career; his work on this Jackson session may be his last on record. Drummer Alvin Johnson was part of the group Jackson brought with him to Prestige, and he isn't known for much beyond his work with Jackson, McDuff, and Jennings, but he knew how to keep things going.

Listening to Prestige: Willis "Gator Tail" Jackson

Recorded at Van Gelder Studio, Hackensack, NJ, May 25, 1959

Willis Jackson, tenor sax; Jack McDuff, organ; Bill Jennings, guitar; Tommy Potter, bass; Alvin Johnson, drums

Tracks recorded: The Gator Jumps (as Gator's Tail); Gil's Pills; Memories of You; A Smooth One; The Man I Love; Please Mr. Jackson; Dinky's Mood; How Deep Is the Ocean; Come Back to Sorrento; Cool Grits; Angel Eyes; Three Little Words; She's Funny That Way; 633 Knock

This is an immense session: the fourteen tunes cut on this date showed up on three immediate releases, and many more over time. Jackson and Co. mix standards and originals, honkers and ballads, providing something for everyone.

I don't think I was much of a fan of organ combos back then. I may have bought a Jimmy Smith album sometime in the '60s, but like many, I was a little put off by organ music, the sound of church and roller rink and radio soap operas. One of the delights of listening carefully and closely to everything recorded for Prestige Records is really coming to understand and appreciate the range and tonality of the Hammond B3 organ in the hands of some jazz virtuosos, and to appreciate how the B3 and the tenor saxophone were, in fact, made for each other.

Please Mr. Jackson, released in 1959, was the first album drawn from this session. It was followed by Cool "Gator" in 1960; "Gator's Tail" and "She's Funny That Way" were held back for a second 1960 release, Blue Gator. The three 45 rpm records to come from this date were

"Please Mr. Jackson"/"Dinky's Mood," "Come Back to Sorrento"/"On the Sunny Side of the Street," and "Cool Grits, Part 1 & 2."

"Gator's Tail," also known as "The Gator Jumps," is a good introduction to this now-classic sound—back then, a new sound, and worth comparing to a tune with almost the same title, the Cootie Williams/Willis Jackson composition that first made Jackson his reputation, and got him his nickname, recorded in 1949 by Williams' orchestra.

Nostalgia tells us that the swing music of the '30s and '40s, made by Duke Ellington stalwarts like Cootie Williams, must be more subtle and sophisticated than the rhythm and blues–derived, simplified hard bop of the soul jazz era, but there's a lot going on in the 1959 version that wouldn't have been dreamed of a decade earlier. The organ of McDuff, for a start—the way it adds shadows and light to Jackson's lead saxophone. The way that Jackson moves from honking to melodic and back again. This is not to knock Williams's swing classic—but Jackson and his quintet have learned a few things from living through the bop era, and from a whole lot of one-nighters together. But what Jackson had in the '40s with Cootie Williams, he still has as he begins a new chapter with Prestige, and it was best described by Jack Kerouac in On the Road: "[Dean] leaped out of the chair and put on a Willie [sic] Jackson record, 'Gator Tail.' He stood before it, socking his palms and rocking and pumping his knees to the beat. 'Whoo! That sonumbitch! First time I heard him I thought he'd die the next night, but he's still alive.'"

Recorded at Van Gelder Studio, Englewood Cliffs, NJ, November 9, 1959

Willis Jackson, tenor sax; Jack McDuff, organ; Bill Jennings, guitar; Wendell Marshall, bass; Alvin Johnson, drums

Tracks recorded: Glad 'a See Ya'; On the Sunny Side of the Street; When I Fall in Love; East Breeze; Blue Strollin'; Medley: September Song / Easy Living / Deep Purple

Willis, Jack, and Bill are back again, and proving once more that they know how to play the music folks want to hear. And proving once again what a blessing it was that Bob Weinstock decided to sign up musicians like Jackson and Hal Singer, bringing what had been marginalized as rhythm and blues into the mainstream of jazz, into the recording cathedral of Rudy Van Gelder, and onto the long-playing record.

The main difference between jazz and rhythm and blues is basically the difference between the jukebox and the jazz radio broadcast, between the 45 rpm record and the LP. Give musicians like Willis Jackson,

Jack McDuff, and Bill Jennings eight minutes instead of three to play a tune like "Cookin' Sherry," and you get the full potential of rhythm and blues: room for three great soloists to open up, stretch out, and develop their solos without sacrificing any of that rhythm and blues intensity. You can dance your ass off to "Cookin' Sherry," or you can snap your fingers and listen to what the soloists are doing, what the two other principals are doing behind the solo, what Wendell Marshall and Alvin Johnson are doing, all the things that make jazz the twentieth century's answer to chamber music, only hotter.

"Cookin' Sherry," "Blue Gator," and "Tu'gether" are the three Jackson originals from the session, with composer credit for "Mellow Blues" given to the three frontline players. But this trio, although they would go their separate ways, made such tight, inventive, and listenable music together that you wouldn't go far wrong in thinking of them as the MJQ of gutbucket. On all of these numbers, they each have solos that complement the others as though they shared one mind or set of guts, while still expressing irrepressible individualism.

They do right by other people's compositions, too. Jackson shows his ballad side on "Try a Little Tenderness," which comes in at just under six minutes and is mostly him, although Jennings contributes a sensitive and unusual guitar solo. Jimmy Dorsey's "Contrasts" brings rhythm and blues to swing, or vice versa, and why not?

Esmond Edwards produced. The session was split up and sprinkled over three albums. "Blue Gator" was on its eponymous album along with "Try a Little Tenderness." "Cookin' Sherry" was also eponymous, joined by "Contrasts" and "Mellow Blues." "Tu'gether" didn't quite manage eponymy, but it came close. It was on the album called Together Again. Three two-sided 45s came out of the session: "Cookin' Sherry," "Blue Gator," and "Tu'gether."

Jackson, with Esmond Edwards and later Ozzie Cadena producing, became one of Prestige's most popular artists. His twenty-four albums between 1959 and 1969 were outdone by Gene Ammons's forty-four, but Ammons started in 1956 and was still turning out new material in 1973, the only artist to continue to record after Prestige was sold to Fantast Records, as his uniquely approachable style fitted in equally with bebop, hard bop, and soul jazz.

Prestige hired other tenormen from the rhythm and blues charts, with varying success. Arnett Cobb recorded seven albums for the label in

1959–60, beginning with a title straight off the rhythm and blues charts: *Blow, Arnett, Blow!* He also participated in a Prestige All Stars session with Coleman Hawkins, Eddie "Lockjaw" Davis, and Buddy Tate. Weinstock brought another rhythm and blues hitmaker to the label in February 1959, Hal Singer, whose "Corn Bread" topped the charts in 1948, but Singer failed to click.

Shirley Scott

Prestige had missed the Jimmy Smith express, but there was a lot more talent to be found in Smith's hometown, Philadelphia. The city was the cauldron from which so many soul jazz organists emerged, and one of the first was a gifted twenty-four-year-old woman named Shirley Scott. She had begun as a young teenager playing piano in her father's basement jazz club, originally on orders from her older brother who needed someone to accompany his tenor sax. She stepped out from her brother's shadow in high school, playing the trumpet, and also, while still in high school, toured briefly as the piano player in a band backing up a rhythm and blues vocal group (also in the combo, a young John Coltrane). Then this young musician fell under the spell of an organ-playing Philadelphian, and decided it was the instrument for her. The inspiration was not Jimmy Smith but Jackie Davis, the pioneer of the Philadelphia jazz organ and a fixture at Philly's Club Harlem. Jackie's inspiration, in turn, was the real trailblazer of the jazz organ sound, Wild Bill Davis, then playing in nearby Atlantic City. Jackie Davis showed her what the organ could sound like; Jimmy Smith showed her that it could hit the big time.

Scott switched over to the Hammond B3, and at twenty-one, she auditioned for Eddie "Lockjaw" Davis, who was intrigued by the idea of a saxophone-organ combo, and liked what he heard from the young Philadelphian. Davis had led a quintet with Sonny Stitt for Roost in 1955, featuring Doc Bagby on organ, and he brought Bagby with him to the larger rhythm and blues independent King Records, where he recorded a few sessions before switching from Bagby to Scott, who recorded her first trio session with him on July 16, 1956. Her first King recordings made up one side of an LP called *Uptown* (Doc Bagby was on the other side). That was followed by *Jazz with a Beat*, which was all Scott. However, King followed the rhythm and blues practice of just crediting the headliner, so her name is not on either of these albums.

That would change when Davis joined Count Basie for a few sessions on Roulette. In December, 1957, Scott received full billing for *Count Basie Presents the Eddie Davis Trio + Joe Newman* on the album cover and in Barry Ulanov's liner notes: "Little Shirley Scott is an astonishing musician . . . as her rhythmic impulse gathers force, it is hard to believe that this girl weighs, at most, 100 pounds. But the power, effective as it is, is not Shirley's most compelling contribution. It is rather, I think, the surrealistic touches with which she decorated the ballads."

Next, there was a session for Roost in early 1958. But the big breakthrough for newcomer Scott—and for veteran Davis—was signing with Prestige. The June 20, 1958, session was released almost immediately; Prestige must have known they had something here, and they were right. *The Eddie*

"Lockjaw" Davis Cookbook with Shirley Scott and Jerome Richardson (George Duvivier on bass and Arthur Edgehill on drums) made it to the market before either the Roulette or the Roost record, and it was a hit. Generally considered to be Davis's most successful record, it made a splash on the jukeboxes too, as nearly every cut was eventually released on 45 rpm. It was followed quickly by *Cookbooks* volumes 2 and 3, and *Smokin'*, which was really a *Cookbook* volume 4.

Weinstock and Edwards knew what they had with the saxophone/organ soul jazz sound of Davis and Scott, but more than that, they recognized what a find they had in Shirley Scott. Even before they recorded the quintet, they had Scott in the studio with Duvivier and Edgehill on May 27, 1958, for a lengthy session that produced seventeen tunes that were released over two albums, one right away and the other in 1961.

Scott knew how to cook, as she proved with Eddie Davis, and she could cook up a tasty soul stew on her own, too, as she demonstrated on her trio sessions. She has said that she was drawn to the organ because "on the organ, no one knows how many different sounds you can get. It's an infinite number of tones. The only problem is taste." She had taste, and it's a good thing she did, because her adventurous nature, her quest to discover and probe a full range of the organ's possibilities, might have been a disastrous cacophony in the hands of someone who did not have her unerring sense of what was right, even at the farthest reaches of the instrument's possibilities. Of all the jazz organists who attained stardom during the soul jazz era of the 1960s, Scott can lay claim to being the most musically advanced. She can deliver the goods with any of them, but she can also consistently surprise.

Scott was even more prolific than Jackson, with twenty-three titles for Prestige under her own name, and ten more with Davis. After ending her partnership with Davis, she formed a new one with tenor saxophonist Stanley Turrentine, whom she married in 1960 (and divorced in 1971). Turrentine was signed to Blue Note, so their joint sessions were divided between the two labels, with the Prestige product released under her name and the Blue Note records under his.

Jack McDuff

Jack McDuff continued to record with Jackson through 1961 (and joined him for a reunion album in 1965), but Weinstock and Edwards wasted little time putting him out front. His first session as leader was January 25, 1960, with Bill Jennings joining him on guitar. He would quickly become one of Prestige's most successful artists. His first album, *Brother Jack*, gave him the name he would be known by for the rest of his career.

McDuff surrounded himself with excellent sidemen. His second album featured cop-turned-jazzman Lem Winchester on vibes. Winchester had signed with Prestige after being discovered by Leonard Feather and showcased at the 1958 Newport Jazz Festival. His life and career were cut short in 1961 when he accidentally shot himself.

McDuff's third album, *The Honeydripper* (1961), featured Grant Green on guitar. Green, who was with him for two more albums, was just breaking out as a major star with Blue Note. *Goodnight, It's Time to Go* saw McDuff's first pairing with Joe Dukes, who would remain with him for the rest of his career, and who would receive general acclaim as the perfect soul jazz drummer. *Brother Jack McDuff Live!* (1963) would provide his biggest hit, and probably his most famous group. The hit was "Rock Candy," a six-minute, fire-breathing romp of pure rhythm and blues, the classic small group swing style forged in the 1940s. The group was McDuff and Dukes, with Red Holloway, a veteran of all styles from small group swing to modern, and with a nineteen-year-old guitarist making his debut: George Benson.

George Benson

Young George Benson had a lot to learn. He recalled in an interview:

> McDuff . . . was very critical. He stayed on me every day—as a matter of fact, he would cuss me out every night. Because I had just started playing chord changes or jazz tunes, and I didn't know very much about what was happening. He would have me play lines in unison or harmony with the saxophone player, and they would be at ridiculous tempos. And by the fact that the saxophone player did them, I didn't question the fact that they could be done. I decided it was just my ability at fault; I'd go home and practice them, play them sideways, until I came up with a way to play these tunes that I didn't even understand. And eventually I began to fit into his repertoire, and became a valuable member of the group; we sold a lot of records, and so

forth. But what had helped me was the way he'd stayed on me all the time, until I learned what to do.

Another good thing about his group was: due to the fact that I couldn't play very well, he would only give me one or two choruses in any song. So whatever I could play, I had to cram it into a chorus or two—which made me learn to fire up very early in my solo. I said: "Well, this is gonna be short," and I'd just rumble away at a lot of notes, and throw in funky things, pretty things, every kind of thing I could think of. And it was good for records, because when I got in the studio I could do that naturally.

McDuff and his longtime drummer Joe Dukes were solid professionals, and very exacting. They would let him have it with both barrels if he didn't measure up, and with no shortage of obscenities:

Finally, after a particularly nasty rant, I snapped: "If y'all don't lay off, I'm gonna take y'all outside and beat y'all old men up! I'm nineteen years old! Y'all can't take me! We're going out in the alley, right now!" McDuff and Dukes just stared at me for a second, then they both pulled out switchblades. But that didn't stop me: "I don't care! Y'all don't scare me! Bring your switchblades into the alley! I'll beat y'all up anyhow!" Fortunately, cooler heads prevailed: nobody went into the alley, and nobody got beaten up. But it got them off my back.

Here's something else Brother Jack told the young guitarist:

I learned the blues from my former boss Brother Jack McDuff. He kept stressing, "Man, put some blues in that stuff, man." I said, "Wait a minute, man, it's not a blues song." He said, "I don't care! Put some blues in it." I asked him why he liked the blues so much, and he told me that no matter where you are in the world—you could be in America or in China—if you play blues, they understand it.

So that's why it's so valuable to me. I've experimented with that philosophy over the years and have found that he's correct. People like the blues no matter where you are all over the world. So it became something that I decided should be a part of everything I did. The blues is like street music. It's like the language of the street.

Benson would remain with McDuff through 1965, and record eight albums with him. (Extra tracks from Benson sessions would continue to appear on McDuff albums for a few years after.) He also cut an album as leader, with a modification of the McDuff group: McDuff and Holloway with Ronnie Boykin on bass and Montego Joe on drums. When he left McDuff's group, he was replaced by Pat Martino, who had originally joined Prestige as a member of Willis Jackson's group. McDuff was with Prestige through 1966 and nineteen recording sessions, which were parceled out over twenty-three albums. Then he moved on to Atlantic and various other labels.

Chapter 19

Prestige's Satellite Labels

As Prestige let go of its bebop and hard bop identity and began to rebrand itself in 1959, Bob Weinstock may have felt a twinge of nostalgia for a simpler musical time. And as he retired from production and talent scouting to concentrate more on the business end of things, he had more time and perspective to find more inventive business solutions. For Weinstock the business solution was diversification: setting up satellite labels for tax purposes. And of course, there were musical considerations also, finding ways to showcase other forms of music that he loved but that did not exactly fit the Prestige or New Jazz brands. He started with a label that showcased jazz stars whose time in the limelight had passed, as first bebop and then its offshoots and successors monopolized the jazz recording industry.

The history of jazz is remarkable for its compression, with so many stylistic and conceptual breakthroughs in such a short time: New Orleans jazz succeeded by swing, succeeded by bebop, by hard bop, by soul jazz, by free jazz . . . all so quickly that Louis Armstrong and Ornette Coleman were contemporaries, and reed player Garvin Bushell could record with self-proclaimed inventor of jazz Jelly Roll Morton and ultramodernists John Coltrane and Eric Dolphy.

One figure who existed in all those eras, and perhaps transcended all of them, was Coleman Hawkins. Hawkins began his career with early blues singer Mamie Smith, recorded with the young Glenn Miller as part of the Mound City Blue Blowers (the group's leader played comb and tissue paper), changed the perception of the tenor saxophone with his breakthrough 1939 recording of "Body and Soul," and participated with Dizzy Gillespie in what is generally regarded as the first bebop record. Hawkins had never exactly gone out of fashion. He had continued to record throughout the 1950s, including a couple of sessions with Prestige. So his August 12, 1959, recording session with a trio led by Red Garland was hardly an unusual move. But it was the first in a series of late 1959 recordings that would be released in early 1960 as the harbingers of new Prestige labels: Swingville, Bluesville, and Moodsville.

Swingville was not at all shy about presenting itself as a new label. The word "Swingville" dominated all of the label's early album covers, in a colorful type design and larger—by far—than the names of the artists or the title of the album. Their second offering, by Tiny Grimes, even incorporated the label into the album's title: *Tiny in Swingville*.

The musicians who recorded for Swingville were serious working musicians who had lived through the bebop era, listened to Charlie Parker, and absorbed what was going on around them. They were playing their music, not Charlie Parker's, but they weren't just going through the motions and recreating what they had done a quarter of a century ago. Some of these recordings combined younger musicians along with the veterans: the Red Garland trio with Coleman Hawkins; Tommy Flanagan with PeeWee Russell; Flanagan, Clark Terry, and Art Taylor with Buddy Tate. On all these records, the still-vigorous veterans of a not-so-long-ago different era showed what they could do, given the chance. Buddy Tate, Rex Stewart, Al Casey, Bud Freeman, Buck Clayton, and Henry "Red" Allen are a few of artists who recorded for Swingville. Coleman Hawkins was its mainstay; ten of the series' forty-two titles featured him.

Who was recording blues in 1959–60? Folkways was the great archivist of indigenous American sounds, and had recorded Lead Belly, Big Bill Broonzy, and other folk blues singers going back to the 1940s. Chess chronicled the blues Great Migration from the Mississippi Delta to Chicago, with Muddy Waters, Howlin' Wolf, Little Walter, and others. Atlantic's Ahmet Ertegun and Jerry Wexler, when they recruited jazz singer Ruth Brown, told her they were starting a new blues label. "What do you want me for?" she demanded. "I don't sing the blues. I hate the blues." "Don't worry," they reassured her. "We're creating a whole new kind of blues" —which they did, with Brown and LaVern Baker, with King Curtis, and especially with Ray Charles. Arhoolie Records was founded in 1960 by Eastern European émigré Chris Strachwitz to record the country blues singers that no one else was recording. Columbia's release of *Robert Johnson: King of the Delta Blues Singers*, credited with setting off the blues craze of the 1960s, would not be released until 1961.

So there wasn't a clear-cut market for the blues, and it wasn't clear that Bob Weinstock, who had created a successful niche market for modern jazz at a time when the conventional wisdom was that the complex and challenging sound of bebop had killed the commercial viability of jazz, had the same vision when it came to blues. Blues singers previously recorded on Prestige included the Cabineers, Ralph Willis, John Bennings, H-Bomb Ferguson, Bobby Harris, Paula Grimes, Rudy Ferguson, the Mello-Moods, Joe "Bebop" Carroll, Bob Kent, Piney Brown, Billy Valentine, and James "Deacon" Ware; if none of these names is familiar to you (it's not the same Piney Brown that Big Joe Turner immortalized in song), that should give you some idea of the measure of Prestige's success in marketing the blues.

Did that change, now that the blues had a label of its own? Well, the first artist to record on Bluesville was Al Smith. And like Prestige's earlier blues singers, he has faded into deep obscurity. It's worth saying, however, that while Prestige's blues artists were never top sellers, that doesn't mean they weren't good singers. Al Smith was a wonderful singer, able to shout the blues or croon the blues, and for his first session he was put together with Eddie "Lockjaw" Davis and Shirley Scott. For his second Bluesville album, he had a band led by King Curtis. There are no other recordings by Al Smith, and he has pretty much been forgotten today.

Subsequent Bluesville artists included Brownie McGhee and Sonny Terry, the Reverend Gary Davis, Willie Dixon, Shakey Jake, Roosevelt Sykes, Lightnin' Hopkins, and Arbee Stidham.

Mildred Anderson had been the vocalist on a 1946 hit record by Gene Ammons, and had made a few rhythm and blues singles in the early 1950s. Rediscovered by Esmond Edwards, she cut two wonderful albums for Prestige, one with Eddie "Lockjaw" Davis and Shirley Scott, the other with Al Sears. Then she disappeared, never to record again.

British journalist Chris Albertson, working as a disc jockey in Philadelphia, discovered Lonnie Johnson, a blues and jazz master whose career dated back to the 1920s and 1930s but had been moribund since a 1948 hit for King Records, "Tomorrow Night." He was working as a janitor in a Philadelphia hotel when Albertson brought him to Bluesville. Albertson produced his record and began a run of several years as a producer for Prestige.

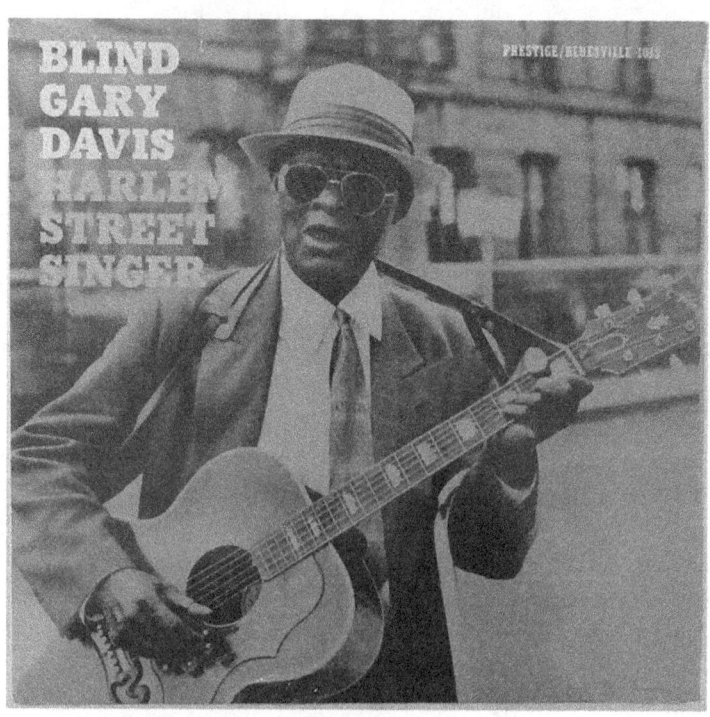

Near the end of Bluesville's existence, Kenneth S. Goldstein, folklorist and producer of a wide range of folk music records, became folk and blues music director for Prestige and was responsible for a number of recordings, including those produced in the field by Samuel Charters, Harry Oster, and Robert "Mack" McCormick, pioneer folklorists and scholars of rural blues.

Both of these labels were discontinued in 1963, and if all this makes them sound like poorly thought-out failures, this would be completely wrong. They made significant and unique contributions to the catalog of American music.

The Bluesville records were approached differently from most recorded blues. There were recordings made in the field by Charters, McCormick, Oster, and others, but most of the rest of them were made in Rudy Van Gelder's cathedral of recorded sound in Englewood Cliffs, New Jersey. And they used the brilliant musicians that were under contract to Prestige, starting with Davis and Scott to back up Al Smith and Mildred Anderson. They had Jack McDuff and Bill Jennings with Chicago blues singer and harmonica player Shakey Jake, bassist Julian Euell with Little Brother Montgomery, and Leonard Gaskin on bass and Belton Evans on drums behind Lightnin' Hopkins.

The third label debut in 1960 was Moodsville, and it's difficult to know what to say about it, not because it was such a sharp break from Prestige's usual modern jazz fare, but because it wasn't. Mood music, later called "Easy Listening" or "MOR" (for "middle of the road"), reached a zenith of sorts with an incredibly popular series of recordings released under Jackie Gleason's name. *Jackie Gleason Presents Music for Lovers Only* featured the superb trumpet playing of Bobby Hackett against the background of a syrupy twenty-seven-piece orchestra. With a sophisticated cover and Gleason's name (what he actually contributed to the music is open to debate; Hackett says he "signed the checks"), it rapidly became the biggest seller in Capitol Records' history up to that point.

Was Moodsville calculated to sell to the mood music crowd? It may have been marketed that way, but Chris Albertson has said (in a discussion on the online *Organissimo* forum):

> As a DJ when these first came out, and later as a Prestige employee, I never thought of them as anything but Prestige albums with a series name.
>
> Sometimes I think that consumers/collectors make more out of such details than the facts call for. When I produced a

session, it was a Prestige session—whether it came out on Prestige, Prestige Bluesville or Prestige Swingville made no difference.

I was never aware of there being any deliberate effort to alter the nature of a Moodsville album from that of, say, somebody's ballad album. If there ever was an instruction from Bob Weinstock to do so, it must have flown off my desk—a desk that saw its share of memos!

As with Swingville, the series title "Moodsville" dominated the early album covers, but the marketing push seems not to have made it unadulterated onto the back liner notes. Ron Eyre put it this way:

> Some years ago, along with the popular acceptance of the long playing high fidelity record, a new vogue was created in the form of "mood music." It was found that there was a definite market for this type of listening and it was not long before there were scores of albums . . . with titles beginning "Music to . . ." Whatever the individuals wanted to do, there was an album of music to do it by . . . we push a button and we turn a knob and we are automatically soothed by lush orchestrations of favorite ballads. Somewhere along the way it seems to us that the feeling behind the fine original compositions of America's lyricists and composers has become a little obscured. We think the PRESTIGE/ MOODSVILLE series will be a welcome departure from "mood" music. The series will feature jazz artists interpreting choice ballads and standards, and original compositions that will fit into the Moodsville series.

The Moodsville catalog reads like a cross between the regular Prestige roster—Garland, Davis and Scott, Yusef Lateef, Lem Winchester, Kenny Burrell, even Miles Davis and John Coltrane (Richard Rodgers's compositions culled from the Contractual Marathon sessions) —and the Swingville catalog, with Hawkins, Taft Jordan, Cootie Williams, Al Casey, and so on. Chris Albertson is right. Nothing in any of these series represents a deviation from Prestige's standards of—if not perfection—spontaneity, improvisation, and swing.

In 1961, Weinstock started one more label, Tru-Sound, which he described as a contemporary rhythm and blues label. He was a little late to the rhythm and blues party, but Tru-Sound put out some good records. Their most successful artist was King Curtis, who had made a name for himself in the 1950s on a series of rhythm and blues hits, mainly by the Coasters. Although rhythm and blues releases did not list the musicians who played on a date, everyone knew the King Curtis sound. He came to Prestige in 1960, recording with Nat Adderley, then a saxophone summit with Oliver Nelson and Jimmy Forrest. He played on several Bluesville sessions. He made four albums for Tru-Sound, including one to capitalize on the twist dance craze (*Doing the Dixie Twist*), perhaps a harbinger of his biggest hit, "Soul Twist," for Harlem entrepreneur Bobby Robinson's Enjoy label. Tru-Sound released records by Juan Amalbert's Latin Jazz Quintet, swing/R&B bandleaders Jesse Powell and Buddy Lucas, vocalists Clea Bradford and Ernestine Allen, and others. They also had a gospel line.

In 1963–64, Prestige Folklore released a number of albums from the flourishing folk music scene of that era, and in retrospect, one has to say their taste was pretty good. These were performers who would more likely have been found hanging out at Izzy Young's Folklore Center in Greenwich Village, or a coffeehouse on Harvard Square, than on network TV's *Hootenanny* show. They included Dave Van Ronk, Bonnie Dobson, Jesse "Lone Cat" Fuller, Tom Rush, Geoff Muldaur, Peggy Seeger, Jack Elliott, and others.

There were also Prestige International (not entirely international; along with the Greek/Italian/Irish/Yiddish compilations, they presented regional Americans like Southerner Obray Ramsay and Westerner Rosalie Sorrels); Prestige Lively Arts (Roddy McDowall reads Lovecraft, Larry Storch reads Philip Roth, James Mason Reads Poe); Prestige Irish; and Prestige Near East. They pretty much touched all bases except rock. These are all worthy endeavors, but really a footnote to the Prestige story.

Chapter 20

Soul Jazz Organists

By 1960, the floodgates had opened, and soul jazz came rushing in, with the Hammond B3 organ leading the torrent, generally in tandem with a tenor saxophone, an electric guitar, or both. Jimmy Smith had started the trend. Alfred Lion and Francis Wolff of Blue Note were sufficiently in awe of his incredible popularity not to sign any other organists, giving Prestige an open field, one that Bob Weinstock took advantage of.

There's no denying Smith's influence, and one who would certainly not deny it was Smith himself. As he put it: "I like all my pupils—Don Patterson, Jack McDuff, Groove Holmes, Shirley Scott, Larry Young, George Fame . . . Freddie Roach is a Jimmy Smith copy . . . John Patton, he's a fair organ player. . . . They're my understudies." One can't imagine Charlie Parker saying the same thing about saxophone players, but circumstances and shifting tastes combined to emphasize Smith's centrality. Because of the boom-and-bust popularity of organ jazz—a sudden rise in the 1960s, equally sudden decline in the next decade (although it continued to be an important sound in rock) —there is a tendency to lump all of the 1960s organists together as a bunch of carbon copies of Jimmy Smith. This is a mistake. They were all individual musicians, each with his or her own approach to the instrument, and to creating jazz music.

We've discussed two important figures, Shirley Scott and Jack McDuff, in chapter 19. They were just the beginning.

Johnny "Hammond" Smith

Johnny "Hammond" Smith had signed with Prestige in 1959, and he would cut seven albums for the label between 1959 and 1962, then return from 1965 to 1970. His nickname was not to distinguish him from other organists, because they all played the Hammond, but to distinguish him from other Johnny Smiths, particularly the acclaimed jazz guitarist. Like many organists, he began on the piano, and like many before him, the sound of a pioneering organ virtuoso inspired him. Since he didn't come from Philadelphia, it wasn't Jimmy Smith. Born in Louisville, Kentucky, Smith moved to Cleveland in 1958, where he first heard Wild Bill Davis. He was working at the time as Nancy Wilson's piano accompanist, but the organ won him over, to the point that when he made his 1959 Prestige debut as a leader, he had already folded "Hammond" into his name.

Smith had a real feeling for the funky qualities of the organ, and he would become known as the instrument's funkmeister as his career developed. He already was plenty funky as he began with Prestige, but he also showed his dexterity with standards, as was expected of an organ group in those days: "The Masquerade Is Over," "Pennies from Heaven," and "Secret Love," not quite a standard yet, although it certainly became one. Smith's was one of the first jazz renditions.

All of the musicians who recorded on Smith's first Prestige session were also new to the label. Guitarist Thornel Schwartz understood and contributed to the guitar-organ dynamic that was developing as an important new thing in jazz. Schwartz was from Philadelphia, and he began his career with Jimmy Smith. He would go on to play with Larry Young, Charles Earland, Jimmy McGriff, and Richard "Groove" Holmes. Bassist George Tucker flew under the radar of publicity during his short life (he died of a brain hemorrhage in 1965, at the age of thirty-eight), but he left a powerful impression as a musician. Tucker had already built an impressive résumé by the time he made his Prestige debut with Smith, working with Curtis Fuller, Bennie Green, John Handy, Slide Hampton, and Melba Liston. He would become a mainstay of Prestige recording during the early 1960s before his death. Drummer Leo Stevens had been with Smith from the beginning, and remained with him for many years. He doesn't appear to have moonlighted beyond his work with Smith, but he was an important part of Smith's jazz-funk sound.

Maybe the best word for Smith's debut recording is "ingratiating." His general attitude seems to be "there's no way you're not gonna like this," and unless you're an unreconstructed organ combo hater, that's going to be pretty much true.

Smith would also work with Oliver Nelson, who was well on his way to becoming one of the most important composer-arrangers of the decade (discussed more in chapter 23). Smith's second Prestige album was also Nelson's second for the label, and it also featured vibraphonist Lem Winchester. Both Winchester and Nelson, two of the brightest talents on the decade's jazz scene, would die young, Winchester at thirty-three of an accidental self-inflicted gunshot wound, and Nelson at forty-three of a heart attack. Nelson would make six records for Prestige before moving on to Impulse! and his greatest success, *Jazz and the Abstract Truth*.

Larry Young

Larry Young made his debut with Prestige in 1960, at the age of twenty. A native of Newark, New Jersey, he was drawn to the Philadelphia organ sphere, and the ubiquitous influence of Jimmy Smith, an influence that could be strongly felt in his three Prestige albums as leader (and two supporting pianist Gildo Mahones). His work for Prestige is powerful, and it still holds up today. But later, when he moved to Blue Note in 1964 (Jimmy Smith had moved on to Verve in 1962), his influence was much more Coltrane than Smith, and he took organ jazz to a whole new place, culminating in *Unity* (1965), with Joe Henderson and Woody Shaw. Young would make another radical change in 1969: *Emergency!*, his Polydor album with drummer Tony Williams, is credited with being one of the seminal albums of jazz-rock fusion.

Richard "Groove" Holmes

Richard "Groove" Holmes was born in Camden, New Jersey, and grew up in the organ-friendly jazz world of neighboring Philadelphia, but he found his first success establishing a Hammond beachhead on the West Coast, recording for Pacific Jazz with Ben Webster in 1961. After five albums and modest success, he returned to the East and signed with Prestige, making his label debut in 1965 with an album called *Soul Message*, in a trio with Gene Edwards on guitar and Jimmie Smith on drums. *Soul Message* included his version of Errol Garner's chestnut "Misty," taken at a brisk danceable tempo and working itself up to all-stops-out rave. Running six minutes on the album, it was also released in a two-minute version on 45 rpm, where it became a smash: a radio and jukebox hit, and a monster seller, making its mark on the pop charts (number 41) as well as jazz and rhythm and blues (number 12). It became one of Prestige's all-time best sellers. Holmes's "Misty" used a familiar arrangement that had originally been written by trombonist Slide Hampton for Lloyd Price's big band, incorporating a Charleston beat as the basis for a more modern sound, and it struck a chord.

Holmes continued to record for Prestige throughout the decade, releasing eleven albums (including one called *Misty*, which included the two-minute version of the song), but *Soul Message* and "Misty" remained his consistent seller, and his signature song.

Don Patterson

Two years after splitting with Shirley Scott, Eddie "Lockjaw" Davis decided to try the saxophone-organ sound again, and hired a trio led by guitarist Paul Weeden. They recorded for Cadet in Chicago, then came east to Prestige in 1962. Davis moved on to other things, but the organist in the group, Don Patterson, along with drummer Billy James, signed with Prestige and became one of their mainstays throughout the decade. Patterson recorded eleven albums as leader and several more with Sonny Stitt and Eric Kloss. His first album, *The Exciting New Organ of Don Patterson*, was a trio session with tenor saxophone and drums. The saxophonist was Booker Ervin, who had signed with the label in 1963, and was fast developing a reputation as one of the important new voices in jazz.

Listening to Prestige:
Don Patterson with Booker Ervin

The Exciting New Organ of Don Patterson

Recorded at Van Gelder Studio, Hackensack, NJ, May 12, 1964

Booker Ervin, tenor sax; Don Patterson, organ; Billy James, drums

Tracks recorded: S'bout Time; Up in Betty's Room; Oeo; When Johnny Comes Marching Home; The Good Life; Hip Cake Walk; Love Me with All Your Heart; People

"S'bout Time" is a Patterson original, and features a soaring Ervin solo, emerging with wings out of the opening riff, and urged on by the organ of Patterson. In his own solo, he lives up to the album title's hype, and also demonstrates what he was talking about when he was quoted as saying, "What I'm trying to do is keep the piano sound when I play the organ." "Up in Betty's Room" is attributed to both Patterson and drummer Billy James, and features some intricate but still funky work by the two lead instruments.

The rest of the album looks elsewhere for musical inspiration, and finds it in a variety of places, some not unexpected (Sonny Rollins's jazz standard "Oleo") and some decidedly unexpected. "When Johnny Comes Marching Home" is a patriotic marching song most closely associated with the Civil War, although the tune is probably even older than that.

> It's a catchy melody, as could be expected from a tune that's lasted that long, but not one that would normally catch the ear of a jazz musician. But catchy is catchy, and Patterson clearly heard something he liked in this one, and it's his baby. He starts out with another patriotic lick, then goes into a funky-slippery interpretation of the familiar melody, with James playing a funky-not-entirely-slippery version of a military snare drum. It takes a while for Ervin to get into the mood, but when he does, he enters with the kind of solo that led his contemporaries to say that you could recognize a Booker Ervin solo after two notes. Patterson and Ervin end up by finding enough inspiration for ten minutes of improvisation on "When Johnny Comes Marching Home," ending up by playing the melody straight. It's quite a performance.

Prestige would continue to put Patterson together with some of its brightest stars. He would record frequently with Pat Martino, Sonny Stitt, and Charles McPherson; other collaborations included David "Fathead" Newman, Houston Person, Howard McGhee, Blue Mitchell, George Coleman, and Grant Green.

Later organists signed to the label were Trudy Pitts (1967) and Charles Earland (1969) (both discussed in chapter 26), Freddie Roach (1966), and Sonny Phillips (1968).

Chapter 21

Moving On

Free Jazz and Eric Dolphy

In 1960, Gigi Gryce's career was just about at its end. Still only thirty-five and at his creative peak, he made three records for Prestige, then one for Mercury near the year's end. Then, disillusioned with the racism and unscrupulous business practices he had encountered, he quit music for good.

But others were just beginning. Wilmington, Delaware, policeman Lem Winchester moonlighted playing jazz vibraphone in local clubs. He'd show up for a gig in uniform, play until it was time for his shift to start, then strap on his gun and head for his nighttime "day job." His discovery by Leonard Feather led to a recording contract with Prestige. A 1959 debut with Benny Golson led to three albums in 1960 as leader, and sessions with Jack McDuff, Shirley Scott, Oliver Nelson, Etta Jones, and Johnny "Hammond" Smith. Then in 1961, as he attempted to show off a gun trick he had learned on the police force, the trick went wrong and Winchester was dead.

Two very good singers recorded for Prestige in 1960: Betty Roché, whose career went nowhere, and Etta Jones, who never surpassed her megahit from her first Prestige album but who continued singing and recording for four decades. Roché had sung with Duke Ellington, with whom she sang what is still widely considered the definitive vocal treatment of "Take the A Train" for a forgettable 1940s movie, *Reveille with Beverly*, but it came in the middle of the Petrillo strike, so it never made it onto a record. Her first album for Prestige had the solid backing of Jack McDuff and Bill Jennings; her second featured more obscure musicians who nonetheless helped her to what later critic Scott Yanow called "arguably . . . her finest all-around recording." After that, nothing at all. Duke Ellington described her singing: "She had a soul inflection in a bop state of intrigue, and every word was understandable despite the sophisticated hip and jive connotations"—which is pretty close to meaningless but has the complex yet flowing swing of an Ellington riff.

Etta Jones was already a show-business veteran by the time she signed with Prestige at the age of thirty-two. She had begun, as so many before her, on Amateur Night at the Apollo in 1943, but unlike Ella Fitzgerald, she did not get universal acclaim. "They almost booed me off the stage," she would recall later. But someone backstage had a more positive take. The male vocalist for popular bandleader Buddy Johnson approached her and told her Buddy was looking for a girl singer; his sister Ella, who had always been his girl singer, was off having a baby. Jones was terrified, sure she wasn't ready, but she went for an audition right there, on the spot, backstage. Another singer was there ahead of her, but Jones knew the lyrics to Johnson's songs, and the other woman did not, so she got the gig. Two days later she was on the road.

Nearly twenty years later, after stints with Barney Bigard, J. C. Heard, and Earl Hines among others, Jones finally got her break with Prestige and, given the sympathetic accompaniment of Frank Wess's flute, produced a record that *Down Beat* critic John Tynan called "a real jazz approach that many other aspiring 'jazz' singers might well note, [making] listening to her a rewarding experience." The album's title song was "Don't Go to Strangers," originally a B-side (to "Secret Love") for the rhythm and blues harmony group the Orioles. Its release as a single became not only her signature song but one of Prestige's biggest hits. It gave her and the label a gold record, something not too common for releases from small jazz labels. She would record several more albums for Prestige, then for other labels with various musical accompaniments, then finally make a very successful partnership with saxophonist Houston Person, with whom she would tour and record for more than thirty years. But this would remain her best-known recording, and her greatest commercial success.

I've written, in *Jazz with a Beat: Small Group Swing, 1940–1960*, about the bifurcation of jazz that took place in the early 1940s, between the jazz that you danced to (Joe Liggins, Roy Milton, Red Prysock) and the jazz that you listened to (Charlie Parker, Dizzy Gillespie, Thelonious Monk). In that book I discussed the former category: music that won the hearts and dancing feet of the public but was unfairly dismissed by the jazz critics of the day. Mike Smith, in his book *In with the In Crowd: Popular Jazz in 1960s Black America*, sees the same phenomenon happening in the early 1960s. The rejection wasn't as extreme; publications like *Down Beat* did review not only Jimmy Smith but also Brother Jack McDuff, Richard "Groove" Holmes, and other practitioners of soul jazz, frequently favorably. But as Smith points out, later historians of the era have tended to give short shrift to the popular performers of the era, completely shutting popular acts like Nancy Wilson and Ramsey Lewis out of their version of the canon.

Without in any way disparaging the crowd-pleasing grooves of the soul jazz performers, it must be said that the adventurous souls who freed jazz from the strictures of chord progressions, daring to risk chaos in search of a new way of making a musical statement, were the newsmakers of the time. This was partly because there's more to write about a revolutionary new approach to any art form (not all of it favorable), so it gave the critics more to do. To a small but committed segment of the music listening public, the more avant-garde movement was the most exciting thing to happen to jazz since Charlie Parker.

Ever since making its debut in 1949 with Lennie Tristano, Prestige had been committed to showcasing the cutting edge of jazz, and they did not shy away from embracing the new forms. Many have called 1959 jazz's greatest year, and part of the reason for that could be found in the breaking of new ground by both familiar and new artists. Miles Davis moved away from the dominance of chord progressions toward what became known as modal jazz. His album for Columbia, *Kind of Blue*, drew near-universal acclaim and broad popular appeal: It is widely considered to be the best-selling album in jazz history. Dave Brubeck, another one of the decade's most popular artists, also broke new ground with his experiments in time signatures, particularly with his album *Time Out*. Bill Evans, Ella Fitzgerald, Charles Mingus, and Chet Baker all released significant new work.

But equally important were the albums that signaled a new and revolutionary shift in the whole concept of jazz. John Coltrane had become a favorite of hard-bop fans with his work with Davis and his sessions as leader with Prestige, but he announced a new and thrilling direction with his 1959 Atlantic release, *Giant Steps*. This was not the total break with the past that would come with his later albums for Impulse!, but it was a significant break. Ornette Coleman made a real break with the past with *The Shape of Jazz to Come*, his 1959 Atlantic debut. Love him or hate him, and there were plenty on either side, he was the biggest story of the year in jazz, and some would say the biggest story of the decade to come.

Coltrane and Coleman are generally considered to be the two central figures of the free jazz movement, but in 1959, another musician moved from Los Angeles to New York: Eric Dolphy. He was soon signed to Prestige Records, where in his short life he would become the third member of a triumvirate that changed jazz in a way that could not be ignored. Dolphy died in 1964, the cause of death uncertain but probably related to undiagnosed diabetes; Dolphy never smoked, drank, or used drugs. But in the space of five years, the first three of them with Prestige, he established himself as one of the foremost originators of the music that was first known as the "new thing," then later, taking the title of an Ornette Coleman record (with Dolphy's participation), "free jazz."

Dolphy grew up in Los Angeles, where he started playing music as a young child. By the time he was in his teens, he was exploring music with a group of like-minded young Angelenos. Next came college, then a stint in the army, before he returned to the LA scene that flourished along Central Avenue and in other venues, too, including his own backyard, where his recording debut two years earlier, on a Prestige session led by John Coltrane. He had since recorded with Cannonball Adderley and Slide Hampton. Pianist Jaki Byard, a prodigious and eclectic talent who would begin leading his own sessions for Prestige the following year, had been around for a decade but had recorded previously only with Boston musicians Charlie Mariano and Herb Pomeroy. Bassist George Tucker was at the beginning of a brief but distinguished career. This was his first recording, but he would be much in demand over the following years, including many sessions for Prestige, before he died of a cerebral hemorrhage in 1965, not long after Dolphy.

Dolphy ran the session, right down to providing both Edwards and Van Gelder with a surprise: "When he pulled out his bass clarinet, Rudy Van Gelder and I did a double take." The bass clarinet is longer than a conventional clarinet and consequently has a deeper tone, about an octave lower. It looks like a clarinet with a saxophone-like curved neck on top, and a smaller version of a saxophone's bell on the bottom. In fact, it was developed by Adolphe Saxe, who would later go on to invent the saxophone. It's an instrument very few jazz musicians have chosen. John Coltrane played it, and the contemporary musician Don Byron. Others, including Gerry Mulligan and Harry Carney, and even Charles Mingus, have played it on occasion. But for Dolphy, its rich tone was a perfect balance to the

flute and alto saxophone. (For Van Gelder, it was a bit of a surprise, but he made the adjustment, and set up a microphone for it.)

The name of the album alone—*Outward Bound*—was enough to serve notice that this was not music to back up the Platters, and it wasn't Chico Hamilton's West Coast jazz, either. But it was a sound that instantly resonated with the critics. Don DeMichael, in *Down Beat*, gave *Outward Bound* five stars right out of the box, saying: "This album is the first extended exposure I've had to the remarkable talent that is Eric Dolphy's. On the strength of what I experienced in the course of absorbing the release, I firmly believe that this man will be one of the most rewarding jazzmen of the coming decade." DeMichael compared Dolphy to Ornette Coleman, becoming the voice of a lot of jazz fans in those early years of the decade: people who wanted to keep up with the new direction in jazz but found Coleman a step farther out than they knew how to go: "It's possible to draw a parallel between Dolphy and Ornette Coleman—similar harmonic conceptions being the most cogent—but, to me, Dolphy's message is the more coherent, and his is the greater talent."

DeMichael recognized the futility of drawing comparisons, and especially the ranking of talents: "Drawing parallels, however, can get out of hand; in the end, the artist must be judged on his own work, though comparisons and contrasts play an important role in shaping any judgment." And Coleman lived long enough to develop and refine his gift, to become a revered elder statesman of jazz. Through 1960, and for the next few years, Dolphy made music that was startling and new but almost impossible not to like. On the other hand, Coleman was making music that was hard to like. I was nineteen in 1959, just the right age to have ears open to everything, and I fell instantly under Ornette Coleman's spell, going down to the Five Spot to hear him again and again. I loved Dolphy, too, falling under his spell right from the first album. In 1961, Dolphy outpolled Coleman in the *Down Beat* readers' alto saxophone poll, while also finishing near the top in the flute and miscellaneous instrument categories.

Another critic of the era, John Tynan, who was able to so clearly and persuasively make a case for Etta Jones, had that same problem with the more forbidding aspects of free jazz, and the same eagerness to latch onto Dolphy as a lifeline. Here's his review (*Down Beat*, March 2, 1961) of an album by another advocate of free jazz, Ken McIntyre (later Makanda Ken McIntyre), *Looking Ahead*, which also featured Dolphy:

> Don't dare listen to this album in a complacent mood or when headache hints; it will shatter your complacency and/or sharpen the headache. Better lend an ear when the need to rebel and

to shake your fist at the stars nags to the point of action. This album, in short, is another dose—almost a purgative—of jazz rebellion.

Admittedly, the two horn men on the firing line fall somewhat short of out-Colemanning Ornette Coleman, for if their emotional approach is similar, their tactics are more formalized. Unlike Coleman, they seem to feel the need of a piano, Walter Bishop Jr. (a blessing in this instance), and they do at least adhere to sets of chord progressions.

Of the two, McIntyre is perhaps the wilder, more unpredictable soloist; and he comes closer than Dolphy to Coleman's intensely personalized expressionism. One feels, for example, that a sudden compulsion to sneeze is translated by him into a musical snort. McIntyre is unafraid of the unexpected and unpredictable: indeed, he appears to delight in exploiting it.

Not that Dolphy is any striped-pants conservative. His alto solo on "They All Laughed" is conclusive testimony to his radicalism. But Dolphy reveals more of a debt, more fealty to musical discipline and consequently less need to gush forth the naked, neurotic cries of a soul in torment than does McIntyre—or Coleman.

Listening to Prestige: Ken McIntyre

Looking Ahead

Recorded at Van Gelder Studio, Englewood Cliffs, NJ, June 28, 1960

Ken McIntyre, flute, alto sax; Eric Dolphy, flute, bass clarinet, alto sax; Walter Bishop Jr., piano; Sam Jones, bass; Art Taylor, drums

Tracks recorded: Geo's Tune; They All Laughed; Dianna; Curtsy; Lautir; Head Shakin'

All but one of the selections are McIntyre originals. The exception is the old Gershwin chestnut "They All Laughed," and it's interesting to see how these modernists take it. They play the head remarkably straight, and they never really lose it. They go far enough out in their improvisations to be satisfying—and because they're that good, to be deeply satisfying—but they always have that "Ha ha ha, who's got the last laugh now?" feeling. Who says the avant-garde can't have a sense of humor? Walter Bishop's solo brings them back into home territory, and they finish up with Gershwin again.

Critic Leonard Feather was another who struggled to come to terms with the new direction in jazz. In the same issue of *Down Beat*, he questioned Dolphy:

LF: For one thing, I would like to make it clear that I don't think I understand . . . as a musician you know certain things I don't understand about what you are doing and I . . . would like to maybe get them clarified in my own mind so that I can make it clear for the average reader . . . what is happening and what people like you are doing harmonically. It's very hard to explain, very hard to analyze. Can you put it into words?

ED: Well, it, you know, it always depends on the subject of what you're improvising on of course, and then, uh . . . Of course if you're playing freer forms and the harmony . . . improvisation is much more freer and you have much more things that you can play . . . the lines are not held to no chord patterns, harmonically.

LF: No, but, what I don't understand is what ARE they held to? I mean what is, what is the difference between the limitations, there must be some limitations otherwise it, you would be arbitrary, you could just play any notes that you like.

ED: Well that's the idea you CAN play every note that you like. Of course, you only can play what you can hear, and quite naturally . . . more or less I guess what I hear is not to your hearing, to what you're hearing. So quite naturally, I hear, uh, more notes on uh, on the same thing that's been said before.

Robert Frost once said that writing free verse is like playing tennis with the net down. Michelangelo Antonioni, in the movie *Blow Up*, went Frost one better, as his mimes played tennis with no net, no rackets, and no ball. Perhaps there's an analogy to free jazz, and perhaps that was why Leonard Feather couldn't get it, and Dolphy couldn't say much more than "I guess what I hear is not to your hearing, to what you're hearing." Only you and whoever you're playing with know where the ball is going and whether you've hit it squarely. But there are spins and trajectories and lobs and smashes that only you can hear. With mimes, you have to take their word for it. With free jazz musicians, they leave a sonic record of their mime tennis game, and sometimes only time sorts out the Serena Williamses from the weekend hackers. In music if you get it right, you're Eric Dolphy and Freddie Hubbard on *Outward Bound*. Get it wrong, and you're just another guy playing out of tune.

Dolphy recorded for Prestige/New Jazz during 1960–61, leading his own groups and occasionally supporting other musicians. His second session, after *Outward Bound*, was the on the Ken McIntyre album, including the conclusive testimony to his radicalism on "They All Laughed."

Dolphy's next album as a leader, *Out There*, was issued on the Prestige subsidiary label, New Jazz. It introduced an important new musician, one whose adeptness and sensitivity to all styles of jazz would make him the most-recorded jazz bassist, perhaps the most recorded jazz musician, of all time: Ron Carter. But it's an unusual debut in that the preeminent bass virtuoso of his era is playing the cello, rather than the bass. The cello has a sparse history in jazz, but it does have a history, going back to W. C. Handy, who used a cellist in his ensemble. During the 1950s, probably the best-known jazz cellist was Fred Katz, who worked with the Chico Hamilton Quintet—a group that included Eric Dolphy. Ron Carter had been trained as a cellist before picking up the bass, but there was never going to be all that much call for a cellist in jazz. Still, it makes a striking debut for him, and this whole session is a striking musical outing.

On *Out There*, Dolphy is really coming into his own, making a kind of music that was so thoroughly his own that it's still hard to describe. As we have noted, the three great innovators of this era were Coltrane, Coleman, and Dolphy, and sometimes they, and the others who pursued experimentation in the same era, like Albert Ayler, Sun Ra, Pharaoh Sanders, and Cecil Taylor, are grouped together as free jazz, but they really were doing very different things. Dolphy is also sometimes labeled as "third stream," which is probably even more difficult to define than free jazz. (His collaborations with John Coltrane were also panned in *Down Beat* as "anti-jazz," but that's just shortsighted and not worth discussing.)

Free jazz, more or less, is generally defined as jazz that is not structured around chord changes. It was a polarizing musical form in the early 1960s as bebop was in the 1940s. Arthur Taylor was compiling his remarkable book of interviews during the years that free jazz (or "freedom music," as he calls it in the book) was in its ascendancy, and he asked a lot of musicians about it. Dexter Gordon said, "My manager told me there would be days like this!" and continued to evade Taylor's every attempt to pin him down on the subject. Randy Weston loved Ornette Coleman but hated the concept of free jazz: "It is completely built up by white writers. . . . My objection is that I don't see how this music is more free than another," and others felt the same way. Philly Joe Jones said that "freedom music doesn't mean anything to me because I've been playing free my whole life." He admired Coltrane and Dolphy: "These men were geniuses. They knew exactly what they were going to do," but he had little use for those for whom "John Coltrane opened the door . . . I call them bag carriers. The bags that they carry their instruments in. . . . They . . . don't know anything about the horn and just make a bunch of noises . . . I think freedom music should be limited to those who can play it." And Ron Carter, in Taylor's interview with him, made an excellent point: "If you hear some guy play freedom who does not know bebop and is not hip to swing, he is just playing off the top of his head. He's not really as free as someone with a musical background."

Third stream is even harder to pin down. *Out There* could be third stream, because you have one guy playing the cello and another guy playing the bass clarinet, except that Gunther Schuller, who invented the term and mostly defined it in terms of what it was not, said that "it is not jazz played on 'classical' instruments. In fact, he said that there was no such thing as third stream jazz—third stream music was a third stream, neither classical nor jazz."

In the space of a very few years, Dolphy created a voice that was one of the most original and expressive in jazz history. Call it third stream, free jazz, freedom music, anti-jazz, or advanced bebop, it is some of the most arresting, nourishing, invigorating music anyone has ever made. The collaboration of cello and whatever instrument Dolphy is playing on any given track could not be richer and more satisfying. Esmond Edwards produced this album, showing that he has some pretty serious range, too, even if it's only to know when to stand back and let Dolphy's genius take over.

Once Edwards and Weinstock found Dolphy, they couldn't get enough of him. In May, he recorded *Screamin' the* Blues, with Oliver Nelson, who would figure in some important collaborations later on. The McIntyre session came in June, and on August 16 he was right back in the studio with the Latin Jazz Quintet, a group of shifting membership but generally centered around conguero Juan Amalbert. Critics haven't been kind to this session, describing it as a mismatch, with Dolphy and the quintet paying little attention to each other. The same criticism was leveled at Charlie Parker's collaborations with Machito, but I don't buy it. Parker in his day, and Dolphy in his, were far too aware, and far too appreciative of a wide range of musical styles, to come into a session so contemptuous of their fellow musicians that they wouldn't listen to what was being put down, or to simply not be able to follow Latin rhythms. Amalbert's quintet have a busy, agitated style of playing for the most part, and Dolphy gets with them and then takes them in directions that are his own. He's a better, more inventive musician than they are, but he's a better and more inventive musician than almost anyone, and he works with them to create something that's musically satisfying. And it must have been sufficiently musically satisfying to all concerned that they agreed to do it again a year later (for the United Artists label).

On September 20, Dolphy recorded with a big band led by soul jazz stalwart Eddie "Lockjaw" Davis, finishing up the year with a December 21 session, which became *Far Cry*. The labels that were taking a chance on the new jazz were not at all shy about marketing its newness. John Coltrane's first step into uncharted territory was one small step for a musician, a giant leap for music, and it was called *Giant Steps*. Ornette Coleman's early Atlantic titles were *Tomorrow Is the Question* and *Change of the Century*. Albert Ayler's debut was *Something Different!!!!!!* (yes, with all the exclamation points). Cecil Taylor put out albums called *Jazz Advance* and *Looking Ahead!*

In 1961, as Dolphy began working extensively with Charles Mingus, Prestige had him back in Englewood Cliffs for one date on March 1, sharing the leader role with Oliver Nelson, for the album *Straight Ahead* (discussed at length in chapter 23). He played sideman for Ron Carter's debut as leader on June 20, and again for Mal Waldron on June 27. On July 16, one of Prestige's rare live recordings caught Dolphy at the Five Spot (with Booker Little, discussed at length in chapter 23). Two LPs came out of this date, one released in 1961, the other in 1963. September 1961 found Dolphy in Europe. Two recording sessions in Copenhagen were released posthumously by Prestige.

After leaving Prestige, Dolphy worked with a number of different musicians, including Charles Mingus and John Coltrane, both of whom he had met while he was still living on the West Coast. He joined Mingus's collective, the Jazz Workshop, in 1960, and the two recorded twelve albums together. Once Dolphy moved to New York, he became close to John Coltrane, and they spurred each other creatively—much to the displeasure of some critics. John Tynan, in a *Down Beat* review of a live performance, wrote:

> At Hollywood's Renaissance club recently, I listened to a horrifying demonstration of what appears to be a growing anti-jazz

trend exemplified by these foremost proponents [Coltrane and Dolphy] of what is termed avant garde music.

I heard a good rhythm section . . . go to waste behind the nihilistic exercises of the two horns. . . . Coltrane and Dolphy seem intent on deliberately destroying [swing]. . . . They seem bent on pursuing an anarchistic course in their music that can but be termed anti-jazz.

Coltrane and Dolphy answered the charge. Dolphy said, "What I'm trying to do I find enjoyable. Inspiring—what it makes me do. It helps me play, this feel. It's like you have no idea what you're going to do next. You have an idea, but there's always that spontaneous thing that happens. This feeling, to me, leads the whole group. When John plays, it might lead into something you had no idea could be done." Coltrane discussed how they got together, and how it affected them musically:

Eric and I have been talking music for quite a few years, since about 1954. We . . . discussed what was being done down through the years, because we love music.

A few months ago Eric was in New York, where the group was working, and . . . I told him to come on down and play, and he did—and turned us all around . . . it was like having another member of the family. He'd found another way to express the same thing we had found one way to do.

After he sat in, we decided to see what it would grow into. We began to play some of the things we had only talked about before. . . . We're playing things that are freer than before.

Coltrane and Dolphy recorded four studio albums together, for Atlantic and Impulse!. After Dolphy's death in 1964, and Coltrane's in 1967, a number of recordings of their live performances were released.

Dolphy also worked with fellow free jazz leader Ornette Coleman. They recorded one album together: 1961's *Free Jazz*, which came out as the debate over the new music, now and henceforth known as "free jazz," was raging. *Down Beat* (January 28, 1962) took the unprecedented step of assigning two reviewers. Pete Welding gave the album five stars: "All things considered, the disc is largely successful. . . . It is a powerful and challenging work of real conviction and honest emotion; it poses questions and provides its own answers to them; it is restless in its re-examination of the role of collective improvisation . . . Needless to say, there is nothing of smugness or complacency about it." John Tynan gave it zero stars: "If nothing else, this witch's brew is the logical end product of a bankrupt philosophy of ultraindividualism in music. 'Collective improvisation?' Nonsense. The only semblance of collectivity lies in the fact that these eight nihilists were collected together in one studio at one time and with one common cause: to destroy the music that gave them birth."

Today . . . free jazz is no longer the "new thing" but a part of jazz history. John Coltrane has attained an almost mystical preeminence that seems to go beyond his status as a jazz musician, but even he is most vividly remembered for a few landmarks: *A Love Supreme; My Favorite Things*. Coleman, for all his eminence and his many recordings and his Pulitzer for *Sound Grammar*, is probably still best known for *The Shape of Jazz to Come* and its haunting, iconic composition "Lonely Woman." Free jazz is still mostly remembered for that moment in time, the very early 1960s, when it turned the jazz world on its head, and Eric Dolphy is still remembered as one of the most important figures in that jazz revolution.

Chapter 22

Dolphy's Peers at Prestige

The musicians Dolphy recorded with are an extraordinary bunch. They'll be discussed in this chapter, but first, it's worth mentioning that Dolphy's avant-garde experiments employed solid base of musicians steeped in the tradition: Roy Haynes, Walter Bishop Jr., Sam Jones, Art Taylor, George Duvivier, and Mal Waldron.

Freddie Hubbard

Freddie Hubbard was Dolphy's roommate when the two of them arrived in New York, and his front line–mate for *Outward Bound*. Hubbard, one of the most important post–Miles Davis trumpeters, was just passing through Prestige, but Prestige was there at the beginning for him. He had made one recording on the West Coast with the Montgomery Brothers, for Pacific Jazz in 1957, and on his arrival in New York, John Coltrane snagged him for a session. He played on one tune, and the session was shelved, not to be released until 1964.

Outward Bound, Hubbard's most memorable Prestige session, was recorded on April 1, 1960. Shortly after that, on June 20, Hubbard made his first recording as a leader for Blue Note. That album was released as *Open Sesame*, and his career was launched. Blue Note, Impulse!, CTI, and Columbia were the main labels he recorded for. He would stop in at Prestige in 1961 and 1963 to assist on albums by two excellent musicians who, for one reason or another, left very light footprints in the path of jazz: Willie Wilson and Ronnie Matthews.

Oliver Nelson

The Eddie "Lockjaw" Davis big band session for the album *Far Cry* in December 1960 is historically significant, not for the contribution of Dolphy, but because it marked the debut of saxophonist Oliver Nelson as an arranger, the role for which he became most notable. Nelson's work would be featured on twenty-three albums for Prestige between 1960 and 1962, six as leader-arranger. Like Dolphy's, his work was advanced yet accessible. Prestige issued his first album as leader in 1959, including four original compositions. The big band session with Davis made critics really sit up and take notice of him as an arranger. He would lead sessions with Johnny "Hammond" Smith, Lem Winchester, and Dolphy, and would have a fiery soul jazz encounter with rhythm and blues legends King Curtis and Jimmy Forrest. Important works included *Afro/American Sketches* (1962), an Ellington-like suite for big band. But his most acclaimed work came when he stepped out to record a session for Impulse! on February 23, 1961. His ensemble featured Dolphy, Hubbard, and Bill Evans. The name of the album was *Blues and the Abstract Truth*.

Don DeMichael, writing in *Down Beat*, declared: "A glance at the personnel of this album might lead one to believe this is another blowing session. It is not. Although there are good, sometimes excellent, solos on every track. Nelson's writing lifts this record out of the ordinary." Nelson's last collaboration with Dolphy was the March 1, 1961, session that produced the album *Straight Ahead*. It featured Dolphy, Nelson, Duvivier, and Haynes, with Richard Wyands on piano. The tunes were all Nelson's, with the exception of Milt Jackson's "Ralph's New Blues." One of them, "Six and Four," so named because it moves from 6/4 to 4/4 time, has become something of a jazz standard. "Straight Ahead" has become, in recent years, a descriptor of a style of jazz that avoids extremes of modernism without being too traditional, either. While Dolphy's presence and his unique improvisational style probably made it sound more avant-garde, today this album would probably be considered straight ahead by most listeners—straight ahead with the touch of Dolphy's genius. The title cut in particular lives up to its name, a rousing five and half minutes of blowing, riffing, and improvising, taken at a bebop tempo. Don DeMichael noted the contrast in Dolphy's and Nelson's playing on this album: "I like the contrast of styles between Dolphy and Nelson—Dolphy comes at you from off the wall, and Nelson usually charges straight at you."

Unlike the meandering Coltrane or Coleman sessions, praised by some, attacked by others, Nelson's arrangements proceeded at a brisk pace. Joe Goldberg, who wrote the liner notes for the album, describes showing up at 3:30, father had built a studio for him. Dolphy's earliest recordings, in 1948 at the age of twenty, were with a large ensemble, Roy Porter's 17 Beboppers, a group of young up-and-coming musicians that included twenty-year-old twin brothers Art and Addison Farmer and twenty-one-year-old Jimmy Knepper. Many of the same musicians, including drummer Porter, also recorded with a twenty-seven-year-old veteran of the Central Avenue scene, Charles Mingus. Mingus's twenty-two-piece Bebop Band also included a couple of other old pros, twenty-four-year-old Art Pepper and twenty-nine-year-old Britt Woodman.

By 1954, a lot of local and visiting musicians were dropping by Dolphy's backyard studio to jam, and one such session was recorded, with Clifford Brown, Richie Powell, Max Roach, and George Morrow. The sound isn't the greatest, but the youthful lyricism of Brown and Dolphy is fun to listen to, even if it doesn't give much of a hint of the Dolphy to come. A 1957 video shows Dolphy playing in a band backing up the popular rhythm and blues vocal harmony group, the Platters. Shortly after that, he got his first big break, joining Chico Hamilton's group in time for its July 1958 appearance at the Newport Jazz Festival. (Dolphy can be seen in the movie *Jazz on a Summer's Day*.) He then returned to LA with Hamilton's group to record for Pacific Jazz and Warner Brothers. His last recording with Hamilton was on May 19, 1959, after which he headed for New York, without much fanfare; there was a considerable disconnect between the two coasts back then.

After he came to New York, Esmond Edwards discovered Dolphy, and he doesn't really remember the details. He told Michael Jarrett, in an interview for Jarrett's *Pressed for All Time: Producing the Great Jazz Albums*: "I remember going to a rehearsal room on Broadway, one of those studios, and I guess whatever group he was playing with was rehearsing. I listened and said, 'Wow!' I approached him about signing. That's my memory of it. I wish I were like Orrin Keepnews and could say, 'Yeah, it was June 25, and he was wearing a polka-dot shirt.'" If Edwards didn't remember the details of the meeting, he certainly remembered the impression Dolphy made on him as an artist fully formed, and ready to step into the spotlight. Asked how much guidance he had given Dolphy in preparing to cut his first album for Prestige, Edward recalls that he did nothing more than give him the time and the date and tell him where to show up, at Rudy Van Gelder's recording cathedral in Englewood Cliffs, New Jersey. As Edwards told Jarrett, "He came with his music and the sidemen he wanted, and that was it."

Dolphy had been in New York long enough to have drawn the attention of the New York jazz world, and his group included veteran drummer Roy Haynes. The others were of Dolphy's generation, young lions ready to embark on major careers of their own. Trumpeter Freddie Hubbard had made his figuring that with a one o'clock session call they'd just be getting through a quick rehearsal and ready to get down to serious recording. Instead, he found the studio empty except for Rudy Van Gelder and Esmond Edwards. The musicians had packed up and gone home. They'd played "Straight Ahead," and they'd played straight ahead, and they'd nailed it the first time through.

Jaki Byard

Jaki Byard made his Prestige debut on *Outward Bound,* and was also the pianist on *Far Cry. Outward Bound* was his first New York recording, and his first with a significant jazz label. It was the recording that got him started on a career that would last through the rest of the century, but he had been around for a while. His first outing, with Boston's Charlie Mariano, had come in 1950, for Imperial, the Los Angeles–based label mostly known for rhythm and blues and rock and roll. Even in 1950, he was hardly wet behind the ears: He was twenty-eight years old, and had been playing professionally for over a decade. Of draftable age during World War II, he spent much of his service time in Florida, where he mentored a couple of young Florida teenagers, Julian and Nat Adderley. Byard recorded with Boston's Herb Pomeroy in 1957. (Pomeroy remembered that when he arrived on the Boston scene as a teenager, the pianist was already "a legend.") Not long after that, he joined Maynard Ferguson's band, which did not give him the musical flexibility he was looking for, but did get him to New York.

Byard certainly found flexibility in Dolphy's company, but he also gave something back. Few musicians could equal Byard's mastery of virtually every style of music, from New Orleans to rhythm and blues to bebop to classical; Ron Carter has described him as "one of the few players I know who can literally play jazz history on the keyboard." But more than that, few could equal his ability to use everything he knew, in unexpected ways, both humorous and profound, in every setting. Byard played and recorded on various keyboard instruments, from organ to celeste; he was talented enough on the saxophone, both alto and tenor, to record on both of those instruments; and he was also skilled on the trumpet, bass, guitar, drums, flute, and vibes.

Byard stayed with Prestige throughout the 1960s, recording eleven albums as leader, fourteen more as sideman. He worked with Dolphy, Don Ellis, Booker Ervin, and Eric Kloss; sidemen who worked with him included Ervin, Joe Farrell, George Benson, Ray Nance, and Roland Kirk. He worked with producers Esmond Edwards, Ozzie Cadena, and Don Schlitten. His records were never big sellers, and he never achieved the top tier of recognition, with no mention at all on the *Down Beat* Readers' Poll until 1965. In 1966 he climbed as high as eleventh, then slipped down into the middle of the pack again. Prestige stayed with him because he was such a formidable talent, and they were right. Byard has mostly dropped off the radar today. Ranker.com, a site that polls contemporary users, has a list of the greatest pianists of all time. There are over seventy names listed as of this writing, and Jaki Byard isn't one of them. But revisiting any of his albums—or visiting one for the first time—will expose the listener to a startlingly original and worthwhile talent.

Listening to Prestige:
Jaki Byard

Out Front!

*Recorded at Van Gelder Studio, Englewood Cliffs, NJ,
May 21 and 28, 1964*

*Quintet: Richard Williams, trumpet; Booker Ervin, tenor sax;
Jaki Byard, piano; Bob Cranshaw, bass; Walter Perkins, drums*

*Tracks recorded: Searchlight; European Episode; Lush Life;
I Like to Lead When I Dance; After the Lights Go Down Low*

Trio (Same without Williams and Ervin): Out Front; Two Different Worlds

> *Out Front!* is Byard's third album as a leader with Prestige. He'd also appeared as a supporting player on several other dates, the most recent one being with Booker Ervin, who returned the favor on the May 21 sessions, along with Richard Williams, another artist well known to Prestige collectors. Williams and Ervin sit out "Lush Life," as well as all of the second session. On bass and drums for both sessions are Bob Cranshaw and Walter Perkins. Cranshaw had made his first Prestige recording just a few weeks earlier, with Shirley Scott and Stanley Turrentine, but he had already begun his long association with Sonny Rollins, including his 1962 recording of *The Bridge* for RCA Victor, the album that heralded Rollins's return from self-imposed exile. Perkins was by this time a familiar face in Prestige sessions.
>
> The album shows a good deal of Byard's range and versatility. In fact, a few different styles and voicings are in evidence on a single cut: "European Episode," at just over twelve minutes more a suite than a single tune. One more facet of his versatility is showcased on "When Sunny Gets Blue," a leftover take from Byard's maiden session for Prestige in 1961, with Ron Carter and Roy Haynes, and featuring Byard on alto sax. Esmond Edwards had produced the earlier session; the two that make up the bulk of this album were produced by Ozzie Cadena. "I Like to Lead When I Dance" and "After the Lights Go Down Low" were not included on the album but made the later CD release.

Booker Little

Dolphy, doomed to a short life, briefly teamed up with another prodigiously talented musician whose life was to be even shorter. Booker Little first recorded with Dolphy at the age of twenty-two; he would not live past twenty-three. Little had already had an extensive musical career by the time he met Dolphy. He was born in 1938 in Memphis, a city with a storied musical heritage, and raised in a musical family: his parents were musicians, and one of his sisters became an opera singer, and a member of the Deutsche Oper Berlin for more than four decades. As a teenager, he began playing with fellow Memphis musician Phineas Newborn. He graduated from high school in 1954, and moved to Chicago to study at the Chicago Conservatory of Music, where he met his first mentor, Sonny Rollins, when both were living at Chicago's YMCA. Rollins introduced him to Max Roach, then reeling from the loss of his close friend and musical collaborator, Clifford Brown. Roach was impressed enough with the teenager to hire him as Brown's replacement, but Little was still in school and couldn't devote full time to the gig, so Roach went with Kenny Dorham instead. But he couldn't forget the talented kid from Chicago, and a couple of years later, Little joined the group to record *Max Roach + 4 on the Chicago Scene*. Chicago was represented by Little and pianist Eddie Baker, but when the group left for New York, Baker stayed and Little went along.

Little continued working with Roach through seven albums; the last one, perhaps appropriately titled *Percussion Bitter Sweet*, was recorded in the first two weeks of August 1961.

In 1960, Little met Dolphy, and they clicked. Their first recording session together came on December 21, 1960. They would have only the two Prestige sessions together, one in the studio and one live, but the musicians who were pioneering this new approach to jazz were a small and often close-knit group, and their paths crisscrossed. They backed up Max Roach's wife Abbey Lincoln for Nat Hentoff's Candid label in January 1961, and in March Little led a sextet including Dolphy for another Candid session, which would be released as *Out Front*. On May 23 and June 7, both Dolphy and Little were part of a twenty-one-piece ensemble brought together in Rudy Van Gelder's studio by John Coltrane. Coltrane had been the first artist signed by the new Impulse! label, and this session was one of the new label's first recordings.

On July 16, 1961, Van Gelder set up his equipment in the Five Spot Café, the Lower East Side night spot that had become a mecca for the new jazz. Opened in 1956, it had begun to set the tone for cutting edge exploration in 1957–58, when Thelonious Monk, who was finally able to play in New York club after being denied a cabaret card for most of the 1950s, opened a residency with a quartet featuring John Coltrane. The Five Spot became Ground Zero for avant-garde jazz in 1959, when Ornette Coleman played his first New York dates there. On this July date, Van Gelder recorded Little's group there.

Prestige did very few live recordings. Weinstock and the label's various producers, as much as they may have strived to capture the spontaneity of a jam session, preferred to do it in the welcoming confines of Van Gelder's studio in Englewood Cliffs. But it is truly fortunate that Esmond Edwards decided to capture this one. Little was rapidly developing as a musician, and his association with Dolphy was spurring him on to new levels of inventiveness. But his musical development, and his life, were rapidly approaching the end. In early August, he did the *Percussion Bitter Sweet* sessions with Max Roach.

On October 5, 1961, he died of complications from uremia. The first *Live at the Five Spot* album was released in December 1961, just two months after Little's death. There was a volume Two released in November 1963, and a final album, titled *Memorial Album*, in 1965, after Dolphy's death.

Chapter 23

Booker Ervin

The first half of the 1960s decade is notable for its practitioners of soul jazz and free jazz, but one of its most important figures, perhaps second only to Dolphy, would not fit easily into either category. Booker Ervin had ties to the jazz forged in the '40s and '50s out of bebop, hard bop, and the cool school—the music that would come to be known as mainstream—but was very much aware of the newest developments in music as well. He had listened to the new sounds in jazz, and absorbed them, but he also knew how to generate old-fashioned excitement.

The late 1940s and early 1950s had welcomed musicians like Zoot Sims who played a sort of hybrid music best described as swing-to-bop, and perhaps the mid-1960s had their own hybrid, straight-ahead-to-free. Ervin could have fitted into this category, had it existed. In Ira Gitler's description, he was "of the '60s but . . . has not lost touch with the tap roots of jazz." Gary Giddins, remarking on his unique approach, said "You know it's him after two notes . . . he is completely himself. . . . It is not avant-garde jazz . . . yet it has the kind of freedom and velocity you might associate with Coltrane."

Ervin arrived in New York fully formed as a musician in 1958, at twenty-eight years old. He was born and raised in Texas, and his earliest influence had been his father, who had played with Buddy Tate. His first instrument was the trombone, but during a stint in the air force, stationed in postwar Okinawa and playing in a service band, he switched to the tenor saxophone. Leaving the service in 1953, he continued his education and apprenticeship in diverse ways, first studying at the Berklee College of

Music in Boston, then returning to the Southwest of his youth, where he joined the territory band of Ernie Fields, playing swing and rhythm and blues.

In New York, Ervin quickly caught the attention of Charles Mingus, with whom he began his recording career in 1959 (he had cut a couple of singles with Fields), a live session that was released as *Jazz Portraits,* by the Charles Mingus Jazz Workshop. His Texas tenorman training with Fields was still very much in evidence in his New York debut, and Nat Hentoff described him in the liner notes to the album as "a player of impassioned force and directness." Ervin remained with Mingus for three years, playing on some of the bassist/composer's most acclaimed albums, including *Mingus Ah Um, Mingus Dynasty,* and *Blues and Roots.* He made his first recording as a leader in 1960 for Bethlehem Records, and led two more sessions during 1960–61, with Savoy and Candid, but during this era, he was still primarily involved with the Mingus Jazz Workshop.

On June 27, 1961, Ervin appeared for the first time on a Prestige recording, on a session led by Mal Waldron, and also featuring Eric Dolphy. Although Dolphy and Ervin had played together with Mingus, they never recorded together with him. One of the tunes chosen for the session was Waldron's "Fire Waltz," which he wrote with Dolphy in mind. It has become a jazz standard, and Dolphy would later record it again, on his *Live at the Five Spot* album with Booker Little. Listening to Dolphy and Ervin working together on this session, particularly this tune, makes one regret that they never had the chance to further explore the partnership.

Bob Weinstock liked to bring a new musician into the studio at least once as a sideman before signing him up as a leader. However, perhaps by 1963 the Waldron session was not fresh enough, because Ervin was next slotted for a session with organist Larry Young that was inexplicably shelved, not to be released until 1999. He was then given cobilling on April 10, 1963, with Roy Haynes. Haynes was already a legendary drummer, entering his third decade as a major figure in jazz. He had led two previous sessions for Prestige/New Jazz, one a near-perfect album called *We Three,* with Phineas Newborn and Paul Chambers, the other nearly as good, with Richard Wyands and Eddie de Haas, called *Just Us.* He would continue his poll-winning, Grammy-winning career well into the twenty-first century. Haynes was the leader on the April session, but "with Booker Ervin" got nearly as prominent a credit on the album, and it was clear that he was a rising star.

Prestige brought Ervin back in the studio on June 19 to make what was, if not his debut album as leader, the album that really established him as a force on the jazz scene. The title of the album was *Exultation!*, and it was an apt one. Ervin was, at this stage, seen by many as the new hope of hard bop: Pete Welding in his *Down Beat* review praised his "hard muscularity, strong swing, and charging force." He also compared him to John Coltrane, but not the Coltrane of 1963: "Listeners will note a strong similarity between Ervin's work and the . . . 'Sheets of Sound' approach evolved by John Coltrane a few years back . . . [but] Coltrane left the approach behind in his move toward . . . the much more convoluted style in which he is currently embroiled. Ervin, however, chose to remain with it and develop it into the strongly personal, emotionally gripping approach that is so forcibly on display in this set."

Ervin continued to build critical acclaim, and to build an audience. He was grounded enough for the mainstream and hard bop fans, and he was advanced enough for the avant-gardists. He created his own sound. This became most apparent with his third Prestige outing as leader, 1964's *The Freedom Book*. It was his first pairing with Jaki Byard, with whose work he was unfamiliar, although both had been at different times part of the Mingus Jazz Workshop. Don Schlitten, who produced the session, talked him into trying out Byard and his trio, with bassist Richard Davis and drummer Alan Dawson. Ervin would continue to work with the three of them for the rest of his tenure at Prestige, although not always together. They were right for where Ervin was going, eclectic musicians who could play in any style, even styles that hadn't been invented yet, that Ervin was maybe making up as he went along. Davis's versatility can be seen in the range of his credits, from Dolphy to Frank Sinatra to Van Morrison. Dawson had worked with Ervin previously, in Boston, of which Ervin said it was "one of the greatest experiences I've had in music . . . with Alan you can forget about the time, go beyond it."

Ervin recorded ten albums altogether for Prestige between 1963 and 1966, with a gap in the middle of that time period; he left for Europe in late 1964, fed up with American racial attitudes, and didn't return until 1966. He made a couple of albums for Pacific Jazz in the latter part of the decade, then returned to the East Coast to make a couple more for Blue Note. His last record date was for Prestige, a session headed by Eric Kloss, in 1969. By then he was in poor health. He died in 1970, of a kidney disease, at the age of thirty-nine.

Listening to Prestige:
Don Patterson with Booker Ervin

Hip Cake Walk

Recorded at Van Gelder Studio, Englewood Cliffs, NJ, July 10, 1964

Booker Ervin, tenor sax; Don Patterson, organ; Billy James, drums

Tracks recorded: Sister Ruth; Donald Duck; Rosetta; Under the Boardwalk; Sentimental Journey; Theme for Dee; Just Friends

This is not your father's organ-saxophone trio album, and anyone looking for Jimmy Smith and Brother Jack McDuff or Shirley Scott and Eddie "Lockjaw" Davis is going to go away scratching their heads . . . these two are going their own way. Booker Ervin already had forged a reputation as one of the most original and important new voices on the jazz scene—not as defiantly antiestablishment as Ornette Coleman or Albert Ayler, but definitely a new sound. Don Patterson was starting to make a name for himself, and the idea that his approach to the organ would mesh well with Booker Ervin's fresh approach resonated with the Prestige brain trust from the start. After putting him on sessions with Eddie "Lockjaw" Davis and Sonny Stitt, they gave him Ervin as a partner for his first session as leader, and it worked well enough to reunite them here.

Perhaps the most interesting result of this pairing comes on "Just Friends." The tune is a sentimental ballad from the 1930s that served as a vehicle for the likes of Kate Smith, Russ Colombo, and Morton Downey, but it became a jazz standard after Charlie Parker included it on his Charlie Parker with Strings album. After that, a number of artists picked it up—it even had a soul jazz organ treatment by Jimmy Smith—but Bird with strings is still the version most jazz fans will think of when they hear the title. It's hard to resist comparing the two versions, especially because Ervin (like every jazz man who came of age in or after the 1940s) is very aware of Bird's recording, and his "Just Friends" is very much of a dialogue with the master. Bird enjoyed the lush romanticism of his string section, but he certainly was not limited by it. And just as Bird both honored and subverted the genre, so Ervin and Patterson both honor and subvert the organ-saxophone soul jazz genre. If there is such a thing as soul jazz-free jazz fusion, they find it here.

Chapter 24

Stars of the Early '60s

The early 1960s were a time of new directions for Prestige, with soul jazz and avant-garde releases, and a time of everything old is new again, with Swingville and Bluesville. Weinstock and his in-studio producers and talent scouts were holding on to the old, reaching out for the new, and finding a variety of jazz styles and gifted musicians. Here are a representative sample, presented in chronological order by first date as a leader for Prestige.

Frank Wess

With all the grasping onto the hot new sounds of the day, and reaching out for what promised to be the trends of the future, the Prestige brain trust was not going to forget to dance with who brung them. Bob Weinstock had founded the label out of the love for a music that was new and different, and his label had survived to see that music embraced (by some, or dismissed by others) as "mainstream." And Prestige still found plenty of room for new musicians playing in the mainstream.

One such was multi-instrumentalist Frank Wess, who had begun a long tenure with Count Basie in 1953, and would always be most closely associated with the Count. He had been hired by Basie as a tenor saxophonist, but his early classical training had also given him virtuoso skills on the flute, and as that instrument began to find its way into the jazz lineup, he became Basie's first-ever flute soloist. Although he would remain with Basie through 1964, he began branching out on his own, recording a few albums for Savoy in 1955–57, and he actually had coleader status with two other tenor saxophonists on a 1957 Prestige album. One of the other horn players on the date was another Basie man, but the other was Prestige's rising star, John Coltrane, who was definitely first among equals. That album was released under the names of the three tenor players—Wess, Coltrane, and Paul Quinichette—by New Jazz, and as the Prestige All-Stars by Prestige, both versions with the title *Wheelin' and Dealin'*. Wess figured in a second Prestige All Stars session the same year. He made two exceptional albums with harpist Dorothy Ashby, where he played flute (see chapter 16). When Weinstock started Swingville Records, he brought Wess in to play on a Joe Newman album for the new label.

On May 9, 1960, Wess got his first date as a leader, fronting a quartet for one of the first Moodsville releases. The official album title was *The Frank Wess Quartet*, but from the prominence that was given to the label name for those early releases, it might as well have been Moodsville 8. Working with Basie, Wess had learned something about how to make music that swung, avoided clichés, and still had popular appeal. With Tommy Flanagan on piano, he brought that touch to a set of ballads that captured a mood without sacrificing creativity. He would make two more albums as leader for Prestige in 1962–63, while also supporting Lem Winchester, Thad Jones, Gene Ammons, and others.

John Wright

John Wright was born in Louisville, Kentucky, but raised in Chicago, and he was Chicagoan to the bone. In 1960, he was playing in a regular Sunday jam session at a club near the hotel where most of the touring big bands stayed; players from the Hampton or Ellington band, or whatever band was passing through Chicago, would come and jam. After one of these sessions, a fellow walked in and said, "I'm from New York, I'm a hiring man for one of the companies in New York, and I've got a spot for you. Would you like to come to New York and record for Prestige?" Wright's response: "Well, I'd heard of Prestige Records and Riverside, Coral, and Blue Note, those were the most prestigious jazz records back in the day. Quite naturally, I said yes. So, he gave me a plane ticket and $500. In August 1960, I went to New York City and that's where I got to record five albums on Prestige Records."

Wright brought his regular trio with him: bassist Wendell Roberts and drummer Walter McCann. And he brought a breath of Chicago with him: not the breath that was hog butcher to the world but the one that came out of the jazz clubs on the South Side. As Wright ran it down in a later interview, the album "was talking about the streets of Chicago; South Side Soul; Sin Corner (Sin Corner was about every corner); Amen Corner (Amen Corner was the churches); 63rd and Cottage Grove; 35th Street Blues; 47th Street (47th street was a red-light district); and LaSalle Street was the financial district. The blocks on State Street, Wentworth, and Cottage Grove, were always storefront churches. It was about two or three storefront churches in every block."

Wright composed the red-light district number, "47th and Calumet," and "63rd and Cottage Grove" for the churches. Wendell Roberts contributed the "35th Street Blues" and the "Amen Corner." "LaSalle Street After Hours" and "Sin Corner" were a natural fit, since who knows what goes on in the financial district of a large metropolis after hours, especially in those days, when the big brokerage offices were macho central? The composer was Chicagoan Armand "Jump" Jackson, a jazz and rhythm and blues drummer and all-around entrepreneur and impresario. "South Side Soul," which became the album's title, Wright's signature song, and part of his name—from then on, he was John "South Side Soul" Wright—appears not to have been written by a Chicagoan at all. Composer credit goes to producer Esmond Edwards, and since Edwards did not make a regular habit of slapping his name on other people's compositions, it seems likely that the credit was deserved.

By the start of the 1960s, Chicago had made a name for itself with the electric blues of Muddy Waters, Howlin' Wolf, and Little Walter, and the North Side piano blues stylings of Ramsey Lewis and Ahmad Jamal. But there was a niche for the mainstream playing of John Wright, too, and his five albums—plus a Bluesville session by Chicago-based traditional bluesman Arbee Stidham.

Wright had left behind the Pentecostal church of his family, making a personal vow that "I was going to play jazz, drink plenty of whiskey, and chase pretty women. I kept that vow, and it almost killed me." He spent some years getting too soaked in whiskey, and his recording career dried up. But there was a happy ending for Wright. He sobered up, married, and made a life for himself in Chicago, where he began what became a tradition: the Wright Gathering. First organized in his suburban home—he had left the South Side by then—it featured his music and the cooking of his third wife, Evelyn, who would prepare the whole year for it, cooking and freezing food for the big day. When Evelyn died in 2007, he thought that would be the end of the Wright Gatherings, but friends and admirers took over the cooking and organizing, and the now-popular event was moved to a nearby park.

Walt Dickerson

Vibraphonist Walt Dickerson came to Prestige in 1961, recommended to Weinstock by John Coltrane. If you don't automatically link Coltrane and the vibes together in the same thought module, listening to Dickerson could change your mind. Don DeMichael, in a *Down Beat* review, described Dickerson's solos "at times spiralling asymmetrically in tangled, biting swirls of notes flying like sparks from a pinwheel; in 1962, *Down Beat* named him the best new jazz artist of the year, and called him "the most important vibraphonist since Milt Jackson."

Dickerson made four albums for New Jazz in 1961–62. The last one, titled *To My Queen* and dedicated to his wife, Liz, is considered by many to be the iconic achievement of his career, partly because of its theme (the title cut took up one side of the LP), but mostly because of its musical direction. Dickerson was always considered one of the most individual stylists on the vibes, but on this album, abetted by his long-time collaborator, the drummer Andrew Cyrille, he moved farther from his bebop-oriented roots to create a freer and more distinctive personal style, finding a direction similar to that of his friend John Coltrane.

Dickerson pulled back from music for several years, starting in the mid-1960s, living in Europe. He eventually starting to record again in 1975, for the Danish Steeplechase label. He returned to the United States in the early 1980s, and while he did play occasionally around his hometown of Philadelphia, he became more and more of a recluse, and he never recorded again. *To My Queen* remained his most notable achievement—one of his Steeplechase albums was titled *To My Queen Revisited*—and he talked about it in a 2003 interview with music critic Hank Shteamer, who had gotten his phone number from Andrew Cyrille:

> Well, there is a way to talk about a person that you find ineffable through music, and my queen being that ineffable person, music was the way that I could express those very beautiful, poignant, intellectual, brilliant, beautiful sides of her. So therefore it couldn't fall in the realm of most songs or most compositions in the

genre but had to escape those restrictions in order to exemplify her. . . . It was a very, very happy experience, and I go back to that periodically. I return to that periodically, restating that which is ongoing in our relationship, which is forever.

The individuals that I chose for that outing knew my queen, and their artistic projections spoke of that. [Pianist] Andrew Hill: beautiful projections. [Bassist] George Tucker: a rock, sensitive. And of course Andrew Cyrille: flourishings, nuances, bracketing the different motifs; he was awesome, and remains to this day, as does Andrew Hill.

Dickerson promised Shteamer that they would talk more, and that perhaps he might even come out of seclusion and do a concert, but Shteamer never heard from him again. He died in 2008. Richard Brody, summing up his career in an obituary in the *New Yorker*, wrote: "Dickerson is, simply, the most innovative vibes player after Lionel Hampton and Milt Jackson; his rapid-fire barrage of short, metallic notes, reminiscent of John Coltrane's 'sheets of sound' and Eric Dolphy's frenetic flurries (Dickerson and Dolphy were close friends), extracted surprising harmonic riches from familiar tunes, and often did so with a puckish humor that belied the tenderness with which he could caress a melody."

Ahmed Abdul-Malik

Ahmed Abdul-Malik, like Yusef Lateef and Randy Weston, was one of the first jazz musicians to incorporate Middle Eastern and North African influences. Lateef found his way into Middle Eastern music in Detroit, through his conversion to Islam, and his friendship with Arab immigrant factory workers on the auto assembly lines. Weston and Abdul-Malik grew up in Brooklyn, where there was an Arabic population around Atlantic Avenue, and an exciting ethnic musical scene.

Brooklyn in the 1950s was part of the city, but it still had a provincial feel. It wasn't the Big Apple. Old time residents recall the days when the Brooklyn Dodger stars lived in the neighborhood, would carpool to the games, and go to neighborhood block parties. The big jazz stars sometimes played clubs in Brooklyn, especially Thelonious Monk, who had been stripped of his cabaret card and couldn't play any of the well-known Manhattan clubs like the Five Spot. They couldn't advertise him when he played in Brooklyn, so no one was looking, and he could get away with it. Jazz Historian Jimmy Morton, a fixture on that Brooklyn scene, once photographed Miles Davis, Monk, Mingus, and Roach backing up Etta Jones at Tony's, one of Brooklyn's most popular jazz spots.

Brooklyn also has a long African American tradition. Urban archaeologists have only recently rediscovered Weeksville, one of the first neighborhoods of Black homeowners in America. And it was the borough where young men like Ahmed Abdul-Malik and Bilal Abdurrahman met, discovered Islam, discovered jazz, and did their apprenticeship. Abdurrahman, in his memoir *In the Key of Me*, lists twenty-four jazz clubs active in Brooklyn at that time.

Abdul-Malik—as a young violin and viola prodigy at New York's High School of Music and Art and still called Jonathan Tim Jr.—played in the All-City Orchestra. Switching to the bass, and taking up jazz in the 1940s, he played with Art Blakey, Coleman Hawkins, and Don Byas. He got his first recording gigs in 1956 with Weston, on Riverside and on the short-lived Dawn label; in the same year, he recorded with ultrahip German pianist Jutta Hipp for Blue Note. The following year, he joined Thelonious Monk's quartet; perhaps they had met during Monk's sojourns in Brooklyn. Abdul-Malik also paid his dues in the Arabic music scene, working with two Lebanese vocalists, Mohammed el Bakkar and Djamal Aslan, both of whom were also known for their virtuosity on the oud, a Middle Eastern instrument similar to the lute, one that Abdul-Malik would take up and master. El Bakkar, in particular, was a huge star throughout the Middle East, and had played a featured role (as an Oriental rug seller) in the hit Broadway musical *Fanny*. To further his immersion in what would come to be called world music, a field in which he was certainly a pioneer, Abdul-Malik worked in the 1940s with the popular calypso artist MacBeth the Great. (Abdul-Malik's parents were immigrants from the British West Indies, although he claimed for a while that they were from Sudan.)

In 1957, Abdul-Malik began working regularly at the Five Spot in New York, most notably a five-month gig in a group led by Monk and featuring John Coltrane, during the brief period when Monk had regained his cabaret card (he would lose it again in 1958). Both Monk and Coltrane encouraged him to pursue his interest in Middle Eastern and North African music, and Coltrane particularly encouraged him to keep studying the oud. Later in the year, he formed his first group, using both mainstream jazz musicians and Arabic musicians. This group, being predominantly Muslim, mostly eschewed the usual jazz clubs, because liquor was served there. That made gigs hard to come by, so in early 1958, they came back to Brooklyn, as Abdurrahman and his wife opened an African restaurant—Brooklyn's first—called the African Quarter.

By the time Abdul-Malik made his first album as leader (for Riverside) later in the year, his apprenticeship on the oud had borne fruit, and it had become an essential part of his music. The titles of his Riverside album and one in 1959 for RCA Victor are evocative of the kind of music he was already making: *Jazz Sahara* and *East Meets West*.

> ### Listening to Prestige: Ahmed Abdul-Malik
>
> *The Music of Ahmed Abdul-Malik*
>
> Recorded at Van Gelder Studio, Englewood Cliffs, NJ, May 23, 1961
>
> Tommy Turrentine, trumpet; Bilal Abdurrahman, clarinet, percussion; Eric Dixon, tenor saxophone; Ahmed Abdul-Malik, bass, oud; Calo Scott, cello; Andrew Cyrille, drums
>
> Tracks recorded: La Ibkey; The Hustlers; Hannibal's Carnivals; Out of Nowhere; Nights on Saturn; Don't Blame Me; Oud Blues
>
> With this album, Prestige would become Abdul-Malik's home for most of his career as leader. Esmond Edwards produced it for New Jazz.
>
> Abdul-Malik had experimented with different groupings of musicians on his first two albums, and for this session he pulled together a different and striking combination. Bilal Abdurrahman had been with him from the beginning, playing the duf (tambourine) on Jazz Sahara, the darabeka (or darbouka, or goblet drum) on East Meets West, the clarinet, and various percussion instruments on this session. Abdurrahman would go on to teach and record several albums of Middle Eastern music for young people. Tommy Turrentine, older brother of saxophonist Stanley Turrentine, had pretty much a mainstream background, playing in the bands of Max Roach, Benny Carter, Earl Bostic, Charles Mingus, Billy Eckstine, Dizzy Gillespie, and Count Basie. He had not recorded a lot before this album, but Abdul-Malik was crafting his sound carefully, and liked what Turrentine could contribute. Eric Dixon, best known for a long career with Basie, had appeared on two Prestige albums in the mid-1950s, with Bennie Green and Mal Waldron. Andrew Cyrille, a Brooklyn native, was new on the scene but already establishing a reputation as one of the most inventive drummers of jazz experimentalism, a reputation that would only grow through his

work with Walt Dickerson, Cecil Taylor, Oliver Lake, David Murray, and others.

Cuban-born Caio Scott's jazz career was limited by his choice of instrument—a cello doesn't fit into every Jazz ensemble. But when he was used—by Gato Barbieri, Carla Bley, Archie Shepp, Mal Waldron, and others—he delivered. No doubt inspired by his jazz cohorts, he frequently played the cello standing up (he used a saxophonist's neck strap to help steady the instrument). He was in demand for a wide range of avant-garde venues in New York, particularly working with dance troupes.

Abdul-Malik does so many things on this album, even dipping into his calypso background for "Hannibal's Carnivals," combining his own blend of calypso with high life, a jazz-influenced updating of a traditional West African folk form that had burst into popularity in Nigeria in 1960. "Oud Blues" is just that: a blues played on the oud, primarily a duet between Abdul-Malik and Scott's pizzicato cello. "Nights in Saturn" is a space-age workout that gives the horn players an opportunity to flex their avant-garde muscles but also gives the lead to Abdurrahman on a Korean reed instrument so obscure, according to the album's liner notes, that neither he nor Abdul-Malik knew exactly what it was (it was later determined to be a peri). There's even a standard ballad on the set, "Don't Blame Me," by Jimmy McHugh and Dorothy Fields, recorded by many in the jazz and pop fields, including another Afrocentric performer, Randy Weston. This version has a beautiful bowed cello solo by Scott, and some intricate duet work between Abdul Malik and Scott playing pizzicato. "La Ibkey" is adapted from a traditional Arabic folk song, full of rhythmic ingenuity, broken down by University of Hawaii professor Njoroge M. Njoroge in his book Chocolate Surrealism: Music, Movement, Memory, and History in the Circum-Caribbean: "The drums play in 7/4 while the soloists alternate between 3/4 and 4/4 and multiples thereof." "The Hustlers" and "La Ibkey" were released on 45. I don't know if they got much jukebox play, or if they were too far out. I like to think they commanded a few nickels in Brooklyn.

Abdul-Malik continued to delve into the forward-looking sounds that would one day be lauded as world music on his final two albums for Prestige. *Sounds of Africa*, recorded after a visit to Nigeria, utilized a ten-piece band including two African-influenced percussionists, Montego Joe and Chief Bey. *The Eastern Moods of Ahmed Abdul-Malik* was a trio album with Abdurrahman playing a variety of reed and woodwind instruments of various cultures, and percussionist William Henry Allen. In addition to Adbul-Malik's original compositions, they played a very Middle Eastern version of George Gershwin's "Summertime."

During the early 1960s, Abdul-Malik was in demand as a bassist, and played with a wide range of musicians. After 1965, with his last albums frankly ahead of their time, and meeting with less than enthusiastic reviews and poor sales, he played very little, but the range was still there, from Earl Hines to Randy Weston. He devoted most of his energy to education, giving lessons in his Brooklyn neighborhood and later teaching at New York University. He suffered a stroke in 1993, and died at the age of sixty-six.

Rahsaan Roland Kirk

Rahsaan Roland Kirk is one of the most innovative and multitalented instrumentalists in jazz. Even in his rhythm and blues days, he was already experimenting with his exotic instruments, and with playing more than one horn at the same time. And if this was originally presented as a gimmick, it was never a gimmick. Hank Crawford first heard him playing as a fourteen-year-old on the rhythm and blues circuit, and remembers: "He would be like this 14 year-old blind kid playing two horns at once. They would bring him out and he would tear the joint up. . . . Now they had him doing all kinds of goofy stuff but he was playing the two horns and he was playing the shit out of them. He was an original from the beginning."

The other horns Kirk primarily used were the manzello and the stritch. The manzello is Kirk's modification of the saxello, itself a modification of the soprano saxophone. The stritch is a modified alto sax, straight like a soprano rather than curving into a bell like a conventional alto (the manzello adds a bell to the conventional soprano structure). Playing all three at once, he could do something no other horn player could do: make chords. But he was also a brilliant flute player, and he made use of all sorts of sound-making devices, in the manner of Yusef Lateef (or Spike Jones), but playing all of them himself.

Listening to Prestige:
Roland Kirk-Jack McDuff

Kirk's Work

Recorded at Van Gelder Studio, Englewood Cliffs, NJ, July 11, 1961

Roland Kirk, tenor sax, manzello, stritch, flute, siren; Jack McDuff, organ; Joe Benjamin, bass; Art Taylor, drums

Tracked recorded: Three for Dizzy; Makin' Whoopee; Funk Underneath; Kirk's Work; Doin' the Sixty-Eight; Too Lat Now; Skaters Waltz

Roland Kirk would make this one recording for Prestige, right at the beginning of his career, and then move on; there would not be another Prestige date for seven years. He had been in the studio only twice before, first in 1956 with a rhythm and blues session for King, then for Chicago-based Argo in 1960, with Ira Sullivan. Kirk's musical knowledge and influences stretched from rhythm and blues to classical, from ragtime to electronic music. So it was interesting that Prestige paired him with Jack McDuff, a guy who essentially played one style, though he did it very well.

But why not? I have a theory: given jazz musicians of quality and imagination, there's no such thing as a bad pairing. Prestige paired Eric Dolphy with Juan Amalbert's Latin Jazz Quintet, a session often criticized as a mismatch (see chapter 22). The same criticism was leveled at Charlie Parker playing with Machito, or at Sonny Rollins with the Modern Jazz Quartet, and it was never true in any of those cases. Just listen, and you'll hear how they're relating to each other. One of the most delightful jazz singles ever is "Slim's Jam," featuring a dead serious avant-gardist (Charlie Parker), an irreverent cutup (Slim Gaillard), and a rhythm and bluesman (Jack McVouty, in Gaillard's language, McVea in anyone else's). And how about the *Birth of the Cool* nonet, who made some of the tightest, most trailblazing music in jazz history, led by Miles Davis, Lee Konitz, Gerry Mulligan, and John Lewis, all of whom came from very different places and went in very separate ways? Jazz is all about reaching out of your comfort zone, so putting together great musicians from different schools is always going to be worth listening to.

Although Kirk could draw on almost any musical language you cared to name, he had a solid grounding in soul jazz. You're certainly going to get things here that you would not necessarily get on any other Jack McDuff album, but you're going to get that jazz with a beat and that down-home sound. Kirk plays the flute in addition to his big three instruments, and also uses a siren. Four of the numbers here are Kirk originals. Two are standards: "Makin' Whoopee" and "Too Late Now." And there's one that you really wouldn't expect to find on a Jack McDuff soul jazz album, "The Skater's Waltz," by nineteenth-century French composer Charles Émile Waldteufel. I'm not sure Waldteufel would recognize what these guys do to it, but he might also be given pause if he could visit the midtwentieth century and hear his "Estudiantina Waltz" sung as "My beer is Rheingold, the dry beer."

Joe Benjamin and Art Taylor round out the quartet. Taylor is a veteran of many, many Prestige sessions, and if you think of him as primarily a bop-era drummer, from his work with Miles, Red Garland, and others, prepare to think again. He establishes himself here as a giant of funk drumming. The album was called *Kirk's Work*. It was later released as *Roland Kirk—Pre-Rahsaan*, which in fact it was. The name Rahsaan would come later, not out of Islamic religious leanings (he was never a Muslim) but because the name came to him in a dream. Even this early in his career, though, he had already been named by an oneirological impulse. His birth name was Ronald, but a dream told him to switch the letters around.

Kirk was out of the Prestige orbit until 1968, when he returned for a truly memorable pairing with Jaki Byard, abetted by Richard Davis, bass, and Alan Dawson, drums. He was still simply Roland at this point; his Rahsaan dream would not come until the following year. Scott Yanow, reviewing for the AllMusic website, gave the album five stars and said: "Jaki Byard and the wondrous Roland Kirk (here switching between tenor, clarinet, and manzello) were two of the few jazz musicians who could play in literally every jazz style, from New Orleans to bop and free form." Kirk introduces another instrument of his own design here, the kirkbam, also a modification of a saxophone. It apparently didn't satisfy him as much as the manzello or the stritch, because there's no record of him using it again. Don Schlitten, who produced the session, had this to say about it: "The beauty in all this music contains an ingredient that's lacking in much of today's jazz, and that's a sense of humor." It's a special kind of humor, one that could only have come from two musicians with such an encyclopedic knowledge of music, and the kind of deep respect that allows for a little irreverence.

Dave Pike

Dave Pike was a Protean talent who seemingly had to keep exploring new jazz styles, so his three albums for Prestige are as good a place as any to go for a representative sample of his work—which is to say, they barely scratch the surface.

Pike's family moved from Detroit to Los Angeles when he was fourteen. Perhaps growing up in a city where there were many gifted musicians but no coalescing style was its own sort of influence. One can only imagine how he might have evolved if the family had stayed in Detroit. His first record date was with avant-gardist Paul Bley. Then, moving to New York, he began working with Herbie Mann, who was himself evolving from bebop to Middle Eastern sounds and Latin rhythms. Pike also recorded with Olatunji, whose sound was heavily influenced by Africa.

At around this time, he made his first album as leader, *It's Time for Dave Pike*, for Riverside, more or less discarding Bley, Mann, and any other cutting-edge musical styles to make a more-or-less traditional bebop album with Detroiter Barry Harris. Reviewers called the work promising but unfocused. The *Penguin Guide to Jazz on CD* was less kind to this album—and to Pike's whole career—saying "the record feels like it's going nowhere, which is what Pike did."

One could as easily say that Pike went everywhere. His time with Mann affected him deeply; he noted, "Musically speaking, the best experience gained from Herbie's group has been learning to play in widely varied styles. African music. Brazilian music. Hebrew music and Afro-Cuban combined with jazz." His first album for New Jazz, *Bossa Nova Carnival*, saw him delving into the music of Brazil. But Pike was no dilettante. Brazil and the bossa nova were popular in 1962, and everyone was recording the songs of Antônio Carlos Jobim, so Pike bypassed Jobim and explored the compositions of João Donato, more experimental and challenging than Jobim, although you might not have guessed that from the title Prestige gave to the album. The label continued to push the commercial side of Pike's music, a commercial side that really wasn't there, with the title of his next New Jazz release: *Limbo Carnival*, which made the album sound as though it were in competition with Chubby Checker's contemporaneous release, "Limbo Rock." Which was, in fact, one of the tunes included. The album, like *Bossa Nova Carnival*, was produced by Eliot Mazer, the son of Weinstock's next-door neighbors in Teaneck, New Jersey. Mazer would soon go on to produce pop and rock acts, including Chubby Checker, for other labels.

If this sounds like a recipe for disaster, it wasn't. Pike's immersive musicianship, plus the percussion of Willie Bobo and Ray Barreto, made even "Limbo Rock," to say nothing of "La Bamba" and "Jamaica Farewell," listenable.

But what was Prestige trying to do with Pike, exactly? A three-record deal was Weinstock's typical initial contract with an artist. By Pike's third studio session, the Latin fad had run its course, but jazzed-up versions of Broadway musical scores had achieved some popularity. Jonah Jones, lightly regarded in jazz circles but with some impressive album sales, had done a couple. *My Fair Lady* had received different jazz interpretations by Andre Previn and Billy Taylor with Quincy Jones. So why not have Dave Pike do *Oliver!*? As it turned out, there was no particular demand for a jazz version of *Oliver!* Was this another of Eliot Mazer's ideas? But he was gone, and Don Schlitten produced. And perhaps it was Pike's idea—he was constantly searching in new directions. He told interviewer Max Barker about this project, "What I tried to do was to capture the emotionally strong content of the show, which then made it ideal for jazz interpretation." Sidemen on the date were Tommy Flanagan, Jimmy Raney, George Tucker, and Walter Perkins, so the music was good. The album was released on Moodsville, which suggests that the Prestige brain trust may not have seen it as breaking new ground. After this release, Pike left Prestige and left the country, spending the next several years in Europe, where he returned to his experimental roots.

Gildo Mahones

Gildo Mahones rarely took the reins as a leader on a session, so he never acquired the name recognition of his piano playing contemporaries like Tommy Flanagan and Red Garland. However, he had a storied career, starting with joining Joe Morris's rhythm and blues band as a teenager, and playing on Morris's rhythm and blues hit "Any Time, Any Place, Anywhere." He was recruited by Kenny Clarke in 1949 to succeed Billy Taylor as pianist in the house band at Minton's. He was rarely short of work, and in 1959 became the piano player for Lambert, Hendricks, and Ross (Jaki Byard succeeded him at Minton's), and stayed with them until they broke up in 1964, at which point he moved to the West Coast.

Mahones's first Prestige gig was backing up Ted Curson on the trumpeter's only session for the label, and after that the label used him a lot. Prestige never had formal arrangements with "house instrumentalists," but they did have guys they called on over and over; Mahones was one of their regulars, as long as he was based in New York and not out on the road with LHR. He played behind Willis Jackson, Frank Wess, Jimmy Witherspoon twice, Booker Ervin twice, and Kenny Burrell.

Mahones's first album as leader was made whenever they could fit him in, with whomever they could round up. It was recorded over three dates: February 4, August 15, and September 3, 1963. The first date was the tail end of an Etta Jones session. Mahones was not on the Jones session, but Larry Young, George Tucker, and drummer Jimmie Smith were, so they were loaned to Mahones for three tunes, one of which was never used; and let's hope they got paid for two sessions. August 15 appears actually to have been a Mahones date, with Kenny Burrell, Tucker, and Smith; Leo Wright played alto sax, and a vocalist named Ozzie Beck, who seems never to have been called upon for another recording by anyone, sang one song. There still wasn't quite enough for an album, so Tucker and Smith came back on September 3. June 4, 1964, was a day actually devoted to Mahones; working with Tucker again, and drummer Sonny Brown, they recorded sixteen tunes.

The first album, *I'm Shooting High*, was supposed to be a New Jazz release, but Weinstock decided to fold New Jazz just before its release, so it was hastily put out under Prestige, but not as one of their regular releases, and it quickly disappeared. The second album was called *The Great Gildo*, and it got more of a treatment; they even took all sixteen tunes, plus one from the earlier session, and made it a double album, which was exceedingly rare for Prestige. The music was excellent; Mahones's style harkened back to an earlier era—and don't forget, eras were only a few years long in those days, if that—when pianists like Red Garland were making tasteful, intelligent, swinging trio albums. Mahones was not competing with the soul jazz makers, and perhaps he should have. There was no great demand for a third album. He did do one more, on a tiny independent label, then decamped for the West Coast, where he had a long and successful career as a studio musician and sideman.

Jimmy Witherspoon

Perhaps as good a word as any to describe Prestige Records in the mid-1960s would be potluck. When Bob Weinstock started the label he was young, and he could feel, with good reason, that he was in the vanguard of a new generation of jazz fans, and jazz entrepreneurs, who were bringing what had been a fringe movement of the 1940s into the mainstream of jazz. By 1963, Weinstock was no longer quite so young, and he was now responsible for making the business decisions for a business that had become successful on the fringes of the entertainment industry: "a farm team for the major labels," as Weinstock put it.

So the sources of the music were different. It came from new guys in town, like Dave Pike, studio guys ready to take a shot at making their own music, like Gildo Mahones, or guys who had been around for a while, maybe quite a while, but who still had something to say. Weinstock created Swingville and Bluesville to showcase some of those musicians—and also as a business decision, to diversify his income stream. Now he was getting ready to contract again; both subsidiary labels would be gone by 1964. But there were still veteran musicians who came along, who deserved to be recorded and might still have sales potential. One of those was Jimmy Witherspoon.

Perhaps Weinstock decided to release Witherspoon's first album on Prestige rather than Bluesville because he knew Bluesville was going to be shut down soon, and he had long-term plans for the singer. That seems far-fetched, because in the potluck atmosphere of 1963, who knew which musicians were going to be sticking around? Or perhaps it was because Witherspoon was so much more than a blues singer. In fact, Witherspoon was arguably the most eclectic singer of his generation, and a quick rundown of his recent outings before Prestige barely scratches the surface. Living out on the West Coast through most of the 1950s, he had done a live album of blues standards at a local jazz club, accompanied by Gerry Mulligan and Ben Webster; an album of standards for Frank Sinatra's Reprise label, with West Coast legends Teddy Edwards and Gerald Wiggins; a couple of albums for the rhythm and blues label Crown; and a live session in Paris with a group of jazz traditionalists led by Buck Clayton. For his Prestige debut, he worked with alto saxophonist Leo Wright and a rhythm section of Kenny Burrell, Gildo Mahones, George Tucker, and drummer Jimmie Smith. They did rhythm and blues hits ("Bad, Bad Whiskey"), a Joe Turner Kansas City blues ("Rocks in My Bed"), and a curious tour de force that became the title song of the album. "Baby, Baby, Baby" was written by Hollywood tunesmiths Mack David and Jay ("Mr. Ed") Livingston to be sung by brassy Teresa Brewer in a musical called *Those Redheads from Seattle*; Witherspoon turns it into what sounds for all the world like an authentic blues, a long way from Seattle and those redheads.

Witherspoon was equal parts down home and sophisticated, and he had a following. He remained with Prestige for seven albums through 1965, featuring a wide range of songs, a wide range of musicians, and even a wide range of locales—one album was made in Sweden with an orchestra conducted by Benny Golson. He would continue performing into the 1990s.

Red Holloway

Red Holloway came to Prestige with Jack McDuff, and he was featured on thirteen McDuff albums for the label. He accompanied Gene Ammons on four albums. But he also made his mark as a leader, with four albums under his own name. These could be categorized along with the soul jazz of McDuff, or with the blues-drenched mainstream jazz of Gene Ammons. But perhaps the most likely style to associate him with is the Chicago version of jazz with a beat, which was the music of his roots: Before signing on with McDuff, he had played and recorded with Sunnyland Slim, Otis Rush, Roosevelt Sykes, Chuck Berry, Willie Dixon, Junior Parker, Lloyd Price, and Bobby Bland, to name a few. His first session for Prestige (two tunes, one of them rejected) used musicians associated with the Chicago rhythm and blues scene (Hobart Dotson, trumpet; George Butcher, organ; Charles Lindsey, guitar; Thomas Palmer, bass; Bobby Durham, drums). The next one brought in New York players—Big John Patton, organ; Eric Gale, guitar—who otherwise had little or no connection to Prestige.

Holloway's albums, to quote the interchangeable teenager who reviewed new records for Dick Clark's *American Bandstand*, had "a good beat—you could dance to them." Francis Squibb, a frequent contributor of liner notes to Prestige albums, said much the same thing, although one could argue that the Bandstand Teenager said it better:

> WARNING—When you play this LP at your next party, you'd better roll up the rugs first! You and your friends will probably find yourselves dancing to this music—dancing so hard the rugs will surely catch fire if you've left them down. Some pails of water to cool the dancers' feet might come in handy, but certainly you don't need to worry the janitor about the radiators—there's enough heat on this record to warm every room in a 20-room house.

Bobby Timmons

One generally associates Bobby Timmons with other labels: Blue Note, because he was so closely associated with Art Blakey and the Jazz Messengers, for whom he composed "Moanin'"; and Riverside, for his association with Cannonball Adderley, for whom he composed "This Here" and "Dat Dere." Or, to put it another way, one generally associates Bobby Timmons with "Moanin'," "This Here," and "Dat Dere." But there was a good deal more to him, much of it with Prestige.

Timmons's recording debut came in 1956 for Blue Note in a group led by Kenny Dorham. They were captured live at New York's Café Bohemia. His first recording as coleader of a group came the following year, for Prestige, with saxophonists John Jenkins and Clifford Jordan. He never was given his own album at Blue Note, although he appeared often on albums by others between 1956 and 1960; he had four albums as leader for Riverside. But Timmons was best known in those years as a sideman, chiefly with Art Blakey (twenty-two albums altogether, fourteen of them with Blue Note), but also with Chet Baker, Kenny Dorham, Frank Morgan, Maynard Ferguson, Curtis Fuller, Hank Mobley, Sonny Stitt, Pepper Adams, Kenny Burrell, Benny Golson, Cannonball Adderley, Art Farmer, Nat Adderley, Joe Alexander, Arnett Cobb, Johnny Griffin, Sam Jones, Dizzy Reece, and Lee Morgan . . . that's a jawbreaking list. But it makes a point . . . two points, actually: The first is that Timmons was very much in demand; the second is that this list—and there were a few more—covers the years 1956 to 1960. After that, nothing. It's quite remarkable. Virtually no one wanted to hire him.

A large part of the reason was Timmons's growing reputation for unreliability due to an increasingly serious heroin addiction. You couldn't tour with him, or rely on him for an extended club date. But he was also starting to get a reputation as a composer of simple tunes (as though that were an easy thing to do), and a pianist of limited range. But soul jazz was still popular, and his work with Blakey and Adderley—and his authorship of three soul classics—had made him a marketable name. He recorded six albums as leader for Riverside between 1960 and 1964, with titles that exploited that reputation, like *Soul Time* and *This Here Is Bobby Timmons* (which included new versions of "Moanin'," "This Here," and "Dat Dere"). If there was more to him than that, maybe no one wanted to know. A 1962 album is noted by a present-day reviewer, Stewart Mason for *AllMusic*, as a pleasant anomaly, "an unusual record for Bobby Timmons," with the pianist's approach compared to Bud Powell and Bill Evans. But the album appears to have been marketed to Timmons's core image: its title is *Sweet and Soulful Sounds*.

Prestige had been derisively referred to in the 1950s, fairly or unfairly, as "the junkie label," because of (per detractors) a propensity to exploit vulnerable musicians, or (to supporters) a willingness to give a second chance to valued musicians like Miles Davis when no one else would. Although those days were long behind them, they did take a chance on Bobby Timmons in 1964. Their first recording session with him came on June 18, and if the album's liner notes by Joel Dorn are to be believed, it's amazing that there was a second. According to Dorn, the session was to have been a quintet, but only bassist Sam Jones showed up for the date. After two hours of indecision and wasted studio time, they were ready to cancel the date, when "someone remembered that Ray Lucas was in town," and the

session was saved. It took two hours, in New York, music capital of the world, for a bunch of jazz professionals to come up with the name of one drummer? And that was hardly the extent of their problems. Dorn says: "Producing a record involves a high degree of empathy between the artist, the A&R man, and the engineer. On this particular session not only was there a lack of empathy, there was an air of antagonism." Dorn doesn't specify the nature or source of the antagonism, and he doesn't identify the A&R man. By the mid-sixties, "A&R" (for "artists and repertoire") had largely vanished as a job descriptor in the music business, replaced by "producer." The producer for this session, according to Dorn's liner notes, was . . . Joel Dorn, with "supervision by" Ozzie Cadena. The twenty-two-year-old Dorn had been lobbying Nesuhi Ertegun in a series of letters, beginning when he was fourteen, for a position producing records for Atlantic. Ertegun had finally given him a shot at producing a debut album for Hubert Laws, and apparently he had talked his way into this gig with Prestige while Atlantic waited to see how the Laws record would do. So, while there's no way of knowing what the nature of the antagonism was or who exactly was the source of it, Dorn left Prestige after this session was done, never to return, going on to a highly successful and honorable career at Atlantic. Cadena continued to work with Timmons on his next three albums; most sources list him as the producer for this session.

Ray Lucas was King Curtis's regular drummer. He had never played with either Timmons or Jones before, so it took some adjusting, and a couple of takes that were unusable before the three of them found a groove. All but one of the tunes selected for the session were Timmons originals. It's interesting to speculate on what the album would have sounded like if the planned-for quintet had materialized. Certainly Timmons did not come prepared to be the only soloist, and to carry the whole session. Quite likely the five new tunes he brought with him were written with a quintet, and a couple more soloists, in mind. The surprise trio alignment meant that he would not be able to rely on a few catchy, "Moanin'"-type riffs. If he were really the pianist of limited range that his detractors made him out to be, he would have been in trouble.

As it turned out, he was up for the challenge. There's plenty of soul on this album, and Jones and Lucas, once they got used to each other, provided a propulsive rhythmic base, and Timmons's improvisation was thoughtful and often daring.

Prestige got what they wanted, a soul album that could be packaged and marketed as such. The title was, if anything, less subtle than the titles of his Riverside albums: *Little Barefoot Soul*. It was successful enough that Prestige booked six more sessions for Timmons over the next two years, three more with Cadena, and three with multifaceted producer Cal Lampley. Most of them had titles chosen with a specific audience in mind: *Workin' Out!*, *Chicken & Dumplin's*, *The Soul Man!*, *Soul Food*, and, for Christmas, *Holiday Soul*.

Time shrinks the catalogs of most artists, not just musical artists, to a few greatest hits. John Steinbeck will mostly be remembered for *The Grapes of Wrath* and *Of Mice and Men*; Marcel Duchamp for "Nude Descending a Staircase"; Chubby Checker for "The Twist"; and Bobby Timmons for the sideman work with Blakey and Adderley that produced his three big hits. Not so much for the Prestige albums. But CD reissues and streaming services keep everything in print, and those who listen to the work that Timmons produced for Prestige between 1964 and 1966—mostly in a trio setting (Wayne Shorter is added for *The Soul Man!*), working with different musicians on almost every session—will understand why his supporters call him the most underrated of jazz musicians. The music on all of these albums, even *Holiday Soul*, is soulful and catchy, but also richly musical and rewarding.

Chapter 25

Final Days

When Bob Weinstock ultimately sold Prestige to Fantasy Records in 1971, part of his stated reason for wanting to get out of the record business was the changing face of music: the jazz he had fallen in love with, that had made him want to start a record company in the first place, just didn't exist anymore. That may have been an exaggeration, but it wasn't much of an exaggeration, and it's easy to see why Weinstock felt that way. What's more, the slippery slope that led to Weinstock's departure was already taking shape by the midpoint of the 1960s.

Jazz held shifting sociocultural roles throughout the middle decades of the twentieth century. In the 1940s, when modern jazz was the outer edge of the avant-garde, the stereotype of the jazz fan was a shady outsider, the "hipster" who sported dark glasses, a beret, and a goatee, in imitation of Dizzy Gillespie. The hipster was seen as living in some kind of alternate reality, like the unfathomable music he listened to. A hipster joke—and there were many, like the Polish jokes of a different era—reflected this: A hipster is walking across the Sahara Desert wearing sunglasses, a beret, bathing trunks, and swim fins. A passerby shouts: "What are you doing? There's no ocean here." Hipster: "Yeah, but dig that crazy beach!" Or the hipster is seen as somehow privy to a level of enlightenment, next to which the rest of the world was square, most famously in the joke where the square approaches the hipster in midtown Manhattan and asks, "How do I get to Carnegie Hall?" Hipster: "Practice, man, practice." Or this one. Square: "Crosstown buses run all night?" Hipster: "Doo-dah, doo-dah."

In the 1950s, jazz didn't change that much. There were new developments, many of them deriving from Miles Davis's 1949 *Birth of the Cool* nonet, Gerry Mulligan's West Coast cool jazz, and John Lewis's chamber jazz, among them. Still, much of what was played in the decade was a natural extension of the revolutionary new ideas that had been brought to jazz in the 1940s.

But the image of the typical jazz fan changed quite a lot.

Television was partly responsible. *Stars of Jazz*, hosted by Bobby Troup on KABC in Los Angeles, was syndicated nationally. Steve Allen featured jazz musicians on his popular entertainment and late-night talk shows. The male musicians, both Black and white, dressed conservatively in suits or sport jackets and ties for these appearances—no berets or Cab Calloway–style zoot suits. The female performers wore evening gowns. And for many, the face of jazz on TV was Cary Grant look-alike Craig Stevens who played immaculately dressed private eye Peter Gunn, habitué of an upscale Bohemian jazz club, equally at home with high society and the outcasts of society. So who was the typical 1950s jazz fan? Well, when Miles Davis was harassed, beaten, and arrested by cops outside of Birdland, the person who intervened and tried to help him was his good friend and fervent fan, the Broadway columnist and radio/TV personality Dorothy Kilgallen.

But perhaps the biggest game changer in the perception of jazz in the 1950s was *Playboy* magazine. Started in 1952 by Hugh Hefner, it rapidly became a tastemaker for a generation. The *Playboy* man was the new archetype of sophistication, in the know about hand-tooled Italian shoes and Bill Blass suits, AR stereo speakers, Ferraris and bachelor pads . . . and jazz. Jazz was a part of what that sophisticate-to-be aspired to. *Playboy* began its jazz poll in 1957, and since their circulation was over a million and *Down Beat*'s was around eighty thousand, it became, at least by the numbers, the most influential poll. The poll drew over sixteen thousand votes, about five times the number who voted in *Down Beat*'s poll. *Playboy* did not make a distinction between living and dead musicians, so Charlie Parker won the alto sax category, and Duke Ellington bassist Jimmy Blanton, who had died in 1942, finished third in his category, but otherwise the results were not markedly different from *Down Beat*'s results. *Playboy Jazz All-Stars Vol. 1*, released on the Playboy label (which was founded specifically to release this album, and lasted only a couple of years), made an impact on the *Billboard* charts, and was probably the first jazz purchase made by a lot of young men of the era. The Playboy Jazz Festival, launched in Chicago in 1959 (and still going, now in Los Angeles) drew seventy thousand people in its inaugural year, compared with about thirteen thousand at the Newport Jazz Festival.

Things would change again in the 1960s. The new decade brought the election of John F. Kennedy, in the eyes of many the apotheosis of the *Playboy* image: young, stylish, modern, socially progressive. JFK wasn't into jazz, but if he had been, he would have been at home with the jazz that was being made during his presidency. It was still Bob Weinstock's kind of music. The free jazz revolution started by Ornette Coleman may have been a little jarring, but Weinstock had entered the jazz world after the epiphany of Thelonious Monk and Charlie Parker; the idea of the rule-bending avant-garde was very much in his wheelhouse. And soul jazz combined the hard bop he had championed with the rhythm and blues he had always liked.

The era that people look back on as the '60s really began somewhere in the middle of the decade and went through the end of the Vietnam War in 1975. The 1963 assassination of President Kennedy was a jolt, but the musically and cultural game changer came the following summer, when the Beatles arrived in America. After that, change was accelerated. In 1965, the Playboy Jazz Poll became the Playboy Jazz and Pop poll. Paul McCartney, not Paul Chambers, was the reigning poll winner on bass, and there were no more *Playboy Jazz All-Stars* recordings. In 1967, *Rolling Stone* magazine debuted, with former *Down Beat* editor Ralph J. Gleason as one of its founding editors.

There's an episode of the early twenty-first-century TV show *Mad Men* set in the mid-1960s. Main character Don Draper, Korean war veteran and hotshot advertising agency executive, is relaxing in his stylish Manhattan bachelor apartment. Still dressed in his designer suit, he puts a record on the turntable of his state-of-the-art stereo system, and sheds his designer jacket. In his Kennedy-image shirtsleeves, he sits in his recliner, kicks off his hand-stitched Italian shoes, sips his single-malt Scotch, and listens to . . . the Beatles' new record, *Revolver*, and "Tomorrow Never Knows." Draper tries to like it, but it's a losing battle. The camera cuts to Peggy Olsen, Draper's young assistant, smoking a joint as she works late in the office. She, the cut suggests, is the target audience for *Revolver*. Draper takes the record off, but he can't stop the cultural tidal shift. It is a perfect tableau of the twilight of the *Playboy* man.

The suave '50s jazz fan, the Peter Gunn–Don Draper sophisticate, became an anachronism. The jazz-appreciating, rock and roll disdaining musical trendsetter is a forgotten image as rock becomes the new cultural touchstone, and *Rolling Stone,* with its Greil Marcuses and Hunter S. Thompsons, becomes its chronicler.

If this meant a marked change for Prestige, it wasn't immediately apparent, and it wasn't abrupt. The label's early releases in 1966 were familiar acts: Johnny "Hammond" Smith, Jaki Byard, Bobby Timmons, and Brother Jack Mcduff. Their first significant new artist of the year was a blind sixteen-year-old alto saxophonist, Eric Kloss. Kloss fit in with Prestige's sound of the 1960s—hard bop, soul jazz—but later on he would wholeheartedly embrace the jazz fusion sound. The organ-saxophone sound was showing a bit of wear by this time, but there was still a demand for it, and Kloss was matched with Don Patterson and with another organist who had already developed a strong reputation but was making his Prestige debut, Richard "Groove" Holmes.

Much of the new product from Prestige was handled by Cal Lampley, a onetime piano prodigy and Juilliard graduate who had performed at Carnegie Hall. Lampley had been producing for Columbia, and had come to Prestige in 1963, taking over as head of production when Ozzie Cadena left to start his own label in 1964. Although Lampley's most significant credit to that point had been producing Miles Davis's *Porgy and Bess* for Columbia, he was given the responsibility of developing the new soul jazz line and developing acts that would have a broader market appeal, while Don Schlitten handled the jazz purist stuff.

Lampley found rousing success in his mandate to give the label more of a pop sensibility when he brought Holmes a new arrangement of a much-loved standard, Errol Garner's "Misty," which had been a hit for Garner and, with lyrics added, for Johnny Mathis. Holmes and Lampley put a six-minute version of the tune on his debut album, *Soul Message*, and a pared-down version, at 1:48, was released as a 45 rpm single. The single version, with its new danceable tempo and soulful organ, caught on. It became the biggest selling record in Prestige's history, and helped to focus the attention of the music world on the possibility that there was money to be made in giving a pop spin to jazz. "Misty," of course, was a jazz tune, but the gates were opening. Grant Green's recording of John Lennon and Paul McCartney's "I Want to Hold Your Hand" became the title cut of his 1966 Blue Note album, and as the decade went on, the Beatles would find their way into more and more jazz sessions, with Prestige alumnus George Benson taking on an entire Beatles album in 1970's *The Other Side of Abbey Road*, on A&M.

Another artist debuting in 1966 was Houston Person, whose brand of audience-pleasing soul jazz would make him one of the most popular jazz artists of the next two decades, both at the helm of his own groups and with vocalist Etta Jones. Person's career is not unlike that of Jonah Jones of the previous decade: a good player, but more popular with the nonjazz or casual jazz audience than the hard core.

The year 1966 was a kind of zenith for soul jazz, as Cannonball Adderley's *Mercy, Mercy, Mercy! Live at "The Club"* became a huge best seller for Capitol, and remains among the top twenty best-selling jazz albums of all time. It was a breakthrough year for Herbie Hancock and Wayne Shorter, who were starting to experiment with new sounds that would place them in the forefront of the jazz fusion movement. They were both still part of the Miles Davis Second Quintet but were also releasing albums under their own names. It was something of a marking time year for Prestige. They had their biggest hit in Holmes's "Misty," but their new artists, Kloss, Holmes, and Person, while all would go on to have successful jazz careers, are not the people jazz historians look back on as significant names in the development of jazz.

The year 1967 marked Pat Martino's long overdue debut as a leader. He had been a sideman to Willis Jackson, Don Patterson, and Brother Jack McDuff. When Prestige introduced sixteen-year-old Eric Kloss, Martino was in his group, and when they introduced Trudy Pitts, the last of their stable of soul jazz organists, Martino was her guitarist. Pitts was a solid talent, but she came a little late to the game, and never quite made the impact that she might have. Pitts was part of the ensemble when Martino finally got his shot as front man. Between 1967 and 1970 he was one of Prestige's most active players, with five albums under his own name, and adding his guitar to albums by Kloss, McDuff, Patterson, Holmes, and also Charles McPherson and Sonny Stitt. Martino continued to be among the top jazz guitarists until 1980, when brain surgery left him an amnesiac, with no memory at all of ever having been able to play the guitar. He set out to learn all over again, and by the turn of the century he was once acclaimed as one of the great jazz guitarists. He continued to play until a couple of years before his death in 2021.

The year 1968 saw even more retrenching. Albums by Prestige regulars were released, including Martino, Sonny Criss, Charles McPherson, Johnny "Hammond" Smith, Richard "Groove" Holmes, Houston Person, and Eric Kloss. A Willis Jackson session saw him reunited with Bill Jennings (now Wild Bill Jennings), with the organ part originally taken in the early years by Jack McDuff now given to Trudy Pitts, whose youthful enthusiasm is welcome.

Jaki Byard released a new album, and Byard was never one to repeat himself. This one was called *Jaki Byard with Strings!* and it was not your father's string section: Ray Nance, violin; George Benson, guitar; Ron Carter, cello; and Richard Davis; bass. Alan Dawson doubles on drums and vibes, and Byard plays organ as well as piano.

Harold Mabern, who had begun making a reputation as one of the important new pianists of the decade, described by critic Gary Giddins as a combination of McCoy Tyner and Art Tatum, had been playing and recording with Art Farmer, Jimmy Heath, Lee Morgan, Wes Montgomery, and others. He had his first leader date with Prestige in 1968, and would make three more albums with the label between 1968 and 1970.

Weinstock, never forgetful of his roots, still reached out to older musicians. Illinois Jacquet was tabbed for a session, produced by Don Schlitten, that a few years earlier would have been issued on Swingville. A February 1968, session in Germany by longtime expatriate Don Byas with the Spanish pianist Tete Montoliu and visiting Americans Ben Webster and Tootie

Heath was licensed from its original German label and released by Prestige in 1969. This was just the first of a series of German sessions featuring veteran American jazz stars. In April, Oscar Peterson, working solo and with a trio, recorded three different sessions that were imported by Prestige. In May and again in August, it was another longtime expatriate, Kenny Clarke, whose Clarke–Francy Boland big band had delighted European audiences for decades. June saw a session led by Lee Konitz, Phil Woods, and Pony Poindexter. Teddy Wilson was never an expat, but he toured and performed in Europe extensively, and a December session in Denmark became the last of the year's European imports.

If one looks over lists made by twenty-first-century listmakers of the top jazz albums of those years, what one doesn't find are any records issued by Prestige. In fact, there are next to no albums by any independent label. Blue Note records are there in abundance, but Blue Note, in 1966, had been purchased by Liberty Records, which in 1971 became part of United Artists Records; Pacific Jazz had gone the same route. Atlantic had been acquired by Warner Brothers in 1967. Impulse! was a part of ABC–Paramount. Other independent jazz labels had folded. Riverside, the most important of them, had gone under in 1964.

Prestige's releases of 1969 were dominated by artists who, even if they were still young, seemed to be a part of jazz's ancient history: Sonny Criss, James Moody, Dexter Gordon, Illinois Jacquet, Billy Taylor, Ben Webster, Eddie Jefferson, Tal Farlow, and Barry Harris. This is a Hall of Fame to the serious jazz fan, but not a serious money-making lineup in 1969, a year that was, in any event, more notable for *Abbey Road, Nashville Skyline,* and *Tommy.*

The end of the year, however, was marked by a significant renascence and a hot newcomer. Gene Ammons was released from prison after seven years and took up where he left off. His brand of soul jazz proved to be as popular as ever. And as it turned out, even in 1969 there was room for one more organ god. Charles Earland had gained notice as part of Lou Donaldson's group on Blue Note. When he went out on his own, Blue Note failed to snatch him up, and their loss was Prestige's gain.

As the decade wound down, Prestige was the last independent jazz label in large part because no one wanted to purchase their catalog. The sales success of Holmes, Ammons, and Earland changed that. The West Coast–based Fantasy Records made a serious offer, and Bob Weinstock was ready to listen. There was no longer a climate in which an independent jazz label could thrive. And Weinstock, as he was to recall in later years, was less and less interested in the new kinds of jazz which had supplanted the jazz he fell in love with as a nineteen-year-old. Bob Porter, who had taken over as head of production from Cal Lampley in 1968, gave this account of the end days in his important book *Soul Jazz: Jazz in the Black Community, 1945–1975*:

> With the hits of Gene Ammons, Charles Earland, and others, Prestige became a prime takeover target. Bob Weinstock had seen his distributors shrink from more than twenty to less than half of that. Despite the hits the label was producing, getting paid by those distributors was becoming increasingly difficult. The era of great independent distributers was almost over. There was massive consolidation under way; and the compressing of territories made regional, rather than local, distribution more the norm. Weinstock negotiated a deal with Fantasy Records of Berkeley California and made arrangements to sell the label for a reported 3.2 million dollars. All of a sudden, the AFM threatened to kill the deal until an audit was done regarding back pension and welfare payments. Rather than call a lawyer to handle the dispute, Weinstock called his old friend and former partner Morris Levy. The problem promptly disappeared, and the sale was completed in May 1971.

Epilogue

The years 1949 to 1971 encompass the best years of some of the most important artists in the history of "America's classical music." And if it were not for the work of the independent labels—Prestige and Blue Note, Riverside and Atlantic, Pacific Jazz, Savoy and Bethlehem and Argo/Cadet and Verve and Contemporary and Debut—this great contribution to America's cultural heritage would have gone unrecorded, lost to posterity. Unlike the classical music of previous eras, the improvisations that define jazz can't be preserved as sheet music.

After Prestige was sold to Fantasy, although there were still some new recordings—particularly by Gene Ammons, who had always called the label his home—it became primarily a reissue label. In 1983, as the compact disc was being introduced to the general public, Fantasy started a subsidiary label, Original Jazz Classics, to repackage and rerelease the catalogs of Prestige, Riverside, Contemporary, and other smaller jazz labels they had acquired. In the early years, Original Jazz Classics were also released on vinyl, but the CD revolution brought them to a new generation. In 2004, Fantasy was acquired by a larger conglomerate, Concord Music Group, which continued to develop the OJC line. In 2009, Concord celebrated the sixtieth anniversary of the formation of Prestige with a memorial two-CD "Best of" package.

Bob Weinstock died January 14, 2006, at the age of seventy-seven. His obituary in the *New York Times*, written by Ben Ratliff, describes him with what can only described as qualified praise. It begins by reminding *Times* readers that his records "weren't known for perfection," going on to say that "Mr. Weinstock generally set up recording sessions with no rehearsal time." In an era known for what some would call a soulless insistence on perfection, with autotune as its apotheosis, this sets Weinstock apart, in a way that not all would call negative.

Ratliff goes on to credit Weinstock's contribution to American music: "But Mr. Weinstock did a remarkable job of flooding the market with the work of many of the greatest small-group jazz bandleaders during an exceptionally fertile time for jazz in New York." I'm not sure that "flooding the market" is exactly the language I would use. I have spent the last several years listening to every Prestige session, in chronological order, and writing about the experience in a blog. I consider myself immeasurably enriched by the experience.

Acknowledgments

I am so grateful for the jazz knowledge and editorial skills of Morris Holbrook, who read every chapter, corrected errors, and provided invaluable insights. And I am indebted in everything I ever write to the keen editorial guidance of my brother, Jonathan Richards. I've relied for encouragement, shared love of jazz, and useful insights on Peter Jones, Larry (the Fluff) Audette, and Michael Kaufman. Jim Eigo, jazz publicist extraordinaire, has opened doors for me.

So much research, and so much networking, comes through the internet these days. People I've met through Facebook who have been invaluable: Stephen Cerra, whose painstakingly researched books on jazz musicians and schools of jazz have information you won't find anywhere else; Mark Stryker, chronicler of the rich fountain of jazz from his hometown in Detroit; Dan Gould, who shared with me his hitherto unpublished (and untranscribed) 2004 interview with Bob Weinstock. I have relied frequently on the hive mind on the jazz forums of Organissimo.com. Someone there always had answers I needed. I reached out to Pete Levin, a jazz musician who knows so much more than I do.

And I can't thank Richard Carlin of SUNY Press enough for his openness to my unorthodox approach to jazz history, and his editorial guidance. I can't imagine a better editor.

Thanks to Bill Fallows for constructing the studio/office that is my work retreat.

Thanks to my wife, Pat Richards, for more than I can possibly express.

Works Cited

When you finally sit down to write a book about a subject that you've been interested in for all of your life, a lot of what goes into it is stuff you just know, from books read long ago, or stuff you picked up listening to an interview on TV or radio years ago, or stuff told to you sometime or other by a musician or another journalist or a music industry professional. Any bibliography is going to be incomplete. So thanks to all those distant sources who put facts and factoids and anecdotes into my magpie brain over decades. If it weren't for you there'd be no book. Heck, if it weren't for you there'd be no me.

Sources Accessed Constantly

Discogs.com, for liner notes to many albums.
Down Beat, many issues from 1949 to 1971 for record reviews, annual readers' polls. Individual *Down Beat* articles listed separately.
Jazzdisco.com/prestige-records, for session logs.
Lordisco.com, Tom Lord's online discography, for session logs.

Other Sources

Bernal, Leonardo Camacho. "Miles Davis: The Road to Modal Jazz." Master's thesis, University of North Texas, 2007.
Bjorn, Lars, and Jim Gallert. *Before Motown: A History of Jazz in Detroit*. University of Michigan Press, 2001.
Brody, Richard. Walt Dickerson obituary. https://www.newyorker.com/culture/goings-on/in-memoriam-walt-dickerson, 2008.
"Cal Lampley." All About Jazz. https://www.allaboutjazz.com/musicians/cal-lampley/.
Carr, Ian. *Miles Davis: The Definitive Biography*. Da Capo, 2009.

Cerra, Steven. *A Gerry Mulligan Reader: Writings on a Jazz Original.* Independently published, 2023.

Cerulli, Dom. "Bob Weinstock: A Man with Prestige." *Down Beat,* June 13, 1957.

Coady, Christopher William. "Afro-modernist Compositional Strategies in Selected Works by John Lewis: 1952–1962." Master's thesis, University of New South Wales, 2011.

Cohen, Noal, and Michael Fitzgerald. *Rat Race Blues: The Musical Life of Gigi Gryce.* Current Research in Jazz, 2014.

Courtwright, David, "When Gotham Was Heroin's Capital." 2023. https://www.vitalcitynyc.org/articles/history-of-opioids-in-new-york-city.

Davis, Miles, and Quincy Troupe. *Miles: The Autobiography.* Reissue edition. Simon and Schuster, 2011.

Delaware Public Media. "History Matters: 'Bop Cop' Lem Winchester." https://www.delawarepublic.org/culture-lifestyle-sports/2017-06-23/history-matters-bop-cop-lem-winchester.

Delehant, Jim. "Country Sophisticate," interview with Mose Allison. *Down Beat,* October 17, 1958.

de Lerma, Dominique-René. *Reflections on Afro-American Music.* Kent State University Press, 1970. Excerpted at https://cannonball-adderley.com/article/lerma.htm.

DeMichael, Dom. "John Coltrane and Eric Dolphy Answer the Jazz Critics." *Down Beat,* April 12, 1962.

Edwards, Esmond. Interviewed in The Music Aficionado blog. https://musicaficionado.blog/2020/03/02/the-artistry-of-esmond-edwards/.

Gans, Geoff, ed. Introduction by Ira Gitler. *Prestige Records: The Album Cover Collection.* City Hall Records, 2009.

Goldberg, Joe. *Jazz Masters of the 50s.* Da Capo, 1965.

Gould, Dan. Taped interviews with Bob Weinstock. 2004.

Hentoff, Nat. "I'm in Jazz Because I Like Freedom." Interview with Phil Woods. *Down Beat,* January 23, 1957.

Hentoff, Nat. Interview with John Lewis. *Down Beat,* December 30, 1953.

Hentoff, Nat. Interview with Sonny Rollins. *Down Beat,* November 28, 1965.

Horne, Gerald. *Jazz and Justice: Racism and the Political Economy of the Music.* New York University Press, 2019.

"In Memoriam: Walt Dickerson." Culture Desk, *New Yorker,* August 12, 2008.

Jarrett, Michael. Interview with Bob Weinstock. University of North Carolina Digital Repository, 1995. https://dcr.lib.unc.edu/.

Jarrett, Michael. *Pressed for All Time: Producing the Great Jazz Albums.* University of North Carolina Press, 2016.

Kelley, Robin D. G. *Thelonious Monk: The Life and Times of an American Original.* Aurum Press, 2013.

Lateef, Yusef. *The Gentle Giant.* Morton Books, 2005.

Levy, Aidan. *Saxophone Colossus: The Life and Music of Sonny Rollins.* Da Capo, 2022.

McNamara, Joseph D. "The War the Police Didn't Declare and Can't Win," https://www.cato.org/sites/cato.org/files/pictures/drugwarevent/mcnamara.html.

Mueller, Darren. *At the Vanguard of Vinyl: A Cultural History of the Long-Playing Record in Jazz*. Duke University Press, 2024.

Myers, Marc. Rudy Van Gelder interview. *Jazz Wax*. https://www.jazzwax.com/2012/02/interview-rudy-van-gelder-part-1.html and https://www.jazzwax.com/2012/02/interview-rudy-van-gelder-part-2.html.

Neumann, Jim. Interview with John Lewis. https://youtu.be/kl2K4PsSIgk?si=4P2fL6nM7ahLFuhw.

Persip, Charli. Interview (discusses watching the Miles Davis and Thelonious Monk recording session), 2011. https://www.youtube.com/watch?v=cpRiQuFzjPE.

Placksin, Sally. *American Women in Jazz, 1900–Present*. Penguin, 1955. Quoted in https://www.vinylmeplease.com/blogs/magazine/dorothy-ashby-liner-notes.

Porter, Bob. *Soul Jazz. Jazz in the Black Community, 1945–1975*. XLIBRIS, 2016.

Porter, Lewis. *John Coltrane: His Life and Music*. University of Michigan Press, 2000.

Ramsay, Guthrie P. *Race Music: Black Cultures from Bebop to Hip-Hop*. University of California Press, 2004.

Rogovoy, Seth. "Mose Allison's Idiosyncratic Blues." https://rogovoyreport.com/2016/11/15/mose-allison-seth-rogovoy-interview-2001/.

Rollins, Sonny. Library of Congress interview, 2018.

Rozzi, James. Interview with Bob Weinstock. https://creativeloafing.com/content-164123-prestige-ous-man-again.

Scheiber, Andrew. "Locating Mose Allison within the Blues Tradition." https://arkreview.org/wp-content/uploads/2017/04/46.1-Apr-2015-Scheiber-Mose-Allison.pdf.

Shteamer, Hank. Walt Dickerson interview, 2007. http://darkforcesswing.blogspot.com/2007/06/in-full-1-walt-dickerson.html.

Simosko, Vladimir. *Eric Dolphy: A Musical Biography and Discography*. Da Capo, 1996.

Smith, Mike. *In with the In Crowd: Popular Jazz in 1960s Black America (American Made Music Series)*. University Press of Mississippi, 2024.

Spicer, Daniel. "The Strange World of Ahmed Abdul-Malik." https://thequietus.com/interviews/strange-world-of/ahmed-abdul-malik/.

Stephenson, Sam. "What Happened to Ronnie Free?" http://www.peckmanjazz.com/bios/FREE.HTM.

Stryker, Mark. *Jazz from Detroit*. University of Michigan Press, 2019.

Taylor, Arthur. *Notes and Tones: Musician to Musician Interviews*. Da Capo, 1993.

Tomkins, Les. Interviews with George Benson. National Jazz Archives, 1974–78. https://nationaljazzarchive.org.uk/explore/interviews/1622801-george-benson-interview-1?.

Wilson, Rod. "Rudy Van Gelder: A Signature Sound." *Rod Wilson's Blog*, 2019. https://www.rodneywilson.ca/2019/02/24/rudy-van-gelder-a-signature-sound/.

Wright, Bruce. *Black Justice in a White World*. Barricade Books, 1996.

Zorach, Rebecca. Interview with John Wright. Never the Same. August 2011.

Index

Abdul-Malik, Ahmed, 225
Abdurrahman, Bilal, 226–229

Adams, Pepper, 31, 148, 156, 237
Adderley, Cannonball, 43, 48, 71, 107, 120, 134, 138, 201, 212, 237, 240, 245
Adderley, Nat, 189, 212, 237
"Airegin," 95, 110
Aladdin Records, 4, 5
Albertson, Chris, 186, 187, 188
Aless, Tony, 15, 27
All Day Long, 130, 133
Allen, Ernestine, 189
Allison, Mose, 157–171
Amalbert, Juan, 189, 206, 230
Ammons, Gene, 5, 21–24, 30, 31, 38, 46, 80, 87, 92, 113, 129, 130, 134, 136, 176, 186, 222, 236, 247–249; heroin addiction, 80; post-prison comeback, 247–249
Anderson, Clarence, 24, 25
Anderson, Speed, 152
Anti-jazz, 205–208
Apollo Records, 4
Apollo Theater, 82, 173, 197
Argo Records, 81, 165, 167, 168, 169, 230, 249
Aristocrat Records, 4, 21

Armstrong, Louis, 42, 93, 116, 152, 162, 183
Ashby, Dorothy, 136, 137, 138, 139, 222
Atlantic Records, x, 4, 5, 12, 31, 72–74, 90, 91, 154, 155, 163, 164, 170, 173, 177, 182, 184, 199, 208, 239, 247, 249
Avakian, George, 106, 108, 110, 114–118, 147
Ayler, Albert, 155, 205, 207, 220

Back Country Suite, 158, 160–165
Baker, Chet, 172, 199, 237, 42
Baker, Eddie, 215
Barnet, Charlie, 10, 94
Barreto, Ray, 113, 135, 146, 233
Basie, Count, 7, 23, 35, 42, 45, 59, 80, 83, 146, 173, 178, 221, 222, 227
Bauer, Billy, 9, 10, 26, 30, 33, 45
Beatles, The, 146, 243, 244
Bebop, 1, 4, 6, 7, 8, 11, 13, 15, 20, 22, 23, 25, 29, 31, 32, 34, 36, 38, 40, 42, 43, 45, 46, 47, 51, 61, 63, 66, 67, 70, 72, 83, 91, 94, 98, 103, 104, 120, 128, 129, 132, 136, 148, 157; transformation to hard bop, 29
Beiderbecke, Bix, 76, 93

"Bemsha Swing," 51, 52, 62, 64
Benjamin, Joe, 230, 231
Bennings, John, 86, 185
Benson, George, 23, 180, 182, 212, 244, 246
Berry, Chuck, 163, 236
Best, Denzil, 13, 35, 52
Bethlehem Records, 76, 123, 133, 218, 249
Billboard, 37, 38, 155, 163, 242
Birdland, 29, 43, 67, 103, 242
Bishop Jr., Walter, 14, 28, 47, 82, 88, 203, 210
Blakey, Art, 23, 24, 28, 39, 43, 44, 47, 51, 59, 60, 70, 72, 82, 86, 91, 94, 95, 99, 102, 129, 136, 226, 237, 240
Blue Bird Inn, 35, 53
Blue Train, 149, 150
Bluesville Records, 184, 185, 186, 187, 188, 189, 221, 223, 235
Bluing, 29, 47
Bohemia After Dark, 77, 107, 108, 137, 139, 151, 152, 237, 242
Boland, Francy, 73, 247
Bradford, Clea, 189
Bradford, Perry, 3
Brookmeyer, Bob, 15, 31
Brown Jr., Oscar, 164
Brown, Clifford, 42, 93, 97–99, 101, 127, 128, 172, 200, 215
Brown, Ray, 67, 68
Brown, Roy, 152
Brown, Ruth, 173, 184
Brubeck, Dave, 6, 41, 43, 67, 70, 71, 91, 106, 117, 118, 199
Bryant, Ray, 98, 101, 127
Burrell, Kenny, 15, 113, 120, 129, 130, 131, 133, 134, 135, 148, 188, 234, 235, 237
Byard, Jaki, 201, 212–214, 219, 231, 233, 244, 246

Byas, Don, 10, 87, 226, 246
Byrd, Donald, 31, 113, 120, 125, 129, 130, 133, 136, 146, 154, 156, 158

Cabineers, The, 86, 113, 185
Cadena, Ozzie, 166, 176, 212, 214, 239, 240, 244
Cadet Records, 21, 138, 194, 249
Candid Records, 215, 218
Capitol Records, ix, 8, 11, 27, 30, 40, 41, 47, 48, 66, 83, 105, 187, 245
Carlin, Richard, x, 126
Carnegie Hall, 140, 241, 244
Carney, Harry, 13, 43, 201
Carroll, Barbara, 13
Carter, Benny, 42, 227
Carter, Betty, 38
Carter, Ron, 43, 205, 206, 207, 212, 214, 246
Casey, Al, 184, 188
Central Avenue, 4, 114, 199, 200
Cerulli, Dom, 8, 121, 143, 153, 160
Chaloff, Serge, 13
Chambers, Paul, 43, 99, 107, 108, 109, 131, 134, 144, 145–150, 154, 155, 218, 243
Charles, Ezzard, 37
Charles, Ray, 4
Charles, Teddy, 36, 50, 75, 106, 113, 119, 123, 131, 143, 153
Charters, Samuel, 187
Checker, Chubby, 232, 240
Chess Records, 4, 21, 78, 81, 138, 163, 164, 184
Clarke, Kenny, 6, 7, 10, 17, 31, 38, 53, 61–63, 67, 70, 72, 73, 90, 93–95, 99, 103, 124, 128, 233, 247; bebop rhythm innovations, 6, 8, 13, 15; leaves Modern Jazz Quartet, 46; Clarke–Boland band and European sessions, 246
Clayton, Buck, 117, 184, 235

Cleveland, Jimmy, 128
Clovers, The, 31, 73
Cobb, Arnett, 146, 173, 176, 237
Cobb, Jimmy, 134, 135, 155
Coggins, Gil, 82, 156
Cohn, Al, 13, 14, 47, 48, 94, 113, 157, 158, 164
Cole, Nat "King," 30, 83, 157, 162
Coleman, Earl, 113, 124, 125, 129, 162
Coleman, George, 195
Coleman, Ornette, 5, 155, 183, 199, 202, 203, 205, 207, 208, 209, 211, 215, 220, 243
Coltrane, John, x, 4, 30, 31, 43, 64, 78, 81, 95, 98–100, 107–110, 113, 119, 130, 131, 134, 135, 143–156, 160, 172, 177, 183, 188, 192, 199, 201, 205–211, 215, 217, 219, 222, 224–226; First Quintet, 43, 98, 108; "Tenor Madness," 99; "Sheets of Sound," 147; with Monk, 148; signs with Prestige, 148; Richards discovers jazz, 152; moves to Atlantic, 154; great innovators of free jazz, 205; with Dolphy, answers critics, 208
Columbia Records, x, 3, 19, 64, 65, 71, 76, 81, 89, 106, 108, 110, 111, 112, 114, 116, 117, 118, 123, 143, 144, 163, 164, 184, 199, 210, 244; sign Miles Davis, 106; 'Round about Midnight reviewed, 110
"Conception," 28
Concord Music Group, 249
Concorde, 72, 73, 74, 112
Contractual Marathon, 109–113, 144, 148
Cookin', 110, 144, 148, 176
Copeland, Ray, 53, 59, 60
Coral Records, 123, 157, 222
Corea, Chick, 13, 53

Cranshaw, Bob, 125, 213, 214
Crawford, Hank, 229
Criss, Sonny, 35, 138, 246, 247
Culley, Frank "Floorshow," 73
Cyrille, Andrew, 224, 225, 227

Dameron, Tadd, 83, 113
Davis, Eddie "Lockjaw," 79, 80, 194, 207, 211, 220
Davis, Miles, 2, 4, 8, 27, 29, 30–33, 35, 39, 40–49, 52, 53, 58, 61–68, 71, 77, 82–85, 88, 89, 93, 94, 95, 98, 99, 102, 104, 105, 106, 107, 108, 109, 110, 111, 112, 113, 115, 116, 118, 119, 127, 129, 134, 136, 143, 144, 146, 147, 148, 172, 177, 178, 179, 186, 187, 188, 199, 210, 226, 230, 238, 241, 242, 244, 245, 253; nonet, 8; rejection of nonet sessions, 40; signs with Prestige, 41; kicks heroin, 48; records with Monk, 61–63; *Walkin'*, 103–104; signs with Columbia, 106
Davis, Richard, 219, 231, 246
Davis, Wild Bill, 191
Dawson, Alan, 219, 231, 246
Dearie, Blossom, 15
Debussy, Claude, 32, 67
Dial Records, 5, 35, 41
Dickerson, Walt, 224, 225, 228, 253
"Dig," 29
Dixon, Eric, 132, 227
Dixon, Willie, 163, 164, 186, 236
Django, 68, 69, 71
Dolphy, Eric, 77, 81, 183, 196, 199–219, 225, 230
Donaldson, Lou, 94, 127, 247
Dorham, Kenny, 17, 66, 84, 95, 101, 215, 237
Dorn, Joel, 238, 239
"Doxy," 95
Drew, Kenny, 82, 86, 91, 101, 149

Dukes, Joe, 180, 181
Duvivier, George, 79, 179, 210, 211

Eager, Allen, 14, 115
Eardley, Jon, 113, 120, 122
Earland, Charles, 172, 191, 195, 247, 248
Eastern Sounds, 169, 170
Eckstine, Billy, 21, 35, 227
Eddie "Lockjaw" Davis Cookbook, The, 79, 179
Edgehill, Arthur, 79, 131, 179
Edwards, Esmond, 75, 77, 78, 79, 80, 81, 113, 116, 124, 169, 173, 176, 179, 186, 200, 201, 206, 212, 214, 215, 223, 227; head of production, 78
Edwards, Teddy, 235
Eldridge, Roy, 93
Ellington, Duke, 5, 10, 13, 42, 45, 52, 71, 82, 98, 117, 132, 163, 175, 196, 197, 211, 222, 242, 243
Elliot, Jack, 189
Ellis, Don, 212
Ertegun, Ahmet, 5, 73, 184
Ertegun, Nesuhi, 12, 74, 239
Ervin, Booker, 194, 195, 212, 213, 214, 217–220, 234
Euell, Julian, 131, 132, 148, 187
Evans, Belton, 187
Evans, Bill, 199, 211, 238
Evans, Gil, 27, 32, 33, 40, 66

Farmer, Addison, 200
Farmer, Art, 31, 35, 36, 39, 43, 50, 78, 93, 94, 95, 113, 124, 125, 127–130, 132, 143, 172, 200, 237, 246
Farrell, Joe, 212
Farrow, Ernie, 167, 169
Feather, Leonard, 96, 180, 196, 204
Ferguson, Charlie, 38
Ferguson, H-Bomb, 53, 86, 113, 185

Ferguson, Maynard, 42, 172, 212, 237
Fields, Ernie, 218
52nd Street, 7, 13, 40, 43, 53, 66, 68, 82, 143, 172
Fishkind, Arnold, 10
Fitzgerald, Ella, 71, 197, 199
"Five O'Clock Blues," 114, 116, 156
Five Spot, 51, 148, 202, 207, 215, 216, 218, 225, 226
Flanagan, Tommy, 101, 109, 130, 133, 134, 135, 184, 222, 233
Folkways Records, 142, 184
Forrest, Jimmy, 45, 46, 136, 189, 211
Foster, Frank, 55, 59, 130, 133
"Four Brothers," 13
Freeman, Bud, 184
Free Jazz, 11, 183, 196, 199, 202, 204–206, 208, 209, 217, 220, 243
Freed, Alan, 140, 141, 151
Fuller, Curtis, 129, 146, 149, 191, 237
Fuller, Jesse "Lone Cat," 189

Gaillard, Slim, 230
Galbraith, Barry, 134
Garland, Red, 43, 99, 105, 107, 108, 110, 113, 134, 144–156, 184, 188, 231, 233, 234
Garner, Errol, 51, 81, 146, 193, 244
Gaskin, Leonard, 66, 84, 187
Gershwin, George, 69, 72, 203, 229
Getz, Stan, 13–16, 19, 20, 26, 27, 41–43, 77, 96, 99, 101, 113, 119, 124, 131, 144, 158, 164
Gibbs, Terry, 13–15
Gillespie, Dizzy, 8, 11, 15, 32, 42, 43, 47, 58, 66, 67, 68, 69, 93, 118, 134, 165, 172, 183, 198, 227, 241
Gitler, Ira, 28, 52, 54, 62, 64, 86–89, 93, 96, 100, 109, 113, 147, 153, 154, 160, 217
Giuffre, Jimmy, 13
Gleason, Jackie, 169, 187

Gleason, Ralph J., 74, 110, 243
Goldberg, Joe, 7, 72, 87, 91, 95, 98, 99, 104, 149, 162, 164, 211
Golson, Benny, 94, 127, 128, 129, 196, 236, 237
Gonzalez, Babs, 83
Goodman, Benny, 8, 10, 30, 31, 34, 35, 43, 141, 153, 172
Gordon, Dexter, 16, 35, 67, 83, 109, 147, 205, 247
Granz, Norman, 5, 119
Gray, Wardell, 17, 34, 35, 36, 37, 39, 67, 93, 113, 128
Green, Bennie, 23, 29, 44, 45, 47, 77, 113, 129, 147, 191, 227
Green, Grant, 180, 195, 244
Green, Urbie, 117
Greenlea, Eph, 21, 22
Griffin, Johnny, 237
Grimes, Tiny, 184
Gryce, Gigi, 50, 113, 124–129, 131, 196; starts own publishing company, 126

Haig, Al, 15, 35, 113, 164
Hakim, Sadik, 58
Hallberg, Bengt, 36, 113
Hamilton, Chico, 200, 202, 205
Hampton, Slide, 191, 193, 201
Hancock, Herbie, 13, 43, 92, 118, 245
Handy, John, 191
Hannan, Tom, 76
Hard Bop, 29, 47, 67, 104, 158, 172, 175, 176, 183, 217, 219, 243, 244
Harris, Barry, 113, 129, 169, 170, 232, 247
Harris, Joe, 58
Hawes, Hampton, 35, 113
Hawkins, Coleman, 5, 10, 17, 42, 81, 82, 99, 101, 114, 146, 148, 172, 177, 183, 184, 188, 226
Hawkins, Erskine, 3

Hayes, Louis, 131, 154
Haynes, Roy, 15, 29, 35, 44, 47, 82, 137, 139, 200, 210, 211, 214, 218
Heath, Albert "Tootie," 148, 247
Heath, Jimmy, 89, 246
Heath, Percy, 15, 29, 38, 39, 44, 47, 48, 53, 60, 61, 62, 67, 70, 72, 86, 88, 90, 92, 93, 95, 102, 106, 107, 124, 128
Hendricks, Jon, 38, 39, 53, 124
Hill, Andrew, 225
Hillyer, Lonnie, 41
Hodges, Johnny, 5
Holiday, Billie, 42, 132, 134, 171
Holiday, Joe, 86, 113
Holloway, Red, 180, 182, 236
Holmes, Richard "Groove," 172, 190, 191, 192, 193, 198, 244, 245, 246, 247
Hope, Elmo, 53, 95, 113, 129
Hopkins, Lightnin', 152, 186, 187
Hubbard, Freddie, 138, 155, 200, 205, 210, 211

Jackson, Armand "Jump," 223
Jackson, Chubby, 8, 15, 26, 27
Jackson, Milt, 5, 53, 61, 62, 67, 68, 70, 72, 74, 90, 91, 143, 159, 160, 211, 224, 225
Jackson, Oliver, 167
Jackson, Willis "Gator Tail," 173, 174, 176, 179, 182, 234, 246
Jaspar, Bobby, 131, 133, 148
Jazz Loft, 76, 77
Jazztet, The, 94, 128, 129
Jefferson, Blind Lemon, 3
Jefferson, Eddie, 37, 38, 58, 113, 247
Jenkins, John, 237
Jennings, Bill, 173, 174, 175, 176, 180, 187, 196, 216
Jennings, Richard ("Prophet"), 77
Johnson, Alvin, 174, 175, 176
Johnson, Buddy, 197

Johnson, Lonnie, 186
Johnson, J. J., 17, 20, 26, 46, 53, 66, 76, 77, 83, 84, 85, 103, 107, 113
Johnson, Robert, 3
Jones, Elvin, 106, 132, 170
Jones, Etta, 196, 197, 198, 202, 226, 234, 245
Jones, Hank, 127, 164
Jones, Jo, 21, 22, 23, 113
Jones, Philly Joe, 43, 88, 99, 105, 206, 107, 144, 146, 147, 149
Jones, Jonah, 233
Jones, Quincy, 38, 81, 128, 129
Jones, Sam, 203, 210, 237, 238, 239
Jones, Spike, 168, 229
Jones, Thad, 31, 131, 222
Jones, Willie, 53, 55, 92
Jordan, Clifford, 237
Jordan, Duke, 17, 21, 22, 113
Jordan, Louis, 30, 162
Jordan, Taft, 188

Kay, Connie, 70, 72, 73, 106
Keepnews, Orrin, 43, 65, 86, 148, 200
King, B. B., 174
King Records, 4, 134, 177, 230
King Curtis, 136, 184, 186, 189, 211, 239
King Pleasure, 34–39, 50, 58, 66, 113, 147
Kirk, Andy, 173
Kirk, Roland, 212, 229, 230, 231
Kloss, Eric, 194, 212, 219, 244, 245, 246
Konitz, Lee, 8, 10, 19, 26, 30, 31, 33, 36, 41, 45, 75, 77, 113, 230, 247
Kotick, Teddy, 120, 158

Lacy, Steve, 52, 53, 61
Lake, Oliver, 228
Lambert, Dave, 38, 39, 83

Lambert, Hendricks and Ross, 38, 233
Lamond, Don, 15, 27
Lampley, Cal, 240, 244, 248
Lanphere, Don, 17
Lateef, Yusef, 132, 155, 157, 159, 161, 163, 165, 166, 167, 168, 169, 170, 171, 188, 225, 229
Latin Jazz Quintet, 189, 206, 230
Laws, Hubert, 239
Lawson, Hugh, 167, 168
Lea, Barbara, 15, 113, 120, 153

Lead Belly, 151, 184
Levey, Stan, 15
Levy, Mo, 2, 126, 248
Lewis, Jerry Lee, 161
Lewis, John, 5, 8, 17, 29, 32, 38, 44, 47, 48, 159, 230, 242
Lewis, Mel, 31
Lewis, Ramsay, 198, 223
Lewis, Smiley, 151
Lieber and Stoller, 151
Lion, Alfred, 1, 4, 5, 12, 43, 50, 51, 56, 77, 102, 127, 133, 190
Liston, Melba, 191
Little, Booker, 207, 214, 215, 216, 218
Little Richard, 152, 163
Little Walter, 184, 223
Looking Ahead, 202, 207
"Love Theme from *Spartacus*," 169, 170
Lucas, Buddy, 189
Lucas, Ray, 238, 239

Macero, Teo, 118
Madden, Gail, 27
Mahones, Gildo, 192, 233, 234, 235
Mal-1, 4, 124, 131
Mance, Junior, 24
Mancini, Henry, 71
Mann, Herbie, 113, 133, 232

Manne, Shelley, 10
Mapp, Gary, 51
Mariano, Charlie, 86, 201, 212
Marsh, Warne, 11
Martin, Don, 76
Martino, Pat, 182, 195, 246
Massey, Bill, 21, 22, 24, 25
Mathews, Ronnie, 210
May, Earl, 24, 149
McCormick, Robert "Mack," 187
McDuff, Jack, 172–176, 179–182, 187, 196, 198, 220, 230, 231, 236, 244, 246
McGhee, Brownie, 86, 113, 151, 186
McGhee, Howard, 26, 195
McIntyre, Ken, 202, 203, 205, 206
McKibbon, Al, 8
McLean, Jackie, 27, 28, 29, 47, 77, 82, 85, 107, 113, 115, 116, 120, 129, 130, 136, 143
McPartland, Jimmy, 12
McPherson, Charles, 195, 246
McVea, Jack (McVouty), 230
Mellé, Gil, 56, 129
Miles, Reid, 77
Mingus, Charles, 48, 53, 92, 106, 130, 142, 153, 199, 200, 201, 207, 218, 226, 227
Mingus Jazz Workshop, 219
Minton's Playhouse, 53, 63, 68, 72, 73, 82, 233
"Misty," 193, 195, 244, 245
Mitchell, Blue, 195
Mobley, Hank, 99, 113, 129, 130, 237
Modal Jazz, 32, 66, 199, 253
Modern Jazz Quartet (MJQ), 48, 50, 61, 64, 66–74, 75, 90–92, 95, 98, 106, 107, 112, 160, 230
Monk, Thelonious, 1, 5, 12, 15, 31, 43, 44, 50–55, 56, 59–65, 76, 77, 89, 92–94, 96, 101, 104, 105, 106, 109, 112, 116, 146, 148, 198, 215, 225, 226, 243
Montego Joe, 182, 229
Moodsville Records, 146, 169, 184, 187, 188, 222, 233
Moody, James, 17, 19, 34–37, 58, 94, 113, 247
"Moody's Mood for Love," 23, 38, 39, 50
Moore, Brew, 14, 17
Morrow, George, 101, 200
Mulligan, Gerry, 8, 13, 14, 27, 31, 32, 40–43, 66, 77, 94, 106, 113, 115, 120, 158, 201, 230, 235, 242
Murray, David, 228

Nance, Ray, 212, 246
Navarro, Fats, 17, 83, 172
Newborn, Phineas, 214, 218
"Newk's Fadeaway," 87, 116
Newman, David "Fathead," 195
Newman, Joe, 25, 178, 222
New Yorker, The, 43, 77, 225
"Night Train," 45, 46, 136

"Oleo," 95, 110, 194
Oster, Harry, 187
Out There, 77, 205, 206
Outward Bound, 202, 205, 210, 212
Overton, Hall, 76, 119

Parent, Bob, 74, 77
Parker, Charlie, 5, 9, 10, 11, 13, 15, 17, 20, 23, 32, 35, 36, 38, 39, 42, 47, 66, 67, 77, 85, 86, 88, 89, 96, 101, 103, 105, 114, 120, 142, 144, 146, 172, 184, 190, 198, 206, 220, 230, 236, 242, 243
Patterson, Don, 172, 244, 246
Payne, Cecil, 134, 148, 156
Pepper, Art, 146, 200

Persip, Charli, 63
Person, Houston, 195, 198, 244, 246
Peter Gunn, 7, 71, 242, 243
Peterson, Oscar, 11, 42, 51, 71, 133, 247
Pettiford, Oscar, 13, 86, 129, 139
Pike, Dave, 120, 232, 233, 235
Platters, The, 200, 202
Pollard, Terry, 138, 165, 168
Porter, Bob, 248
Potter, Tommy, 15, 21, 22, 28, 35, 47, 61, 131, 174
Powell, Bud, 15, 20, 26, 50, 51, 82, 84, 85, 146, 238
Powell, Jesse, 189
Powell, Richie, 101, 200
Prestige All Stars, 129, 130, 131, 133, 134, 148, 156, 177, 222
Prestige Folklore, Prestige International, Prestige Lively Arts, 189

Quill, Gene, 122, 131
Quinichette, Paul, 86, 148, 222

Rabkin, Hesh, 126, 127
Ramirez, Ram, 39
Raney, Jimmy, 15, 75, 113, 119, 120, 121, 130, 134, 143, 233
RCA Victor Records, 3, 123, 214, 227
Redd, Freddie, 113, 124
Rhythm and Blues, x, 4, 5, 37, 38, 45, 46, 53, 73, 74, 83, 126, 128, 130, 132, 136, 141, 146, 151, 152, 153, 160, 161, 163, 172, 173, 175, 176, 177, 180, 186, 188, 189, 193, 198, 200, 211, 212, 223, 229, 230, 233, 235, 236, 243
Richardson, Jerome, 79, 130, 133, 179
Roach, Freddie, 190, 195
Roach, Max, 8, 17, 20, 30, 33, 53, 66, 70, 72, 84, 97, 98, 99, 101, 200, 214, 215, 226, 227

Rollins, Sonny, 5, 17, 27–30, 44, 45, 47, 50, 53–55, 59–61, 66, 76, 77, 82–101, 104, 107, 109, 110, 112, 115, 119, 128, 144, 146, 147, 172, 194, 214
'Round About Midnight (record album), 89, 110
Round Midnight (movie), 16, 67
"Round Midnight" (song), 52, 89, 106, 129
Rouse, Charlie, 128
Ross, Annie, x, 38, 113
Royal Roost, 7, 8, 12, 17, 30, 40, 43, 53, 66, 99
Rush, Tom, 189
Russell, Curly, 13, 20, 59, 60
Russell, George, 32, 33, 67
Russell, PeeWee, 184
Russell, Ross, 5

Savoy Records, 4, 5, 20, 38, 83, 94, 119, 123, 134, 155, 165, 166, 167, 168, 169, 218, 222, 249
Saxophone Colossus, 100
Schildkraut, Dave, 103
Schlitten, Don, 79, 117, 125, 212, 219, 231, 233, 244, 246
Schnitzler, Arthur, 70
Schwartz, Thornel, 191
Scott, Caio, 132, 133
Scott, Shirley, 79, 80, 172, 177, 178, 179, 186–190, 194, 196, 197, 214, 220, 227, 228
Seeger, Peggy, 189
Shihab, Sahib, 131, 148
Shorter, Wayne, 43, 240, 245
Silver, Horace, 68, 92, 93, 94, 95, 102, 124, 126, 128, 159
Sims, Zoot, 13, 14, 27, 47, 48, 66, 101, 106, 113, 115, 158, 164, 217
Smith, Al, 185, 186, 187
Smith, Bessie, 3

Smith, Jimmy, 80, 107, 108, 171, 172, 173, 174, 177, 190, 192, 220
Smith, Jimmie, 193, 234, 235
Smith, Johnny "Hammond," 191, 196, 211, 244, 246
Smith, Mamie, 183
Smith, W. Eugene, 76
Stevens, Leo, 191
Stidham, Arbee, 186, 223
Sorrels, Rosalie, 189
Soul Jazz, 80, 136, 171–183, 190, 191, 193, 195, 198, 207, 211, 220, 221, 230, 231, 234, 236, 237, 243–248
Specialty Records, 4, 7, 160, 163
Status Records, 134
Stewart, Rex, 5, 184
Stewart, Teddy, 24
Stitt, Sonny, 17, 20–26, 30, 46, 50, 86, 94, 109, 113, 147, 177, 194, 195, 220, 237, 246
Straight Ahead, 207, 211, 212
Swingville Records, 146, 184, 188, 221, 222, 235, 246
Sulieman, Idrees, 129, 131, 134, 148

Tate, Buddy, 177, 184, 217
Tatum, Art, 42, 51, 246
Taylor, Arthur, 61, 77, 82, 89, 109, 124, 128, 129, 130, 131, 133, 144, 145, 146, 148, 149, 150, 154, 155, 156, 184, 203, 206, 210, 230
Taylor, Billy, 50, 113, 143, 247
Taylor, Cecil, 5, 205, 207, 228
Terry, Clark, 17, 31, 35, 92, 134, 184
Terry, Sonny, 86, 151, 186
Thigpen, Ed, 148
Thompson, Lucky, 103
Third Stream, 205, 206
Timmons, Bobby, 127, 237, 238, 239, 240, 244
"Trinkle Tinkle," 51, 52

Tristano, Lennie, 6, 8, 9, 10, 11, 19, 26, 30, 32, 33, 41, 51, 75, 83 112, 199
Tru-Sound Records, 188, 189
Tucker, George, 191, 201, 225, 233, 234, 235
Turner, Dale, 16, 67
Turner, Joe, 152, 185, 235
Turrentine, Stanley, 138, 179, 214
Turrentine, Tommy, 227
"Twisted," 35, 39
Tyner, McCoy, 246

United Artists Records, 207, 247

Van Gelder, Rudy, 58, 59, 60, 63, 64, 81, 109, 201, 212, 215
Van Gelder Studio, Englewood Cliffs, 59
Van Gelder Studio, Hackensack, 58, 60, 69, 77, 78, 95, 97 *(nb, Since the Van Gelder Studio is in virtually every discographical entry in this book, those references are not included in this index.)*
Village Vanguard, 43, 172

Waldron, Mal, 113, 120, 124, 125, 129, 130, 131, 132, 133, 148, 207, 210, 218, 227, 228
Walkin', 23, 103–105, 145
Wallington, George, 13, 39, 50, 107, 113, 129, 158, 160, 164
Walton, Mercy Dee, 160
Watkins, Doug, 101, 129–136, 143, 148, 156, 169
Watkins, Julius, 53, 54, 55, 60, 92
Webster, Ben, 103, 172, 192, 235, 246, 247
Wein, George, 1
Weinstock, Bob, 1, 2, 5–27, 31, 35–39, 41, 43–48, 50, 52, 60, 61,

Weinstock, Bob *(continued)*
   64, 67, 68, 74–78, 81, 83, 85–87,
   95, 98, 101–109, 112–124, 127,
   129, 130, 133, 135, 141, 143, 144,
   147, 148, 154, 156–162, 167–179,
   183, 185, 188, 190, 206, 215, 218,
   221, 222, 224, 232–235, 241, 243,
   246–251
Wess, Frank, 131, 136–139, 198, 221,
   222, 234
West Coast Jazz, 6, 40, 202
Weston, Randy, 205, 225, 226, 228, 229
When Farmer Met Gryce, 78, 124
Williams, Cootie, 42, 173, 175, 188
Williams, Joe, 164
Williams, Larry, 151
Williams, Mary Lou, 39
Williams, Maurice, 160
Williams, Richard, 213, 214
Williams, Teddy, 21
Williams, Tony, 43, 192
Wilson, Nancy, 191, 198
Wilson, Shadow, 28, 98
Wilson, Willie, 210
Wiltshire, Teacho, 37, 39
Winchester, Lem, 180, 188, 192, 196,
   211, 222
Winding, Kai, 15, 17, 26, 27, 41, 53,
   77, 107, 113
Witherspoon, Jimmy, 234–236
Woodman, Britt, 106, 200
Woods, Phil, 31, 113, 119–123, 129,
   130, 131, 143, 146, 158, 247
Wright, Bruce, 126, 127
Wright, Gene, 24
Wright, Herman, 137, 139, 169, 170
Wright, John, 222–224
Wright, Leo, 234, 235
Wyands, Richard, 211, 218, 251

Young, David X., 75, 76
Young, Lamonte, 141
Young, Larry, 136, 218, 234
Young, Lester, 5, 16, 18, 42, 43, 73,
   86, 94, 99, 101, 145
Young, Webster, 131, 148

www.ingramcontent.com/pod-product-compliance
Lightning Source LLC
Chambersburg PA
CBHW032037150426
43194CB00006B/320